The Demography of Early Modern Towns:
York in the Sixteenth and Seventeenth Centuries

Liverpool Studies in European Population
General Editor DAVID SIDDLE

The Demography of Early Modern Towns: York in the Sixteenth and Seventeenth Centuries

CHRIS GALLEY

LIVERPOOL UNIVERSITY PRESS

First published 1998 by
LIVERPOOL UNIVERSITY PRESS
Senate House, Abercromby Square
Liverpool, L69 3BX

British Library Cataloguing-in-Publication Data
A British Library CIP record is available

ISBN 0–85323–503–1 *cased*
0–85323–513–9 *paper*

Set in Times New Roman by
Northern Phototypesetting Co. Ltd, Bolton
Printed and bound in the European Union by
Bell and Bain Ltd, Glasgow

CONTENTS

LIST OF FIGURES

LIST OF TABLES

ACKNOWLEDGEMENTS

The idea that one day I might wish to write a book about early modern urban demography was first mooted by Bob Woods over a pint of beer following a highly stimulating seminar in Sheffield by Osamu Saito on mortality in nineteenth-century Japan. Bob has been a continual source of enthusiasm and encouragement throughout the years – first as my PhD supervisor, second as my Head of Department and, last but not least, as my friend.

Along the way I have accumulated a series of debts of gratitude which I gratefully acknowledge. John Woodward also acted as my PhD. supervisor in which capacity he provided me with exemplary support and encouragement. Much of the primary research was carried out at The York City Archives and The Borthwick Institute of Historical Research which proved to be an excellent environment in which to undertake academic research. I wish to thank Rita Freeman and Chris Webb for their help in guiding me round their respective archives. My knowledge of historical demography has greatly benefited from discussions with colleagues both in Sheffield and Liverpool particularly, Violetta Hionidou, Graham Mooney, Nicola Shelton and Naomi Williams. Bob Woods, David Siddle and Caitríona Ní Laoire read the whole book while Jill Rudd and Naomi Williams read and commented on chapters at various stages of completion. Collectively they proved to be perceptive critics and the text has been considerably improved by their attention to detail. Sandra Mather drew the figures; her patience and eye for detail are greatly appreciated. I would also like to thank Robin Bloxsidge of Liverpool University Press and Frances Hackeson who meticulously guided me through the process of publication.

The writing of the book was made possible by the award of a three-year British Academy post-doctoral fellowship and subsequently of a one-year fellowship from the Department of Geography, University of Liverpool. I am grateful to both institutions. Parts of the book first appeared in 'A never-ending succession of epidemics? Mortality in early-modern York', *Social History of Medicine* 7 (1994), 29–57 and 'A model of early modern urban demography', *Economic History Review* 48 (1995), 448–69.

Finally I wish to thank my family, in particular my mother from whom I inherited my love of books. I wish to dedicate this book to her memory.

PREFACE

Edeith Byines daughter unto Willim Beines Cowper was baptyzed 16 september (1632)
Edeith Binnes daughter to Willm Binnes 23rd September at mothers coffen end (buried)
Edeith Bynnes wyif unto Willm Binnes Cowper was buried 23 september neire the southe Church doore 1632
Willm Binnes Cowper of this p'she and Susanna Stead servant to mr ffrancis Buckle weire maryed the 29th daye of November (1632)

In the parish register of St Martin-cum-Gregory, York there are four entries that relate to William Binnes. First, his daughter Edith was baptized. A week later, she along with her mother, also named Edith, was buried, presumably having died as a consequence of a difficult birth. Only two months after this tragedy William remarried. Birth, death and marriage often mark the most momentous periods in a person's life and this sad reconstruction illustrates how demographic events could shape the lives of ordinary individuals. Of course, it is not possible to tell how William Binnes was affected by these events; but in a period when fertility was largely unrestricted and only rudimentary medical care existed, most people had little control over their demographic fate, marriage being the exception, to some extent at least. Within any particular locality the experiences of individual families often differed considerably. For instance, in 1637 Thomas Cherry married Judeth Day in the church of St Martin Coney Street, York. They continued to live in that parish and by the time Thomas died 18 years later they had baptized ten children. Only two of Cherry's children were still alive when Judeth died in 1662: five had died in infancy (aged under one); two had died aged two and one aged three. The fortunes of Richard Sowrey and Mercy Murton who married in 1660 in the same church were more favourable. They baptized six children between 1661 and 1670 and at the time of this last baptism all the Sowrey children were alive. The reasons why these two families had such markedly different experiences of infant and childhood mortality cannot be known; however, at the aggregate level of the parish, town or country, the demographic regime – the set of interrelated demographic characteristics that pertain within a population – can be determined and this will allow many of the influences that affected an individual's experience of birth, death and marriage to be examined.

This book is concerned with one particular demographic regime – that of towns and cities in the early modern period (from c.1540 until c.1700). Following Wrigley and Schofield's pioneering work with English parish registers national and indeed rural demographic trends are well established (Wrigley and Schofield, 1981). However, much less is known about urban demography. Few empirical studies have been undertaken largely because urban parish registers are thought to provide a poor guide to the number of demographic events that took place in towns; yet in spite of the general lack of hard demographic evidence there has still been considerable debate as to why urban demography appeared to have differed so radically from that of rural areas.[1] What follows seeks to examine these debates and redress the imbalance by providing a comprehensive analysis of urban demography in the early modern period. Much of the book's focus will be concerned with three issues that need to be resolved in order for the demography of towns to become better understood. The first relates to the relative paucity of information that is available about urban demography and will be addressed by means of a case study of York, England's 'second city', between 1561 and 1700. This approach is in part necessitated by the time-consuming nature of demographic analysis in the parish register period, but it also has advantages. All the relevant demographic material for a single city can be consulted and this will enable any changes to the demographic regime to be identified. At all times emphasis will be placed on explaining how and why the individual components of the demographic regime changed and how York's demography influenced and was influenced by its economy and society. While no single city ever can be considered typical, York possesses many attributes that merit detailed study. Its demographic archive has survived well and the range of material that is available is typical of other English towns. The second set of issues relate to the debate about the nature of urban demography. The results from York will therefore be examined in a wider context; comparable material from other English and European cities will be introduced where appropriate and as a means of resolving some of the current debates a generalized model describing the mechanisms of urban demography will be proposed and justified. Once the dynamics of change within urban demographic regimes have been discussed a third set of wider issues can be addressed. These relate to the impact of urbanization on national demographic regimes and to longer-term urban demographic changes.

To complement this approach, much of the demographic analysis is on three levels: the first is concerned with individual demographic experience, often within families; the second presents aggregate data, mainly from York, and provides a comprehensive account of the demography of a large early modern city; the third sets York within its national and European context, it makes comparisons, draws conclusions and considers wider issues. Likewise, the book is divided into three sections. The introduction sets the scene by reviewing what is known about urban demography and providing some background information about York's economy and society. The central section exploits all available demographic sources to provide a dynamic analysis of York's changing demography. Finally, the conclusion seeks to resolve the issues raised in the introduction. It discusses the importance of urban demography to national population histories, provides a wider context for the case study and seeks to set an agenda for future research. Much will involve the calculation and interpretation of aggregate measures; yet at all times it is important not to lose sight of how these demographic conditions affected individuals – the cumulative experiences of families such as the Binnes, Cherrys and Sowreys provide telling witness to the social conditions endured by those who lived in the many cities of early modern Europe.

1 This is summarized in de Vries (1984), pp. 175–98.

INTRODUCTION

Chapter 1

THE DEMOGRAPHY OF
EARLY MODERN TOWNS

Daniel Defoe travelled the length and breadth of Britain and in describing a visit to Chester in the 1720s he noted five remarkable things about the city

> 1. Its walls, which are very firm and in good repair. 2. The castle, which is also kept up, and has a garrison always in it. 3. The cathedral. 4. The River Dee, and 5. the bridge over it.[1]

In concentrating on Chester's most impressive physical and structural features Defoe was highlighting some of the main characteristics of urban places. The most distinctive feature of many early modern towns, at least to approaching visitors, was their walls. Gates provided entry, but these could be locked and the town separated from the surrounding countryside. By the seventeenth century some town walls had fallen into disrepair and suburbs had developed; nevertheless, most of England was still rural and its towns provided striking contrasts with their rural hinterlands.[2] By mentioning the castle and cathedral Defoe reveals that some towns developed because they were military or ecclesiastical centres and if they were both, like Chester, they were likely to become major cities. The livelihoods of virtually all early modern towns depended upon trade, hence the importance of bridges and rivers. Towns were also distribution centres and to emphasize that Chester's economy was thriving, Defoe's description contains accounts of its Rows (long galleries which connect the houses and shops alongside the main streets), shops, broad streets, warehouses which had just been destroyed by a flood and the recent introduction of piped water. Chester is revealed to be an important regional centre with a thriving economy: a 'modern' city with an ancient history. The format of Defoe's description of Chester is similar to many of the other towns and cities included in his Tours, and after reading these it is clear why they proved to be so attractive to the many visitors, traders and migrants who flocked to them each year.

Towns may be relatively easy to identify, but providing a working definition of 'urban' proves to be less so. Within a pre-industrial context, Clark and Slack provide the best attempt.[3] They do not offer a definition as such; instead they indicate five primary characteristics that towns should have: a concentration of population, an economic function, a complex social structure, a political structure and an influence beyond their immediate boundaries. The simplest way of defining 'urban' is by pop-

---

1 Defoe (1971), p. 392. Defoe's *Tour* does not report an actual itinerary since in some instances visits had been made up to 40 years previously; see pp. 15–16.

2 Contemporary prints, drawings and paintings often depict seventeenth-century towns almost as oases set in a rural landscape. For some examples, see Murray *et al.* (1990), pp. 14, 132–33, 135, 140.

ulation size with arbitrary cut-offs of 5,000 or 10,000 often being used.[4] In order to survive, towns needed an economic role – they were all market places and many were also centres for specialized trades and manufacture. Towns exerted an influence over large areas or in London's case throughout the whole country; hence, they were centres of opportunity and a focus for migrants. Political structures developed in order to regulate town life and conspicuous wealth was often displayed alongside abject poverty, even if sufficient charity was usually available to help those in greatest need. Here it is not necessary to discuss the relative merits of defining towns by these different characteristics, although it should be pointed out that there is no absolute way of differentiating urban from rural. For the demographer the consequences of large numbers of people living together, often in close proximity, is the crucial feature of urban settlements and the demography of towns is generally considered to have differed radically from that within their immediate rural hinterland. There are three main reasons for this. First, towns were often subject to high rates of growth. During the seventeenth and eighteenth centuries many towns expanded rapidly which caused England to evolve into a predominantly urban society.[5] Secondly, all towns experienced high levels of migration, although much of it was only temporary. A large proportion of the urban population was therefore in a state of flux and their demographic characteristics are consequently difficult to determine. Thirdly, high population densities created the conditions in which disease could spread easily. Mortality rates in early modern towns were high and usually exceeded those in rural areas, the frequent outbreaks of bubonic plague that periodically decimated early modern urban populations being the most obvious example of this phenomenon. Towns could also be centres for medical help, charity and poor relief, and these may have mitigated the consequences of high levels of disease for some people at least.[6] All early modern cities were unhealthy places; but however high levels of mortality were, the economic benefits of urban life outweighed any additional threat to life. Most towns flourished and increasing levels of urbanization ensured that national population patterns were increasingly influenced by what happened in the urban sector.

3 Clark and Slack (1976), pp. 4–6. Perhaps the most famous discussion is Sjoberg (1960). Cities were usually differentiated from towns by having cathedrals, although often the term is used to describe large towns and here the two terms will be used interchangeably.

4 Such definitions are time- and place-specific; for instance, some places with a population of 10,000 may only qualify as villages today.

5 This process accelerated during the nineteenth century and by 1851 over 50 per cent of the population of England and Wales could be considered urban; Law (1967). Law's definition was based on a population of 2,500 with additional provisos about nucleation and population density.

6 Towns could also provide a focus for the development of new ideas, some of which may have influenced demographic behaviour, especially with respect to marriage, fertility and the care of children.

THE URBAN HIERARCHY: ENGLAND, 1500–1800

Few urban population listings exist prior to the 1801 census and consequently it is only possible to estimate the population of most early modern towns. These estimates are sometimes based on lists of freemen, partially surviving tax and ecclesiastical counts or parish registers; hence, they need to be treated with caution and some margin of error included alongside the figures. Despite these reservations it is certain that substantial urbanization occurred in England during the period 1500–1800. In 1550 there were just four cities with populations in excess of 10,000; by 1700 that number had risen to 11 and by 1750 there were 21 (de Vries, 1984, pp. 270–71). Table 1.1 indicates how quickly population increase occurred in some English cities. The populations of the largest five towns at each date are given, together with those of towns previously included in the table. London dominated the urban hierarchy at all times, increasing from c.55,000 in 1520 to 200,000 in 1600, 675,000 in 1700 and nearly a million by 1801. London's increase in population was remarkable, although other towns often matched or even exceeded these rates of growth.

Table 1.1: The population (in 000s) of some large English towns, c.1520–1801

c.1520	c.1600	c.1670	c.1700	c.1750	1801
London 55	London 200	London 475	London 575	London 675	London 959
Norwich 12	Norwich 15	Norwich 20	Norwich 30	Bristol 50	Manchester 89
Bristol 10	Bristol 12	Bristol 20	Bristol 21	Norwich 36	Liverpool 83
York 8	York 12	York 12	Newcastle 16	Newcastle 29	Birmingham 74
Exeter 8	Newcastle 10	Newcastle 12	Exeter 14	Birmingham 24	Bristol 60
	Exeter 9	Exeter 9	York 12	Exeter 16	Newcastle 42
				York 11	Norwich 36
					Exeter 17
					York 16

Source: Wrigley (1985b), p. 686.

Norwich grew faster than London during the late seventeenth century, as did Bristol in the first half of the eighteenth century, and the emergence of the northern industrial towns of Birmingham, Manchester and Liverpool after 1750 was truly phenomenal. Not all towns grew, however. While Norwich and Bristol tripled their populations during the seventeenth century, any increase in Exeter, Ipswich and York was only slight. Coventry, together with the much smaller town of Stafford, even lost population.[7] Wrigley has estimated that the proportion of the English population living in towns with a population greater than 5,000 increased from five per cent in 1520 to eight in 1600, 17 in 1700 and 27 in 1801, with London alone accounting for

---

7 Corfield (1977), pp. 41–45; Adey (1973). For population estimates of smaller towns see Clark (1989). There is debate as to the fortunes of provincial towns in the period before 1550. It is difficult to estimate urban populations during this period and any conclusions are likely to remain tentative. For a summary of the debate, see Dyer (1991).

two, five, eleven and eleven per cent of the total at each respective date.[8] Most urban growth was concentrated within London until 1600, but during the seventeenth century many smaller towns began to grow and urbanization continued even when the population of England was in stagnation during the second half of the seventeenth century. Between 1520 and 1700 London was up to 20 times greater than its nearest rival Norwich. Next were a group of provincial capitals with populations in the region of 10,000 and below these came an expanding group of towns such as Worcester, King's Lynn and Chester with populations in excess of 5,000 (Wrigley, 1985, p. 688). Few European capitals dominated provincial cities like London did. In much of Europe there were networks of large provincial cities. Paris had a similar population to London in 1600, but in France there were 13 provincial centres larger than Norwich.[9] Holland, the most urbanized European country at this date, had 19 cities with populations in excess of 10,000, although Amsterdam's population was only 65,000 (de Vries, 1984, pp. 274–76). Likewise on the Italian peninsular there were 58 cities with populations in excess of 10,000, and whilst such comparisons are hardly just, English provincial cities like Norwich, Bristol and York were very small compared with similar European cities such as Lyon, Augsburg or Messina.[10]

Much has been written about how towns were capable of increasing their populations so quickly (Keyfitz, 1980, pp. 142–51). Changes within any population are governed by the basic demographic equation:

$$P_1 = P_0(b - d + i - o)$$

where P_1 and P_0 are populations at two points in time; b = births, d = deaths, i = in-migration and o = out-migration occurring during the interval. Population increase was therefore determined by levels of natural change (the difference between births and deaths) and net migration (the difference between in- and out-migration). For most cities, levels of natural change were insufficient to generate large-scale population increase. The birth rate within a population was capable of variation, but substantial changes usually only occurred over long periods. The death rate was more variable, especially when mortality crises occurred and large numbers died in a short period. Most cities recovered quickly following periods of crisis mortality as migrants flocked to the city. Since the existence of cities was dependent upon their

---

8 Wrigley (1985b), p. 688. The population (in millions) of England, less Monmouth, increased from 2.8 in 1541 to 4.1 in 1600, 5.2 in 1650, 5.0 in 1700 and 8.7 in 1801; see Wrigley and Schofield (1981) pp. 528–29.

9 de Vries (1984), pp. 273–76. Norwich had a population of c.12,000 in 1600. This compares with the following populations (in 000s): Angers (25), Arles (15), Bordeaux (40), Cambrai (12), La Rochelle (23), Lyon (40), Marsaille (40), Metz (19), Nantes (25), Rennes (22), Rouen (60), Strasbourg (28) and Toulouse (>40). At the same time France's population was four to five times greater than that of England; Dupâquier (1979), p. 11.

10 de Vries (1984). In 1600 Lyon had a population of 40,000, Augsburg 48,000 and Messina 50,000. Stockholm and Copenhagen also dominated their provincial cities, but both were much smaller than London.

economic, political and social functions, the size of population that a city could maintain was determined more by these considerations than by purely demographic factors. Put simply, a town's economy could only sustain a certain number of people, and whilst this was subject to variation, especially in times of recession or if the rich were willing to maintain expanding numbers of poor, the only way that a population could increase substantially was following a comparable expansion in its economy. Migration acted as a safety valve and is the key to understanding urban growth; in times of economic growth more people would move into the city and in times of recession people would move away from the city in order to find employment elsewhere. This process occurred independently of levels of natural increase. Of course the demographic characteristics of urban populations (those factors influencing b and d) were also very important. If natural decrease was a permanent feature of some cities' demography then migration would be necessary just to maintain the population. The overall level of that migration was certainly influenced by levels of natural change, but people moved into or out of cities in order to exploit available economic opportunities and the population rose or fell accordingly.[11] The means by which cities were able to grow are only now beginning to be fully understood, but from the middle of the seventeenth century onwards the mechanics of urban demography began to be examined.

URBAN DEMOGRAPHY – CONTEMPORARY VIEWS

In 1662 John Graunt published a small book entitled *Natural and Political Observations made upon the Bills of Mortality*. It provided a rigorous statistical analysis of certain aspects of the London Bills of Mortality and effectively launched the discipline of demography. Amongst the many innovations contained within this work Graunt drew attention to the high levels of mortality in the capital, calculated the amount of migration that was necessary for London to expand and constructed some of the first life tables. Graunt conceded that there were difficulties concerning the accuracy of some of the cause of death information and that 'there have been a neglect in the accounts of the christenings' (Graunt, 1662, p. 30); but despite these shortcomings, he managed to provide an exhaustive analysis of mortality change in the capital. He also noted the main difference between rural and urban demography:

> in the country the christenings exceed the burials, yet, in London they do not. The general reason of this must be, that in London the proportion of those subject to die, unto those capable of breeding is greater than in the country ... or else we must say, that London is more unhealthful, or that it inclines men and women more to barrenness, than the country (Graunt, 1662, pp. 44–45).

Graunt then discussed each of these points in turn. He argued that a number of people who came to London on business, for pleasure or to be cured of diseases left their wives at home in the country; hence, 'the breeders in London are proportionally fewer' (Graunt, 1662, p. 45). Furthermore, many apprentices, who were bound from

11 Rural economic opportunities are also an important influence on whether a person decides to migrate.

marrying from between seven and nine years continued to live in London after their apprenticeships had ended (Graunt, 1662, pp. 45–46). Graunt also argued that high levels of barrenness in London were caused by 'intemperance in feeding', 'adulteries and fornications, supposed more frequent in London' and what virtually amounts to the stresses of urban life.[12] Graunt finally considered some of the reasons for London's high mortality

> As for unhealthfulness it may well be supposed that although seasoned bodies may and do live near as long in London, as elsewhere, yet new-comers and children do not ... otherwise why do sickly persons remove to the countryside (Graunt, 1662, pp. 45–46).

In conclusion Graunt firmly attributed London's burial excess to mortality:

> When I consider that in the country 70 are born for 58 buried, and that before the year 1600 the like happened in London, I considered whether a City, as it becomes more populous, doth not, for that very cause, become more unhealthful, I inclined to believe that London is more unhealthful than heretofore, partly for that it is more populous, but chiefly because I have heard that 60 years ago few sea coals were burnt in London, which are now universally used (Graunt, 1662, p. 70).

Whilst he may have been wrong in inferring that London's high mortality was mainly due to coal-smoke, it is interesting to note that Graunt did not believe that London had always experienced a surplus of burials. To the modern reader Graunt's explanations of London's low levels of fertility and high mortality may appear antiquated; nevertheless, his analysis of London's demography remains both subtle and astute. Graunt realized that large numbers of migrants were needed if London was to expand, he knew that these migrants also affected levels of fertility, but above all he appreciated the risks to life posed by living in an unhealthy city. Without recourse to the tools of modern demographic analysis, Graunt argued that London's peculiar demographic regime, as revealed by the Bills of Mortality, resulted from a combination of high levels of mortality, low fertility and a certain amount of under-registration.

Graunt's book influenced successive generations of demographers, although few tackled the problem with his insight.[13] In 1681 William Petty, whose main work was concerned with the thesis that England would prosper if its population increased, undertook an analysis of the Dublin Bills of Mortality (Hull, 1964, pp. 481–98). Petty compared levels of mortality between London and Dublin. Much of his work is superficial, however and he made no attempt to discuss fertility. Indeed, Petty's thinking was dominated by the high levels of mortality in the capital: 'London would in time decrease quite away, were it not supplied out of the Country balance' (Hull, 1964, p. 482). In particular, Petty viewed plague with horror since if the population of London continued to increase, an outbreak would wipe out 'as many in one year

---

12 Graunt (1662), p. 46; 'the minds of men in London are more thoughtful and full of business than in the country'.

as the whole nation will refurbish in twenty'.[14] A more sophisticated approach was adopted by Edmund Halley, who in 1692 published a study of births and deaths in the city of Breslau. Halley's aim was to produce a comparative life table for a city which unlike London was not affected:

> by reason of the great and casual accession of strangers who die there ... The people we treat of should not at all be changed, but die where they were born, without any adventitious increase from abroad, or decay by migration (Halley, 1669, p. 596).

Halley showed that while Breslau, with a population in excess of 30,000, suffered high levels of mortality (the infant mortality rate was 281 per 1,000 live births), there were still more births than deaths in the city (an annual average of 1,238 births and 1,174 deaths were recorded between 1687 and 1691; Halley, 1692, p. 600) which sharply contrasted with London and Dublin where natural decrease occurred.

Throughout the eighteenth century there was considerable interest in issues relating to demography and in particular there was much debate as to whether England's population was increasing or decreasing. While concern was expressed about the large cities 'which tended to increase more slowly from births within their limits than country districts, if indeed they increase at all',[15] there were few developments in demographic techniques and much work in urban demography now focused on amassing aggregate series of baptisms, burials and marriages, then making conclusions based on levels of natural change. Little attention was given to fertility and the problems caused by under-registration: instead, the implicit assumption was made that the greater the imbalance between baptisms and burials, the higher mortality must have been.[16] This belief typified much of the work of Thomas Short who gathered baptism and burial series for a wide variety of rural and urban settlements and then proceeded to determine why there were differences in mortality between these places (Short, 1750; 1767). By no means all of Short's examples reveal urban natural decrease and while he correctly identified that 'All the registers agree that in Cities and great Towns there is a greater number of Deaths of Infants and Children than in Country Places and the like Situations' (Short, 1750, p. 63), this observation was based only on baptism/burial ratios, not mortality rates. It is difficult to determine exactly how Graunt's more sophisticated account of urban demography evolved into the rather simplistic belief that any excess of urban burials was caused

13 What follows does not attempt to be exhaustive. A useful summary is given in Stangeland (1966).
14 Hull (1964), p. 475. As early as the 1690s Gregory King had identified an urban mortality gradient having calculated that London's crude death rate at 42 per 1,000 inhabitants compared with 33 for lesser cities and 31 for villages; quoted in de Vries (1984), p. 179.
15 Stangeland (1966), p. 159 discussing the work of Charles Davenant who also argued that economic growth was dependent upon population growth. The debate is discussed in Glass (1973a) and reprints of some of the more important documents are contained in Glass (1973c). The debate was only resolved after the results of the 1801 census had been published.
16 Kuczynski (1938) shows that most work on fertility in this period offers little other than a reiteration of Graunt's views.

entirely by high mortality. This notion gained acceptance, however. William White, writing in 1782 about York, argued that since the excess of burials recorded between 1728 and 1735 had given way to an excess of baptisms between 1770 and 1776, then there 'is certainly a great rise in the scale of healthiness' (White, 1782, p. 37). According to White this was due to:

> inoculation ... improvements in the treatment and cure of several disorders, the cool regimen in fevers, the admission in fresh air, the general use of antiseptic medicines and diet ... a general improvement and greater attention to nature in the management of infants (White, 1782, p. 42).

Despite this list the only quantitative evidence given to support this assertion is that the balance between baptisms and burials changed during the period.

During the eighteenth century the German demographer Johann Peter Süssmilch assembled a large quantity of material for many continental cities. He argued that mortality was density-dependent and that cities were a considerable drain on national populations.[17] Malthus made much use of Süssmilch's data and he too concluded that towns were subject to high rates of mortality. In a passage that echoes Graunt, Malthus states:

> There certainly seems to be something in great towns, and even in moderate towns, peculiarly unfavourable to the very early stages of life: and the part of the community on which the mortality principally falls, seems to indicate that it arises more from the closeness and foulness of the air, which may be supposed to be unfavourable to the tender lungs of children, and the greater from the superior degree of luxury and debauchery usually and justly attributed to towns.[18]

Whilst Malthus acknowledged that in large towns 'the whole of the procreative power' is seldom called into action, the theme which constantly recurs throughout his work is that mortality in the great cities was sufficiently high to merit being a considerable check to populations (Malthus, 1970, pp. 255, 106).

By the nineteenth century it was well established that levels of mortality in many cities were high. Much of the work of William Farr, with his urban mortality league tables which he compared with a selection of healthy rural districts, was devoted to publicizing the high levels of mortality in large cities.[19] Farr could calculate actual mortality rates, although by the middle of the nineteenth century English cities no longer experienced natural decrease and mortality rates in most places had been reduced from early modern levels. However, during the eighteenth century, when levels of urban mortality were at their height, there is little evidence to suggest that all cities experienced urban natural decrease. Data from large provincial English cities are scarce and the example of London, which often recorded massive amounts of natural decrease, has tended to dominate thinking. Yet even here Graunt conceded that low fertility and considerable amounts of under-registration complicated the picture. Spurred on initially by the ravages caused by epidemics of plague, much work

---

17 de Vries (1984), p. 179. Süssmilch's influence is the theme of Hecht (1987).
18 Malthus (1973) p. 242. This is also quoted in Woods (1989), p. 80.
19 The work of William Farr is discussed in Eyler (1979).

on urban demography from Graunt through to Malthus has concentrated on assessing levels of mortality in towns, and most demographers would have agreed that 'it appears with how much truth great cities have been called the graves of mankind'.[20]

URBAN DEMOGRAPHY – MODERN VIEWS

The thesis that early modern cities were 'graveyards' experiencing natural population decrease caused principally by high mortality has achieved wide acceptance. According to Barry, 'Generally speaking towns found it hard to maintain their population levels; without migrants their population would have stagnated or fallen rather than grown'.[21] It is also forcefully expressed by Wrigley in his book *Population and History* (1969, pp. 97–99). By means of a mortality contour map he shows how mortality in an imaginary seaport influenced the surrounding area and thereby acted as a demographic sink for the whole of its rural hinterland. In a later article Wrigley elaborates this view:

> Large towns such as York, Bristol, Norwich, Newcastle or, pre-eminently London, often failed to balance their demographic books. More were buried than were born within the city walls and in the surrounding suburbs. Without a steady stream of immigrants many, perhaps most, towns before the 19th century would have lost population.[22]

Wrigley essentially agreed with Graunt that while levels of fertility may have been low, the overriding feature of early modern urban demography was high mortality. Sharlin (1978) challenged this orthodoxy. Sharlin accepted that early modern cities experienced natural decrease, but he argued that this was a direct consequence of migration to cities. Most migrants were young and single and since rates of illegitimate fertility were low, they were responsible for few births, although many died following contact with the urban disease pool. Sharlin's so-called 'temporary migrants' recorded substantial natural decrease and this offset any small measure of natural increase recorded by the 'permanent residents'. To support his argument Sharlin produced a table of natural change for citizens and non-citizens in the city of Frankfurt am Main which he used as surrogates for 'permanent residents' and 'temporary migrants'. These data show that Sharlin may be correct, yet they are not capable of providing conclusive proof for his thesis. Finlay, in a reply to Sharlin, used the results from four parish reconstitutions, and argued that in London 'It is very clear … that insufficient native-born children survived to an age at which they could marry and replace themselves in urban areas'.[23] However, as Sharlin pointed out, it was still theoretically possible that if a relatively high proportion of the population married, then even according to Finlay's data the fertility of London's 'permanent residents' would have exceeded their mortality. At this point in the debate it became obvious

20 Malthus (1970), p. 196 quoting Price (1771), p. 243.
21 Barry (1990), p. 12. According to Goose (1986), p. 179, historians are unanimous in accepting urban natural decrease.
22 Wrigley (1987), pp. 136–37. Also, see Wrigley (1990), pp. 103, 110.
23 Finlay (1981a), p. 172. Also, see Sharlin (1981), pp. 175–80.

that progress was being thwarted by a lack of data with both Sharlin and Finlay being unable to fully specify the demography of urban populations. Sharlin could produce no data which expressly differentiated between 'temporary migrants' and 'permanent residents' within the early modern city, whilst Finlay was unable to provide sufficient information about London's fertility.

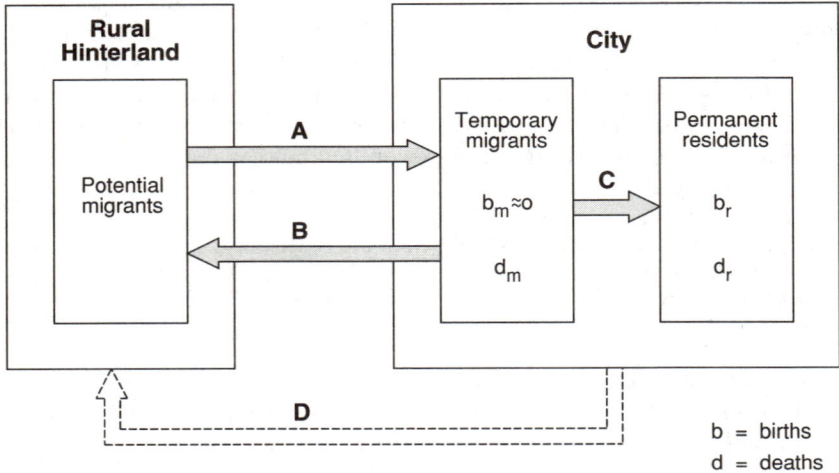

Figure 1.1: Sharlin's model of early modern urban demography

Figure 1.1 summarizes the essential differences between the arguments of Wrigley, Finlay and Sharlin. All agree that natural decrease occurred – the number of deaths of temporary migrants and permanent residents was greater than the number of births in the same groups; i.e. $d_m + d_r < b_m + b_r$, and since few births occurred to temporary migrants this inequality effectively reduces to $d_m + d_r < b_r$. The debate between Sharlin and Finlay hinges on whether the permanent residents also experienced natural decrease, $d_r < b_r$. Finlay argued that the very high levels of mortality in London would have ensured that this was always the case while Sharlin replied that a high proportion married may ensure that $b_r > d_r$. For all cities, migration was essential for their economic and demographic survival. Sharlin accepted that there may have been some movement between temporary migrants and permanent residents (C); but many would move into the city for only short periods and if they survived this experience, they would eventually have moved elsewhere (A→B). For Finlay the city needed migrants in order to survive and many migrants must have settled permanently (A→C). Whilst it is clear that all of the migration streams A, B, C and D occurred, it is not known to what extent each predominated, and without access to the appropriate demographic measures which explicitly differentiate migrants from residents, the debate has languished. In 1989 Woods attempted to revive interest in the topic by posing the question, 'What would one need to know to solve the "natural decrease in early modern cities" problem?'. Here the main enigma of early modern cities is revealed:

> For many of the young migrants there was an urban penalty – the city was an urban graveyard as one would expect it to have been for the old and destitute – but for many more the city was a means of escape, a source of wealth and vitality, a place of hope in which normal family life could be lived albeit at higher risk of infants and children dying prematurely (Woods, 1989, p. 92).

Thus, cities provided a number of economic opportunities for the aspiring migrant and along with these went the opportunity to marry and settle permanently. Sharlin's two groups were therefore by no means mutually exclusive and cities such as London, Bristol, and Norwich could have only expanded at the rate which they did because significant numbers of migrants were able to settle, become permanent residents, and start families. The key to resolving the debate between Finlay and Sharlin lies in being able to differentiate migrants from residents, but as Woods showed it is impossible to fully reconstruct the demography of a city's population without access to a detailed population register. Indeed, many characteristics of the urban migrant remain elusive with virtually nothing being known about out-migration (B and D) and the extent to which this was confined to temporary migrants or involved whole families. Sharlin's main contribution to the debate has been in stressing the important role of migration in explaining the unique features of urban demography, but as he finally points out much still remains to be discovered:

> With better data, perhaps we can leave aside disputing the simple 'what if' thesis which arose from the erroneous interpretation of counts of births and deaths. Regardless of whether cities would or would not have declined in size without migration, posing the question in this way combines and confutes the distinct demographic components of nuptiality, marital fertility, mortality and migration. Thus it would be useful to examine both temporary and permanent migration in early modern cities. How did migration change with fluctuations in bread prices and the economy? What proportions of residents of cities were migrants, both temporary and permanent? What occupations did permanent residents and temporary migrants have? Within cities it is also necessary to investigate the constituent elements of the population patterns – nuptiality, fertility and mortality. Who married in the cities, at what ages, and how many children did they have? What were levels of life expectancy? We know from rural demographic studies that nuptiality, fertility and mortality varied over time. Presumably cities were not different in this regard. If we put aside the question we inherit, we can concentrate on a more subtle understanding of the demographic processes in early modern Europe (Sharlin, 1981, 179–80).

These questions are crucial to a proper understanding of urban demography and while data from English cities may not include sufficient detail to enable a full set of answers to be given, enough exists, as will be demonstrated in the case of York, for many of the issues raised by Sharlin to be addressed. These will continually recur throughout the book and Chapter 6 will seek to reconcile the debate between Sharlin and Finlay by proposing a model of early modern urban demography that stresses the importance of the urban economy in influencing demographic rates. However, before proceeding to examine the demography of York in detail, it is important to summarize what is already known about other English cities.

ENGLISH URBAN DEMOGRAPHY

In order to chart the demographic history of a town it is necessary to have access to accurate data, the most basic being, in the absence of reliable population counts, totals for births, deaths and marriages. Before the civil registration of births, deaths and marriages was established in 1837, this information can be gleaned from parish registers.[24] All parishes were instructed to keep a register of baptisms, burials and marriages from 1538, although few have a complete set covering the period 1538-1837. Furthermore, births and deaths were not recorded directly.[25] Thus, in any ecclesiatical registration system there is likely to be some shortfall, especially of infants who died before baptism and nonconformists who might be excluded from the system.[26] In spite of these drawbacks some parish registers have been shown to provide an accurate reflection of the number of vital events occurring within a parish, although problems such as concentrations of nonconformists, high population turnover and the poor quality of some registers was thought to preclude accurate demographic analysis in many cities. For these reasons no London parish and only 18 out of the 404 (4.5 per cent) parishes selected by Wrigley and Schofield as the basis of their *Population History of England* can be considered urban in the seventeenth century.[27] Consequently, in 1984 de Vries wrote:

> The demographic characteristics of urban populations are not well known. In fact, the impressive advances made in historical demography during the last twenty years have only made more acute our sense of ignorance about fertility, mortality and nuptiality among city-dwellers (de Vries, 1984, p. 175).

Attempts have been made to rectify this situation, most notably with studies of London's demography (Finlay, 1981c; Landers, 1993). Landers' work has primarily focused on mortality, partly due to the richness of material in the Bills of Mortality. He discovered that levels of mortality in the capital were very high, especially at the beginning of the eighteenth century, and argued that London suffered from a 'high

---

24 Bills of Mortality were also compiled for some cities. These sources often included additional information about cause of death, but the system essentially remained a parochial one and their compilation relied upon the cooperation of the parish clerk.

25 For a short period following the Commonwealth Act of 1653, parish clerks were ordered to record births and deaths; Woodward (1975). Finlay (1981b), pp. 6–11 provides a short account of legislation relating to parochial registration.

26 Some nonconformists maintained seperate systems. Vann and Eversley (1992) discuss Quaker demography using such sources.

27 Wrigley and Schofield (1981), pp. 485–89. One of these is in Chester, five in Norwich, four in Shrewsbury and eight in Ipswich. No parish which subsequently developed into a large industrial city was included either.

potential' mortality regime – infant mortality rates were high and the population was sufficiently large to ensure that a number of diseases became endemic, which consequently meant that levels of childhood mortality were also very high.[28]

By comparison with what is known about the demography of London, very little can be gleaned from the work that has been carried out on English provincial towns. However, the first national census in 1801 contains sufficient information to provide a broad comparison of urban trends. In order to determine whether the national population was increasing or decreasing, each parish clerk was required to provide totals of baptisms and burials for the period 1781 to 1800 and then at decadal intervals starting in 1780 and going backwards until 1700. These data were then published as a supplement to the census.[29] There are considerable problems associated with this source. In addition to the omissions that may be associated with all parish registers, many of the returns were themselves inaccurate.[30] Arithmetic errors occurred, some clerks did not comply with the order, little account was given to defective registration, nonconformists were ignored and the data were only published for the ancient geographical unit of the hundred which meant that many towns were included together with a substantial rural hinterland. In Bristol the establishment of four private burial grounds in the second half of the eighteenth century renders Rickman's data largely worthless. In spite of these severe reservations, the returns can illustrate the trend in *some* areas (Table 1.2). Given that these data should be viewed with caution, three facts emerge. First, there is considerable variation between individual years, with 1740 being conspicuous as a year of high mortality. Secondly, with the exception of the small town of Lichfield, where natural increase was usual, the first part of the eighteenth century was generally characterized by natural decrease. Thirdly, by the end of the century a more balanced regime is evident in all cities, and as Corfield points out:

> [During the eighteenth century] the balance of burials in many large towns began to change. In the earlier decades the annual total of burials in many large towns surpassed the number of baptisms. By the end of the century that pattern was no longer so clear-cut in an increasing number of large and small urban centres (Corfield, 1982, p. 107).

Whether this implies that there was comparable variation in the birth/death ratio is difficult to say since the problem of assessing levels of under-registration was not addressed. Finally, while changes to mortality, fertility, or both must have occurred at some point during the eighteenth century, it is not possible to determine which changed or by how much.

---

28 Relatively few studies of fertility and nuptiality in the capital have been undertaken. For exceptions see Landers (1990b); Boulton (1987).
29 *1801 Census Parish Registers* (London, 1802).
30 Wrigley and Schofield (1981), pp. 597–630. Appendix 7 deals with Rickman's parish register returns.

Table 1.2: Baptism/burial ratios from Rickman's parish register returns, 1801

Date	Chester	Exeter	Lichfield	Norwich	York
1700	0.86	0.98	1.23	0.92	0.75
1710	0.90	0.96	1.29	0.50	0.95
1720	0.71	1.09	1.10	0.76	0.83
1730	0.92	0.99	0.91	1.06	0.99
1740	0.79	0.49	1.41	0.90	0.61
1750	1.15	1.01	0.90	1.11	0.88
1760	0.61	0.97	1.27	1.11	1.02
1770	0.89	0.93	1.38	0.93	1.08
1780	0.90	0.72	1.14	1.02	0.90
1781–90	0.98	1.12	1.28	0.99	1.01
1791–1800	0.97	1.09	1.37	1.01	1.00
Population 1801	15,052	17,398	4,712	35,944	16,846

Source: *1801 Census.*

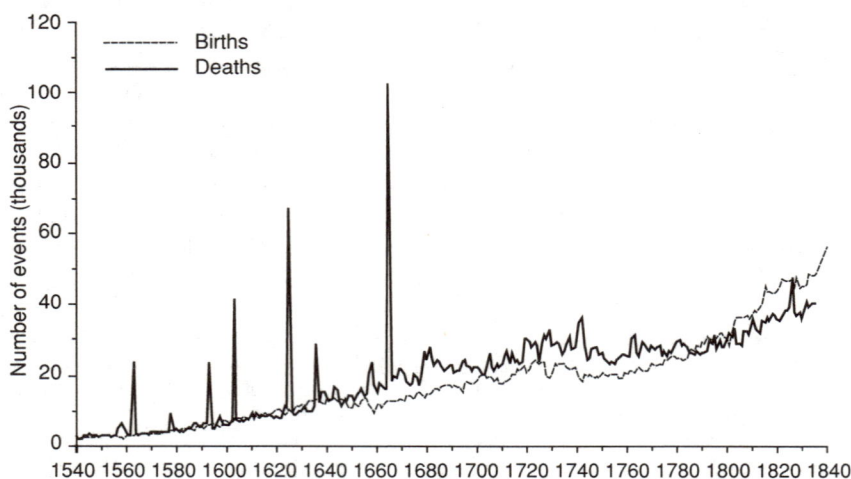

Figure 1.2: Births and deaths, London 1540–1840
Source: see text.

The London Bills of Mortality enable long-term population changes within the capital to be assessed. Wrigley and Schofield used them and by disentangling London from their national figures it is possible to estimate the number of births and deaths in the capital (Fig. 1.2).[31] Three phases in London's demographic history can

31 Figure 1.2 results from a reversal of the process described in Wrigley and Schofield (1981), pp. 77–83 using the data from Table A4.1, pp. 537–52. The graph of baptisms and burials is very similar since the number of births and deaths were calculated by applying national correction ratios to the number of baptisms and burials.

be distinguished. The first lasted until the mid-seventeenth century and is dominated by the effects of one disease – bubonic plague. Periodic outbreaks caused huge increases in the number of deaths, although in non-epidemic years, at least until the 1640s, births matched or even exceeded deaths. Immediately following periods of crisis mortality it was usual for levels of nuptiality and fertility to increase sharply. According to Graunt (1662, p. 38), following an outbreak of plague in 1625 'London was repeopled within two years' with most of this being due to large amounts of in-migration. While it is difficult to determine the long-term consequences of such levels of migration, it appears from Figure 1.2 that in the absence of plague London may have been able to maintain a balanced demography. The second phase, from c.1640 to c.1790, is one of universal natural decrease. After the Great Plague of 1665, surges in mortality become less pronounced, there was a decrease in the number of births between 1640 and 1660 and in each year deaths outnumbered births, often by 30 per cent. From the 1790s natural increase occurred in nearly every year. Landers has shown that mortality increased during the first half of the eighteenth century, then it fell; but clearly substantial changes to both mortality and fertility must have occurred before this date.[32] The fall in the number of births between 1640 and 1660 may however have been due to an increase in birth under-registration. Boulton, in a study of returns from the Marriage Duty Act of 1695 in London, concluded that:

> Few individuals would have escaped burial registration in the capital at the end of the seventeenth century ... Birth registration, on the other hand, caused by religious dissent, may have been running at 17 per cent in the late seventeenth century (Boulton, 1992, p. 252).

Furthermore, since Boulton's conclusions do not take into account any omissions due to unbaptized burials and infant mortality rates were in the region of 300 per 1,000 live births, the gap between baptisms and burials may need to be narrowed even further. London's demographic regime was clearly complex and more work needs to be undertaken in order for it to become fully understood, especially in the period before 1700.

Much less is known about the demography of smaller English towns and cities, although the pattern described above for London may be typical. By the sixteenth century plague was primarily an urban disease striking in what often appeared to be a random manner. Ports and towns in the South East were particularly affected and it is likely that no large English town escaped infection entirely during the early modern period. All cities were not affected equally, however. York suffered only one major outbreak between 1560 and 1670, while Norwich suffered seven and Bristol five (Slack, 1985, pp. 61–62). Norwich was so badly affected by outbreaks that it is virtually impossible to determine any underlying demographic trend in the city (Fig. 1.3). In some years natural increase even occurred. A short-term boost to fertility in

---

32 Landers (1993), pp. 193–95. Outbreaks of plague tend to complicate any attempts to determine underlying levels of mortality, see Finlay (1981c), pp. 111–32; Glass (1972).

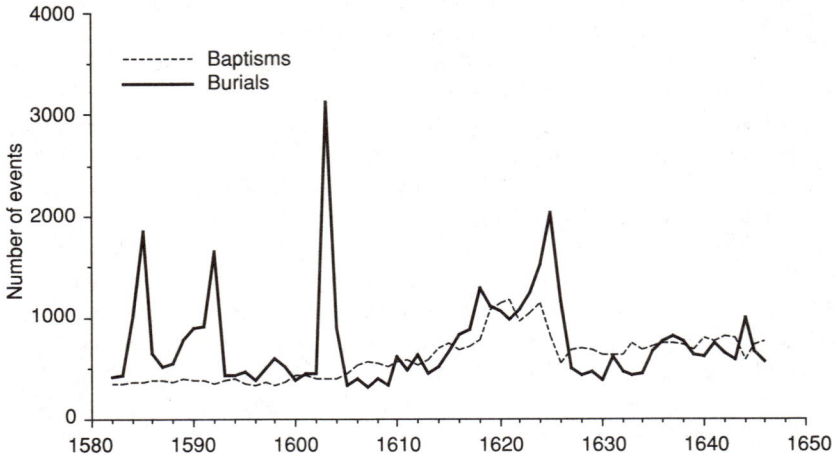

Figure 1.3: Baptisms and burials, Norwich 1582–1646
Source: Allison (1955), p. 607.

the period of recovery following plague may explain the natural increase between 1605 and 1610; yet, natural increase is also evident for most of the period 1627–46 which suggests that Norwich's demography, like that of London, may have been more balanced if plague had been absent.[33] Bubonic plague was a fearsome disease and it could have a devastating impact on a city, with sometimes between a quarter and a third of the inhabitants dying within months. Many also fled from the disease and only returned after an epidemic had subsided. Thus, even though some cities were able to stay free from epidemics for decades, it is unlikely that any large provincial city was able to record overall natural increase during the plague period.

In the post-plague period and between outbreaks of plague it was not unusual for large cities to record more baptisms than burials. Colchester, Ipswich and Reading were all able to produce a surplus of baptisms until at least the early seventeenth century (Goose, 1986, p. 179; 1994, p. 280). Ipswich in particular managed natural increase throughout the entire period 1540-1740 (Reed, 1981, p. 95). Hull, with a population of c.5,000 in 1600, also managed natural increase until the mid-seventeenth century, as did Worcester.[34] Less is known about the demography of the larger provincial cities. One long series of vital events can be constructed and this shows

33 During the eighteenth century Norwich experienced natural decrease until c. 1760; then until the end of the century there was an approximate balance between baptisms and burials when natural increase then became the norm; Edwards (1969).

34 Forster (1969), p. 157; Dyer, (1973), p. 22. This pattern may also have applied to Bristol, since Slack indicates that natural increase occurred in certain parishes of that city; Slack (1977), p. 58.

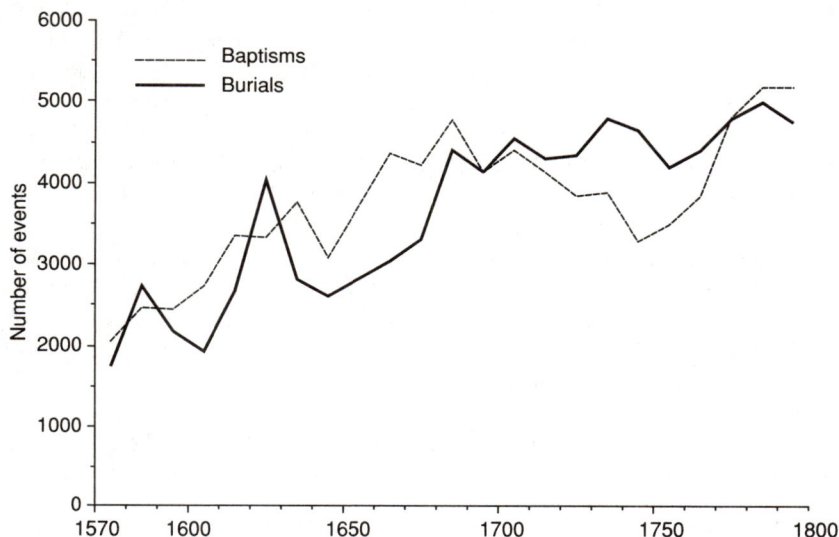

Figure 1.4: Decadal baptisms and burials, Exeter 1570–1800
Source: Pickard (1947), p. 18.

that in Exeter between 1570 and 1700 natural increase was substantial (Fig. 1.4). The data for Exeter are only available in the form of decadal averages and consequently any short-term variations in mortality are smoothed.[35] Natural increase was the norm in most years, although this gave way to natural decrease during the eighteenth century. Exeter appears to show a similar pattern to London and it is interesting to note that the number of baptisms seems to fall even though the population increased between 1700 and 1750. After 1790 natural increase once again occurred. Smaller towns with populations of c.2,000 also appear to have experienced a variety of demographic fortunes. For example, Dewsbury recorded substantial natural increase during the seventeenth century while the fishing port of Bridlington suffered mixed fortunes, recording natural decrease for at least part of the period.[36] Likewise, Barnstaple, Stafford, Gloucester and Portsmouth recorded natural increase and Plymouth, Crediton and Maldon natural decrease (Clark and Slack, 1976, pp. 85–87). During the sixteenth century, Rye experienced substantial natural decrease, although this appears to have been largely due to a succession of severe epidemics (Mayhew, 1976, pp. 45, 270). It would therefore appear that there was no simple urban demographic pattern at least with respect to natural change. Before 1800 it is certain that

35 Slack (1985), p. 62 indicates that Exeter suffered outbreaks of plague in 1590–91 and 1625.
36 Original parish register data supplied by the Cambridge Group for Population and Social Structure.

universal urban natural decrease did not occur, and by the nineteenth century natural increase had become virtually universal. The pattern described for London may have occurred in other cities, although the incidence of plague complicates the picture. Most of the evidence concerning urban natural decrease comes from the late-seventeenth and eighteenth centuries. Mortality decreased between 1750 and 1850 throughout England, and while starting from much higher levels it may have decreased at a greater rate in cities (Wrigley and Schofield, 1981, pp. 241–43; Landers, 1993, pp. 193–95). In London, mortality increased from 1700, although it is not known whether a similar increase affected other cities. Levels of urban mortality changed, and while mortality was a powerful influence on levels of natural change, it was by no means the only one. It is also a source of concern that under-registration may have increased at the same time that natural decrease began to be the norm for many towns. Furthermore, very little is known about levels of urban fertility. Clearly it is difficult to make too many generalizations concerning patterns of natural change in early modern cities. Van der Woude in an analysis of population developments in the northern Netherlands argues similarly that there was no law of 'urban natural decrease'. Instead he proposes that:

> just as the eighteenth century urban surpluses of deaths changed in the first half of the nineteenth century into a balance between births and deaths and even into a surplus of births, why should this have been impossible during the 1575–1650/1675 period that also witnessed a steep growth in the number of urban dwellers? Is it perhaps possible that the very conception of the city as a graveyard for the nation has been based on our knowledge of only a peculiar urban demographic situation or period, i.e. the so-called 17th century demographic crisis with its generally unfavourable relationship between births and deaths? It is likely that a better knowledge of sixteenth century urban demography would cast doubt on the idea of the inevitability of the urban surplus of deaths (van der Woude, 1982, p. 60).

With under-registration being severe in some cities and urban fertility rates by no means constant, it is perhaps not surprising that natural change, being a measure of the relative number of births and deaths in a population, should also be subject to change. Therefore, rather than relying on a measure such as natural change, mortality, fertility and under-registration must be examined separately in order to understand the demographic characteristics of an urban population.

MIGRATION AND URBAN DEMOGRAPHY

Migration, the life blood of all urban communities, is perhaps the most important and least understood aspect of early modern urban demography. Net migration rates can be calculated relatively simply by subtracting natural change from overall population change; but, since little evidence about migration away from towns exists, gross migration rates are virtually impossible to determine.[37] Thus, knowledge of urban migration is limited by the source material, and while it may be possible to infer that

---

37 Where annual population listings have survived, such calculations are straightforward; Reher (1990), pp. 249–63.

most adults would have migrated at some stage in their lives, simple facts, such as the proportion of the urban population who were migrants and the numbers remaining permanently or eventually moving elsewhere, are likely to remain unknown, for English cities at least.[38] Before 1841, when information about birthplace is readily available in the census, a range of quantitative sources such as apprenticeship registers, court depositions, Freemen's and marriage registers may give information about place of origin, thereby revealing the extent of migration fields. Such sources are selective however; they ignore some marginal sections of the population who may be highly mobile and they tend to reinforce the view that most migration to cities was by single people from the countryside.[39] Court deposition data can be more useful since witnesses were sometimes asked to give a short account of their lives and migration histories can then be compiled.[40] Diaries have the potential to be a more illuminating source, but they are socially selective, few in number and were usually written by males (Clark and Souden, 1987, pp. 11–12; Ben-Amos, 1994, pp. 69–83). Two further problems complicate the study of urban migration. One is technical and concerns the area under study. The smaller the area, the higher the rate of mobility is likely to be, since almost every move will result in the crossing of a boundary. This problem often becomes acute when the unit of observation is a small urban parish, since turnover rates could be very high. The second problem concerns the relative lack of source material about female migration. Some women became apprentices and freemen, but they did so in such small numbers to make the quantitative analysis of these data difficult. Deposition data are more helpful, but with little information available about female servants and some women moving to cities after becoming widows the complexities of female migration are likely to remain hidden (Hill, 1994, p. 187). With a few exceptions, complete histories cannot be constructed and consequently the limitations of the source material ensure that only a rudimentary and possibly biased picture of migration is likely to emerge.

According to Clark (1979, p. 59) the reasons why people migrated were twofold: some were forced by necessity while others moved to exploit economic opportunities that were not readily available in their locality; these he classified as 'subsistence' and 'betterment' respectively. The subsistence migrant might have been forced to move for any number of reasons: unemployment, eviction or even, in exceptional circumstances, the threat of famine. Movement was often directed towards towns and cities where prospects for work and charity were greater than in the countryside. In times of stress, especially towards the end of the sixteenth century, citizens viewed any sudden influx of migrants with concern and took measures

---

38 This is not the case for some European cities; de Vries (1984), p. 191. There has been a comparative dearth of published work on migration in recent years, Clark and Souden (1987) being the last major publication in the field, and this consists mainly of reprinted articles.

39 Patten (1973), pp. 11–22. Where a particularly detailed population listing has survived, a different dimension to the subject can be given; Schofield (1970). Unfortunately, no comparable urban listings from the early modern period are known to have survived.

40 Clark (1972) and Goldberg (1992a), make use of this source.

to remove casual migrants in order to exclude them from poor relief (Clark, 1985, pp. 50–54). Surveys of the poor were carried out in many cities, vagrants were regularly moved on, although during the seventeenth century, following economic expansion and increasing levels of urbanization, the perceived threat that vagrants and poor migrants might overwhelm some cities appears to have diminished.[41] Most migration occurred by choice as employment opportunities were taken up in cities. These types of migrant are best exemplified by the apprentice. These so-called 'life-cycle' migrants were young, they often came from rural areas and many moved elsewhere, sometimes returning home, once their period of training had come to an end. Some were eventually able to become 'free' and trade on their own account while others found work as journeymen. Once secure employment had been achieved, marriage became a possibility for many and the transition into urban life was made more permanent. The classification of migrants into 'subsistence' and 'betterment' has its limitations, however. Both 'push' and 'pull' factors certainly affected overall levels of migration, but much of the population could be classified as potential migrants; that is, given the right conditions or opportunities they would be willing to move.[42] This explains why cities were repopulated so quickly following outbreaks of plague. With casual employment easy to obtain in towns and cheap lodgings plentiful, the move to town was a more informal process than is often acknowledged. Reher's work on the small Spanish town of Cuenca has shown that annual turnover rates were near to ten per cent, 'migration levels were extremely intense for people of all ages, sexes and social categories', and he concludes that the whole population shared a common 'culture of mobility' (Reher, 1990, p. 302). This phenomenon may also have applied to English early modern towns, but if it did, it is likely to remain obscured by the sources. The extent to which whole families moved has hardly been addressed in an English context, and in the rapidly expanding towns and cities of the seventeenth and eighteenth centuries a wide range of opportunities must have been available. Many women moved into towns, often to the extent that they outnumbered men. They were frequently employed in some form of service, yet it is difficult to view this as 'betterment', especially when compared with the opportunities available to men. Furthermore, the extent to which women wished to marry and the likelihood of finding a suitable partner were probably important factors influencing the decision to migrate. Many people needed to visit towns in order to use their services, and with some developing into centres of entertainment for the social elite it often became fashionable to own or rent an urban residence. This meant that towns had many visitors and for some, seasonal migration became increasingly important. The reasons why people migrated were diverse, yet for most the decision to migrate was an economic one with the most important influence on the type and level of migration to a particular city being the nature and state of its economy.

---

41 The most famous survey of the poor was conducted in Norwich; Pound (1971). Vagrancy and urban poverty still occurred in the seventeenth century, although its worst effects were mitigated by the Poor Law. For overviews of these topics see Beier (1985) and Slack (1988).

42 The concept of potential migration is discussed in de Vries (1984), pp. 214–17.

Table 1.3: The population of Lichfield, 1695

Age	Bachelors	Spinsters	Husbands	Wives	Widowers	Widows	Total
0-	167	201					368
5-	227	183					410
10-	156	127					283
15-	136	170		1			307
20-	44	125	15	22			206
25-	49	72	38	69	1	3	232
30-	9	25	68	81	7	5	195
35-	6	22	105	87	7	29	256
40-	1	3	52	43	4	16	119
45-	1	1	66	46	6	13	133
50-	1	2	21	22	3	12	61
55-	4		37	38	8	25	112
60-	2	1	17	23	3	22	68
65-		1	21	10	8	41	81
70-			2	1	2	9	14
75-	1				4	5	10
80-					1	2	3
85-					1	1	2
90-							0
95-						1	1
Total	804	933	442	443	55	184	2,861

Source: Glass (1965), p. 181.

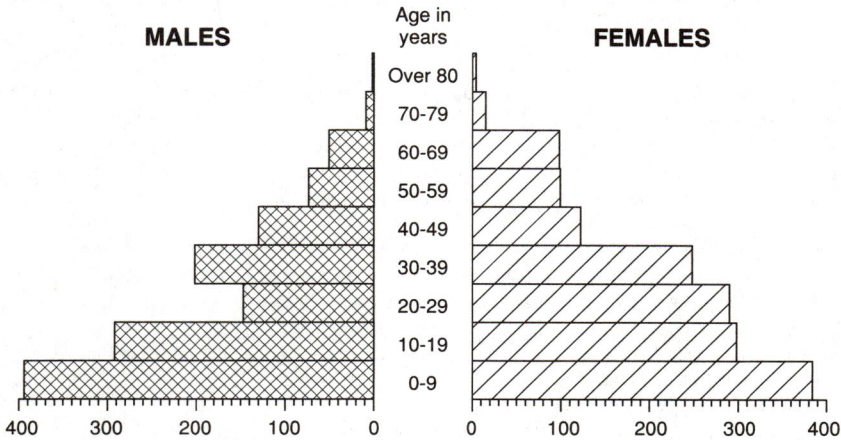

Figure 1.5: The age-sex structure of Litchfield, 1695
Source: See Table 1.3.

Without access to the types of register that are available for Scandinavian populations, the effect of migration on urban demographic regimes cannot be fully determined.[43] Some of its consequences can be inferred, however. Much migration was both age- and sex-specific and this often caused distortions in urban age-sex structures. Figure 1.5 shows the population structure of Lichfield, the largest seventeenth-century city for which such evidence exists.[44] Due to high levels of mortality and fertility, most early modern populations will have had age-sex structures that resemble a pyramid and in Lichfield it appears that large numbers of males in their 20s were missing.[45] It could be concluded from this that most would have been apprentices who had moved out on a temporary basis in order to obtain training, but once the population is divided up by marital status a more complex picture emerges (Table 1.3). The overall sex ratio of the population was 83 males per 100 females and for adults (over 15) this figure decreases to 72. The excess females, not surprisingly, were mainly young single women, although there were also a large number of older widows 'who resort to great Towns for Conveniency of Living'.[46] Only eight spinsters aged over 40 were recorded and for most women wishing to live permanently in Lichfield it would appear that marriage was necessary even though widows seem to have experienced no such problems. King's alternative figures give additional information.[47] These show that there was a greater demand for female rather than male servants and more daughters were able to remain at home. The core of Lichfield's population comprised those who were married together with their children (77 per cent); in addition there were servants (eight per cent), sojourners (six per cent) and the once married (nine per cent). These classifications are somewhat crude; they do not mention apprentices and do not allow for some widows or children being employed as servants. The age-sex profile of Lichfield does, however, illustrate the extent to which age- and sex-specific patterns of in- and out-migration, presumably resulting from internal economic demand, may affect the overall composition of the population. Lichfield's marriage market appears to have been dynamic even, though

43 In addition to recording vital events, Swedish population registers note movements into and out of parishes; see Kälvemark (1977).

44 King (1973), p.93. The figures quoted are for the city, excluding the Cathedral Close. The enumeration appears to have been made by King himself, in part to verify the accuracy of returns for the city made as result of the Marriage Duty Act. This alternative enumeration gives 2,833 for the city and 205 for the Cathedral Close (see p. 91).

45 King appears to have made considerable effort to ensure the accuracy of the Lichfield listing. There are some problems with the age data, however. Only 48 infants were recorded compared with 70 aged one and 103 aged two, although this was partly a consequence of a recent smallpox epidemic. There was also some age heaping since there were greater numbers with ages ending 5, 6, 7, 8, 9 compared with those ending 0, 1, 2, 3, 4; King (1973), p. 93. King performed several calculations aimed at adjusting Lichfield's age-sex structure; see Glass (1965), pp. 207–10.

46 Letter from King quoted in Glass (1965), p. 206.

47 King (1973), pp. 90–91 provides the following breakdown: Houses – 616; People – 2,833; Males – 1,273; Females – 1,560; Husbands – 462; Wives – 462; Widowers – 52; Widows – 191; Sons – 582; Daughters – 684; Men Servants – 96; Female Servants – 143; Single People or Sojourners: male – 81; female – 80.

remarriage for widows was difficult and those spinsters unable to find marriage partners eventually moved elsewhere.[48] The ease with which marriage was possible, either through the availability of suitable marriage partners or the existence of favourable economic conditions for the establishment of new households, was therefore both an important consequence and determinant of migration (Smith, 1981a). Furthermore, the number of couples who marry and the age at which they do so were crucial in determining overall levels of fertility and a small increase in the numbers getting married, especially if they are young, could have a considerable effect on overall levels of fertility.[49]

Table 1.4: Urban sex-ratios (males per 100 females)

Place	Date	Sex-ratio
Coventry* (adults only)	1523	72.0
Bristol	1696	80.2
Gloucester	1696	81.0
Lichfield	1696	81.4
Ipswich	1695	82.0
Southampton	1696	82.4
Bury St Edmonds	1695	85.7
London† (40 parishes)	1695	86.7
Leicester	1696–99	87.1
Norwich	1696	92.5

Sources: * Phythian-Adams (1979), p. 200.
       † Glass (1972), p. 278.
      Rest – Souden (1984), p. 150.

Complete population listings giving status and exact ages do not exist for other early modern towns, although it is possible to determine the sex-ratios of some English cities (Table 1.4). All had excess females in their populations and since most of the figures in Table 1.4 refer to the sex-ratio of the whole population, as with Lichfield, any imbalance is likely to have been greatest amongst sections of the adult population. The sex-ratio at birth is about 105 males per 100 females in most populations, and while males generally suffered higher rates of mortality at all ages, there should still be an approximate balance between male and female children (Pressat and Wilson, 1985, pp. 205–07). The late seventeenth century was a period of population stagnation throughout England and it is uncertain whether the excess

48 Schofield (1984a), p. 14 infers that the proportion of females remaining celibate by age 45 in this period was near to 10 per cent.
49 With low levels of illegitimacy, most births were confined to marriage. The proportion of married females under 45 was 303 out of 2,861 (10.6 per cent).

Table 1.5: Sex-ratios at burial from Rickman's parish register returns, 1801

Date	Chester	Exeter	Lichfield	Norwich	York
1700	83	88	77	93	100
1710	79	94	78	106	98
1720	89	97	98	101	99
1730	87	89	77	129	100
1740	103	88	97	98	99
1750	86	93	188	85	91
1760	140	78	53	106	93
1770	110	84	82	92	105
1780	102	99	115	114	86
1781–90	94	89	103	93	94
1791–1800	95	90	115	93	99

Source: *1801 Census.*

of women in cities was simply caused by the employment of a greater number of female domestic servants or whether more opportunities existed for males in rural areas and towns were consequently forced to recruit more females.[50] It is therefore particularly unfortunate that most early modern urban listings have survived from this period. Evidence from late fourteenth-century Poll Tax Returns suggests that some urban populations were more balanced, although there were considerable variations (Goldberg, 1992b, pp. 372–73). Souden examined sex-ratios at burial and inferred a similar situation during the early part of the seventeenth century.[51] By the eighteenth century the sex-structure of cities varied and was subject to change (Table 1.5). For much of the eighteenth century York appears to have had a balanced population, Norwich one that favoured males, while in Chester, Exeter and Lichfield there were greater numbers of females. However, all these figures are based on small numbers of burials. There was also some volatility; the composition of Lichfield's population appears to have changed in a relatively short time, as did Chester's, although in opposite directions. Given high turnover rates, patterns of migration could change relatively quickly, thereby significantly altering the age/sex structure of urban populations. This could create a situation where for some, marriage opportunities became limited; alternatively, the opposite may easily have occurred. Whatever happened in individual cities, migration had the potential to be an important influence on urban demographic regimes. The presence of any temporary migrants created a greater

50 Souden (1984b), p. 150 showed that the sex ratio was 100 for 33 villages in Northamptonshire, Wiltshire and Kent villages during the same period.

51 Souden (1984b), p. 158. Souden's conclusion was based on data from the following urban parishes: Bristol St Augustine, Banbury, Bury St Edmunds St James, Ludlow, Otterly St Mary. By analysing Rickman's parish register returns Souden concluded that in the eighteenth century and probably before, there were distinctive regional patterns in the balance between the sexes. Souden (1987).

population at risk and consequently a greater number of deaths occurred. Furthermore, it is likely that some of these individuals would not have acquired immunity from the diseases common or endemic in cities and mortality rates within the migrant population may have been higher than in the resident population.[52] Migration also has the potential to affect fertility rates.[53] A migration flow resulting in a particularly skewed sex-ratio may affect the overall proportion married, but with the 'reproductive value' of migrants being high – their ability to marry and have children when they arrive in cities – the numbers who marry, the age at which they do so and the length of time they remain in the city unmarried are all factors which may alter the demographic balance. The links between migration and nuptiality are complex, however. Within a city experiencing considerable economic expansion it might be assumed that there would be plenty of opportunities to set up new businesses and marry. While the desire to marry may be evident, the ability to marry is dependent on a number of factors, not the least of which is finding a suitable partner. Given an almost unending stream of young migrants circulating through early modern cities it might be thought that it would be easy to find a spouse. For some at least this was true. However, given a distorted age-sex structure resulting from a skewed migration stream this may result in only a relatively small proportion of the population being able to marry. These issues are clearly inter-related and it is probable that they cannot be entirely resolved given the limitations of the source material. Nevertheless, the number of migrants who marry will substantially affect the level of births, deaths and natural change in early modern urban populations.

CONCLUSION: CITIES AND ENGLISH POPULATION HISTORY

Throughout the early modern period the demography of towns differed considerably from most of the rest of the country and increasing levels of urbanization will therefore have serious consequences for English population history if insufficient weight is given to the urban sector.[54] Table 1.6 illustrates some of the consequences of urban growth between 1600 and 1800.[55] If all towns with populations greater than 5,000 did not experience natural increase, then this growth could only have been possible

52 For a discussion of mortality theories see Landers (1993), pp. 7–39; McNeill (1980).
53 For the effects of migration on the fertility of a pre-industrial town it is instructive to look at some Japanese examples. Saito (1990), p. 219 maintains that changing employment practices affected demographic patterns, 'while the existence of servants and apprentices tended to create an imbalance in the marriage market, casualized labour was likely to be associated with more balanced sex-ratios and higher proportions married among people of childbearing age and consequently with higher overall birth rates'. Sasaki (1985), p. 153 also shows that in addition to high levels of mortality, the city of Takayama experienced low levels of fertility.
54 For the nineteenth century see Woods (1985).
55 Woods (1989), Table 6.1 compares London's growth with that in provincial England. Some population estimates used in Table 1.6 may be subject to error; but this does not alter the conclusion that substantial urban growth occurred throughout the period. For a discussion of London's population, see Harding (1990).

Table 1.6: Urban growth and natural increase

a) The urban population of England (in 000s)

Date	London	Towns >5,000
1600	200	135
1675	475	205
1700	575	275
1750	675	540
1801	960	1,420

b) The consequences of urban growth (in 000s)

Period	Population increase		Natural increase London	Required rural–urban migration	Natural increase provincial England
	London	Other towns			
1600–75	275	70	−331	676	1,499
1675–1700	100	70	−181	351	93
1701–50	100	265	−336	701	771
1751–1801	285	880	−198	1,363	2,196

Sources: Wrigley (1985b), p. 688; Wrigley and Schofield (1981), Table 6.5, p. 168.

through in-migration and hence must have been dependent on natural increase in the rest of England, assuming that large-scale immigration did not occur.[56] For much of the period urban growth was accommodated by the natural increase within provincial England. The period 1675–1700 was an exception, however, since London and the towns could only have continued to grow, assuming the figures for population and natural change are correct, if there was considerable rural depopulation. While London's migration field encompassed the whole country, as migration horizons contracted towards the end of the seventeenth century the effects on some of the parishes immediately surrounding the capital must have been staggering (Boulton, 1987b, p. 108; Dobson, 1989). Moreover, while some who migrated in the period 1675–1700 will have been born in the earlier period, those who did were the survivors from a larger cohort.[57] Thus, at all times urbanization soaked up at least half the natural increase in the country and between 1675 and 1750 this must have resulted in rural depopulation. Furthermore, if smaller towns also experienced substantial levels of natural decrease, then the 'cost' to the rest of the country would have been even greater. While the figures given in Table 1.6 can only be approxi-

56 Wrigley and Schofield (1981), pp. 528–29 show that net emigration occurred in the period.
57 This point is made in Wrigley (1967). Such calculations are based on net migration rates and the estimates need to be inflated to take into account those moving to towns on a temporary basis.

mate, one thing is certain – urban demography had an increasing influence on national population trends, and the greater the difference between town and country, the greater the impact of urbanization becomes. Moreover, with London experiencing considerable changes in its demography during the period, similar changes in the smaller towns may compound these effects, especially given the excessive mortality in the capital at the beginning of the eighteenth century. A greater knowledge of the demography of provincial towns will clearly help to clarify some of these issues, but before this is attempted via a case study of York, a synthesis of what is already known about urban demography needs to be given.

Two aspects of urban demography have tended to dominate much that is written about the subject: natural population decrease and high mortality, with the link between both being stressed in most cases. Mortality rates were considerably higher in towns compared with the majority of rural areas.[58] This rural-urban gradient persisted until the twentieth century and its cause is relatively simple to determine. A combination of extremely insanitary conditions coupled with high levels of population density meant that transmission of disease was easy; infant and childhood mortality rates were high, although once an individual had been exposed to the urban disease pool there is the possibility that adult urban mortality rates, about which very little is known, may not have been significantly higher than rural ones.[59] The relative abundance of material about mortality has led to a consequent neglect of fertility. Few urban fertility rates have been calculated and, more importantly, the extent to which nuptiality and differential population structures influenced overall levels of fertility still remains obscured as high turnover rates compound the problem. Evidence from a variety of cities suggests that urban natural decrease was by no means universal, and whilst it is difficult to generalize, three phases in a city's demographic history are usually apparent, as indeed occurred in London. Until c.1670 the demography of English towns was dominated by the effects of plague, with mortality rates of 25–33 per cent in a single year being not unusual. In non-plague years natural increase may have occurred especially in smaller cities, and while many towns experienced long periods without the disease, a single outbreak could wipe out any accumulated natural increase almost instantaneously. From 1650 to c.1750 most cities experienced natural decrease, although during this period there is the possibility that substantial under-registration affected some places. Even though levels of under-registration probably increased further after 1750, baptism/burial ratios show that natural decrease gradually gave way to natural increase during the second half of the eighteenth century in all places. The explanation for these changes must be that levels of mortality, fertility, under-registration or some combination of all three varied during the period. While such changes have been well documented at the national

58 There were exceptions of course, most notably in the Fens where mortality rates matched or even exceeded those in cities; Dobson (1992), pp. 81–89.
59 High rates of turnover mean that few adults were born and buried in the same parish and reconstitution studies reveal little about adult mortality rates which then usually have to be inferred from model life tables. For the problems inherent in this method, see Woods (1993).

level, the pattern in cities is less apparent, although clearly there were likely to have been considerable local variations (Wrigley and Schofield, 1981). Whatever levels of mortality and natural change were, the fortunes of individual cities were largely independent of their demography. London suffered the highest mortality rates yet it still managed spectacular growth. Urbanization continued without interruption from the mid-sixteenth century, even during periods of national population stagnation. The key variable appears to have been the state of the urban economy, and given favourable conditions there always appear to have been sufficient potential migrants ready, willing and able to take their chance in the city. Throughout the early modern period cities were attractive to migrants at all times, many urban economies grew and this provided a powerful stimulus to the whole country.[60]

60 See Wrigley (1978) for a discussion of the economic relationship between towns and the countryside.

Chapter 2

ECONOMY AND SOCIETY: YORK, 1500–1800

York ... next to London claimeth Priority of all other Cities in England; a place of great antiquity and fame ... a fair, large and beautiful City, adorned with many splendid buildings, both publick and private, is very populous, much resorted unto and well inhabited by Gentry, and wealthy Trades-men.[1]

York's success resulted in part from its location. Situated on a moraine at the confluence of the Foss and the Ouse, it lies at the heart of a low-lying, pastoral area known as the Vale of York. With most of Yorkshire's river system draining through the Vale and the Great North Road passing only a few miles to the west, direct and easy access was available to an area stretching from Cumbria to the north Midlands. York was a natural focus for the region and its sphere of influence extended in varying degrees throughout the north. The city provided a market place for local agricultural produce and merchants congregated there, transporting their goods down the tidal Ouse to Hull and often on to London or the continent. By the medieval period York was recognized as England's second city with Richard II coming close to making it his capital and the government removing there for a short period at the beginning of the fourteenth century (Tillot, 1961, p. 54). Despite a period of decline in the late fifteenth and early sixteenth centuries York recovered and developed into an important administrative and social centre. Throughout the whole of the sixteenth and seventeenth centuries it remained one of England's largest and most important cities.

John Speed's map, engraved in 1610, shows the topography of York during the early Stuart period (Fig. 2.1).[2] The walled city is approximately square with each side measuring about two-thirds of a mile. Opposite the main gates were small suburban developments which contained roughly 15 per cent of York's total population at this time. Speed's map was accurately surveyed, but only the main thoroughfares are shown and many of the smaller alleys are missing; nevertheless, it is clear that the centre was densely populated whilst towards the walls, especially in the south and east, there were many open spaces, fields and orchards. The parishes near the walls and in the suburbs would therefore have provided a striking contrast with the more affluent built-up central parishes (Palliser, 1982, pp. 88–89; 1983, p. 205). Speed's map highlights how the city was physically dominated by the Minster, which together with its archbishop, courts and large administrative structure made York an

---

1 Richard Blome (1673), quoted in Palliser and Palliser (1979), p. 23.
2 This is the earliest map of the whole city. Other maps are discussed in Royal Commission on Historical Monuments (1972), pp. xxxii–xxxvi.

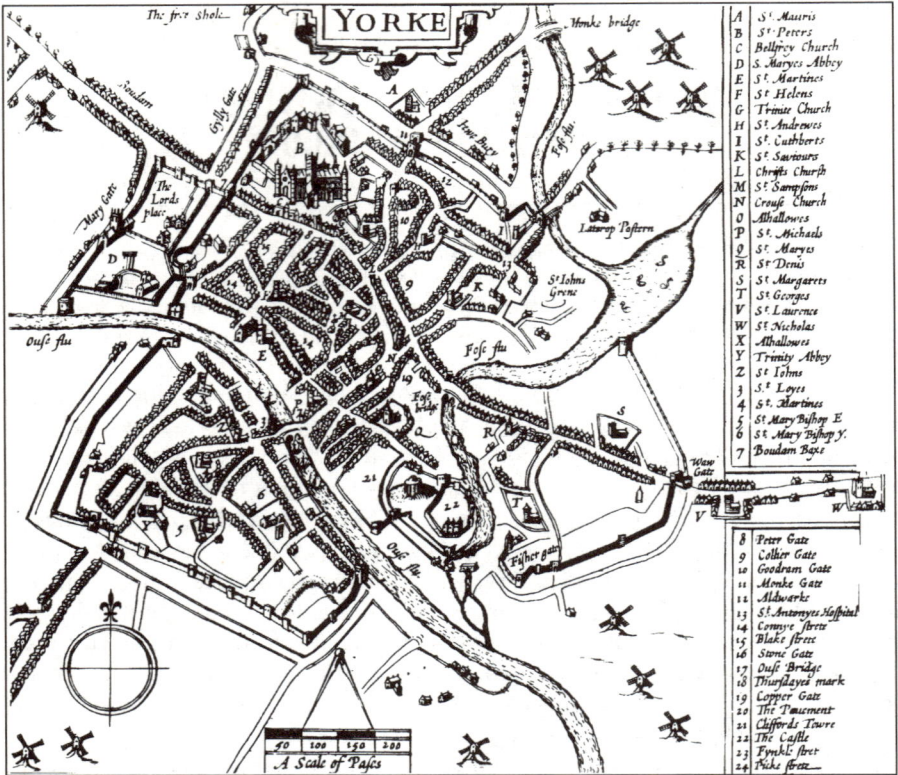

Figure 2.1: John Speed's map of York, c.1610

ecclesiastical centre second only to London. The other dominant building in York was Clifford's Tower, which stood on a mound alongside the Castle. Together, these formed the legal and military heart of the city. Varying numbers of troops were garrisoned in the Castle, which also housed the city's principal gaol. Apart from the parish churches and St Mary's Abbey, the remaining building of importance was the King's Manor.[3] In 1561 this became the permanent home to the King's Council in the Northern Parts, a powerful court which controlled the north of England on behalf of the Privy Council. The Minster, Castle and King's Manor made York the most important provincial administrative centre. They also brought much business to the city and helped it to recover from the recession of the early sixteenth century. Relatively few people were directly involved in administration, however. Instead, in common with most early modern towns, most of the population was employed in

---

3 This is marked as the Lord's Place on Speed's Map.

either manufacture or distribution. This ensured that most of York's economy was broadly based with its various sectors being of local, regional, national and even international importance.

YORK'S CHANGING ECONOMY 1500–1800

During the medieval and early modern periods York experienced fluctuating economic fortunes. Throughout it remained a regional capital and a major trading and distribution centre, but at various times it was also an important centre for industrial manufacture, administration and the social elite. By the beginning of the fifteenth century York's economy was based on the manufacture and distribution of woollens; merchants moved into the city, exports increased and trades serving consumer demand flourished.[4] York's prosperity proved to be short-lived, however. By the 1460s most of its manufacturing capacity had relocated to the West Riding, where conditions for clothmaking were more favourable, and in 1561 only ten weavers were employed in the city and these worked in linen, not wool (Dickens, 1961, p. 125). There was also some loss of overseas trade and by the first half of the sixteenth century the city was in recession. Recovery occurred slowly from around 1560 as trade increased steadily and exports via Hull recovered (Palliser, 1979, pp. 260–87). Throughout the seventeenth century York's economy remained successful, although problems occurred in the wake of the Civil War when disruption to trade and the abolition of the two courts caused a short period of recession (Wilson, 1967, pp. 281–83). York's market economy remained strong, however, and slowly the city developed into an entertainment centre for the social elite, a role in which it became pre-eminent during the eighteenth century.

In spite of periods of growth and recession for much of the sixteenth and seventeenth centuries, York's economic base remained fundamentally the same. Without recourse to measures which may indicate the amount of trade carried out in York, the simplest method of investigating York's economy is to examine its occupational structure via an analysis of admissions to the Freedom (Collins, 1900). The admissions register is not an ideal source, however.[5] While up to a half of households were headed by Freemen, it is difficult to know how non-Freemen were employed. The Register also omits females almost entirely, since between 1500 and 1603 only 44 women out of a total of 6,231 were enroled. Many would have been widows carrying on their husbands' trade, and with females being employed in a wide variety of occupations, it is difficult to quantify their overall contribution to the economy.[6] Furthermore, most Freemen listed only their principal occupation, yet bi-employment

4 Between 1331 and 1371 there was a sixteenfold increase in traders associated with wool; see Bartlett, (1959), p. 23.
5 See Dobson (1973), pp. 1–22 for a discussion of this source. Swanson (1989) employs a range of additional sources in order to examine York's occupational structure, although Palliser (1979), p. 148 shows that the Freemen's Register still provides a good indication of York's occupational structure.
6 For York in the medieval period see Goldberg (1983); Thwaites (1984); Willen (1988); Wright (1985 and 1989).

Table 2.1: Percentage admissions to the Freedom by trading group, York 1500–1699

Trade	1500–24	1525–49	1550–74	1575–99	1600–24	1625–49	1650–74	1675–99
Textiles	9.7	8.3	6.3	3.8	6.0	7.5	7.4	5.7
Clothing	10.1	10.1	12.8	13.6	16.8	13.6	11.0	4.9
Leather	13.9	14.8	17.3	17.4	16.4	17.2	18.9	15.7
Building	6.0	5.7	6.2	6.1	5.0	3.8	7.0	8.5
Woodwork	4.2	4.5	3.2	4.2	4.8	4.8	4.5	6.4
Metal	9.8	10.9	11.5	9.9	8.2	6.3	8.6	10.0
Distributive	15.3	16.5	13.3	20.0	18.9	21.4	16.8	17.6
Transport	3.1	2.7	2.6	3.3	1.8	1.0	2.8	2.8
Food and drink	16.8	18.0	18.3	18.3	17.1	17.1	13.2	14.5
Professional	6.4	3.1	2.7	0.6	1.6	1.7	2.8	3.7
Miscellaneous	4.6	5.5	6.0	3.0	3.3	5.6	7.1	10.2

Source: see Appendix 1.

was commonplace.[7] An example of this is to be found in the brewing trade which was essentially a domestic occupation often carried out by women. A list from 1596 of York innholders, tiplers and brewers records at least 75 per cent having had a second occupation and it is often more useful to consider the whole family as the unit of production rather than just the head of household.[8] Despite these reservations, the Freemen's Register is still useful since it indicates the most important occupations in York (Table 2.1). Considerable stability occurred throughout the period 1500–1700, with the food and drink, clothing, leather and distribution trades accounting for over 50 per cent of Freemen admissions, figures that are typical of many smaller English market towns.[9] Significant numbers were also employed in the building and metal working trades with smaller numbers in textiles and woodwork. Compositional effects caused some of the changes within Table 2.1. The increasing importance of the miscellaneous section was partly due to a diversification of trade, but also to the success of the Labourer's guild which became involved in the organization and control of labour towards the end of the seventeenth century. The clothing trades show a decline after 1650 which was largely a consequence of the formation of the Merchant Taylors who were involved with the distribution of cloth both at home and abroad.[10] Ignoring these effects, there were few changes to York's occupational struc-

---

7 Swanson (1989) shows that many craftsmen had to resort to other occupations in order to survive. Also, see Pelling (1982).

8 Cooper (1928–29), pp. 292–301. Of the 251 individuals listed, 229 were male, 21 were described as 'widow' and one as 'singlewoman'.

9 Clarkson (1971), pp. 88–89. Alternate groupings are possible and it is sometimes difficult to decide where to place certain trades; for instance, do shoemakers (cordwainers) belong with the leather or clothing trades? For a complete analysis of the registers see Appendix 1.

10 With the formation of the Merchant Taylors there was a fall in the number of both merchants and tailors gaining the Freedom. Even though there was little change in the actual work being carried out, the problem of choosing where to place the Merchant Taylors illustrates the difficulty of assigning trades to particular groupings.

ture during the sixteenth and seventeenth centuries. Table 2.1 reveals that York was principally a service centre with its food and drink sectors being particularly important.[11]

Table 2.2: Ten most common occupations from York's Freemen's register

	1500–24			*1525–49*			*1550–74*	
1.	Merchant	94	Tailor	112	Tailor	154
2.	Tailor	85	Merchant	109	Merchant	111
3.	Cordwainer	62	Tapiter	68	Baker	78
4.	Fisher	46	Cordwainer	65	Cordwainer	69
5.	Butcher	44	Tanner	62	Tanner	62
6.	Baker	43	Baker	51	Butcher	61
7.	Tanner	39	Butcher	49	Glover	45
8.	Tapiter	38	Miller	43	Innholder	40
9.	Haberdasher	35	Grocer	42	Carpenter	36
10.	Miller	30	Fisher	38	Tiler	36

	1575–99			*1600–24*			*1625–49*	
1.	Tailor	170	Tailor	220	Tailor	190
2.	Merchant	157	Merchant	126	Merchant	169
3.	Cordwainer	80	Cordwainer	90	Cordwainer	117
4.	Baker	76	Butcher	75	Baker	91
5.	Innholder	70	Innholder	71	Tanner	71
6.	Tanner	65	Baker	70	Butcher	58
7.	Butcher	60	Tanner	69	Miller	53
8.	Glover	54	Glover	56	Mercer	53
9.	Draper	40	Joiner	48	Labourer	48
10	Joiner	38	Haberdasher	46	Glover	41
			Mercer	46		

	1650–74			*1675–99*	
1.	Tailor	193	Labourer	105
2.	Cordwainer	142	Cordwainer	101
3.	Tanner	95	Baker	82
4.	Baker	88	Merchant Taylor	77
5.	Labourer	77	Tanner	69
6.	Merchant	76	Carpenter	68
7.	Butcher	70	Bricklayer	68
8.	Mercer	65	Butcher	61
9.	Bricklayer	62	Tailor	59
10.	Carpenter	57	Merchant	54

Source: see Appendix 1.

11 Clarkson (1971), pp. 88–89. This was also true of other regional capitals.

The ten leading occupations in the Freemen's lists are given in Table 2.2.[12] At the head of each list are the tailors and merchants, although the prevalence of these trades is once again complicated after 1662 by the Merchant Taylors. Table 2.2 shows the importance of the cloth trade to York's economy even though it was no longer manufactured in the city. Cloth was often transported over long distances to the city and merchants were frequently the richest members of society, dominating the council until at least 1660 (Wilson, 1967, pp. 43–71). The need to feed and clothe an urban population is reflected in each list by the butchers and bakers and the leather trades of cordwainer and tanner. Labourers make their first appearance after 1625 and by 1675–99 they are the leading craft. Interestingly, innholders only appear between 1550 and 1624, coinciding with the Council in the North's residency in York. The building trades of carpenter, bricklayer and joiner frequently appear and throughout the table there is a remarkable consistency. With the exception of merchants and those trading in cloth, most of York's leading trades were those that catered to the local market. York was a major regional centre and had large numbers of traditional specialized occupations such as goldsmiths, glaziers and musicians. By 1700 it was also home to a thriving book trade and had a number of craftsmen manufacturing luxury consumer goods like rugs, clocks, and tobacco-pipes (Appendix 1; Forster, 1961, p. 167). There is little evidence of industrial development or of significant changes within York's occupational structure, and this remains the key to understanding why its population was not able to increase substantially until the second half of the eighteenth century. Despite problems, York's market economy remained strong and resilient throughout most of the period 1500–1800.

With its civil and ecclesiastical courts, the county gaol and, at times, a sizeable garrison, York had always been an important administrative centre and this brought considerable benefits to the city. Twice-yearly assizes, accompanied by many social gatherings, were held at the Castle and these led the gentry to visit York regularly. The Castle also housed the county gaol which in 1606 had as many as 140 prisoners; it was also a defensive stronghold and acted as the legal and military focal point of the city (Palliser, 1982, pp. 94–95). In 1569 as a result of the rising of the northern Earls a force of 3,000 was stationed in York to protect the city and even larger numbers of troops were sent to the city during the Civil War (Palliser, 1979, pp. 4, 88, 270). Above all, between 1561 and 1641, the most important court outside London, the Kings Council in the North, together with its religious equivalent, the Ecclesiastical Commission, were based in the city.[13] Initially, the Council had transferred from town to town throughout the north; but in 1561 it became permanently established in York at the King's Manor. The responsibility of the Council was the day-to-day administration of northern England while the Ecclesiastical Commission was a new body specifically set up to enforce the religious settlement following the accession

---

12 Also, see Palliser (1979), p. 159. The discrepancies between Palliser's figures and those in Appendix 1 result from a slightly different periodization and some grouping together of trades. Any differences are slight, however.
13 The standard history of the Council in the North is Reid (1921).

of Elizabeth in 1558. Both courts were busy, they attracted much business to the city and the establishment of these courts must be seen as one of the primary reasons why York was able to achieve economic recovery during the late sixteenth century.[14] Without records it is difficult to quantify the economic gain that the courts brought to the city, but it has been estimated that the Council in the North alone heard between 1,000 and 2,000 cases each year (Palliser, 1979, p. 4; Reid, 1921, pp. 344, 359). Perhaps 400 cases per year were brought before the Ecclesiastical Commission, while one of several minor church courts heard 243 cases between 20 October 1585 and 13 January 1586.[15] Each case would have required at least one visit for any non-York resident claimants, and with the majority of the litigants being better-off, this influx of relatively wealthy visitors caused money to flow into the city. The hospitality trades had always been an important feature of York's economy and the city had an enormous capacity for lodging travellers. A survey as early as 1537 reveals that there were 1,035 beds for hire, coupled with others in the city liberties and perhaps another 200–300 kept by merchants (Palliser, 1979, p. 166). In 1596 there were 68 innholders, 79 brewers and 104 tiplers licensed in the city and these figures rose sharply over the next decade.[16] By 1606 the number of tiplers had risen to 156 and while many inns and ale-houses were probably small, one inn alone had the capacity for stabling over 200 horses (Palliser, 1979, p. 167). It is therefore no coincidence to discover that the food and drink trades were of greatest importance when the courts were in residence (Table 2.1). The Council had a permanent staff of around 30 to organize the proceedings and in all 'there were probably over 100 people connected with the service of the Council'.[17] Solicitors and lawyers were needed to prepare cases and a number of new wealthy households must have been set up in the city whose presence would have provided a further stimulus to trade. The housing of the Council in the King's Manor also meant substantial rebuilding which gave a boost to the building trades at a time when little new public building had been taking place. Few people were directly employed by the courts, but their contribution to York's economy was such that it is not surprising to discover that when they were abolished, the city corporation made frequent appeals for their restoration. The church courts also continued to thrive until the 1640s when they were discontinued following the collapse of royal rule. In 1660 the ordinary church courts, but not the Ecclesiastical Commission, were restored with the new King. Business was once again brisk, although it never quite matched the period before 1640 (Sharpe, 1980, p. 8).

---

14 Palliser (1979), pp. 260–87. During the same period the traditional church and secular courts also increased their workloads; see Marchant (1969), p. 1.

15 Palliser (1979), p. 5; Sharpe (1980), p. 6. Numbers of causes entering York's Consistory and Chancery courts are given in Marchant (1969), pp. 62, 68.

16 Cooper (1928–29), pp. 292–301. Over ten per cent of York's households must have been connected with the drink trade.

17 Brookes (1954), p. 7. The President of the Council had an annual salary of £1,000 and brought with him a very large and prosperous household. For instance, in 1561 he asked for stabling for 36 horses when he made a trip to Newcastle.

By the early eighteenth century Drake, York's eminent historian, could write that:

> What has been, and is, the chief support of the city ... is the resort to and residence of several
> country gentlemen with their families in it ... there is no place, out of London, so polite and ele-
> gant to live in.[18]

With its race meetings, riverside walks and many fine buildings, York was a natural
meeting place for the social elite. Some had permanent residences in the city, others
made frequent visits. Gradually a fashionable 'season' developed around the assizes
which caused a considerable influx of wealth which stimulated the luxury trades and
created new leisure facilities. According to Borsay:

> Among the provincial capitals the most prestigious rendezvous was York ... By the early eigh-
> teenth century pleasure, and those who sought it, were critical to York's livelihood ... The city's
> position as the fashionable metropolis of the North was strengthened in the 1730s by a burst of
> civic and commercial investment in a theatre, race-course, assembly room, and walk (Borsay,
> 1989, pp. 30–31).

To some extent, York had always been an important social centre. With its fine
churches and Minster, York had attracted visitors and tourists since medieval times.[19]
At the beginning of Elizabeth's reign there were 447 gentry families living in Yorkshire, and according to Palliser 'they would regularly come to York for the assizes,
the election of knights of the shire or simply to meet socially and buy in the shops'
(Palliser, 1979, p. 15). By 1642 this number had risen to 679, and visits to York for
a variety of reasons had become commonplace (Palliser, 1979, pp. 15–18). The
national courts further stimulated gentry involvement in the city and the diary of
Lady Margaret Hoby, whose husband was a member of the Council in the North,
gives a good example of this process (Meads, 1930). She records going to York
mainly for social reasons although also to shop, consult lawyers, obtain medical
advice and by 1600 the Hobys had purchased a town house because of her husband's
business commitments. Throughout the seventeenth century York increased in
importance as a social centre and at the beginning of the Civil War there were at least
24 nobles and gentry who owned property in the city (Palliser, 1979, pp. 27–28).
Some of these residences were large with the 1674 Hearth Tax return showing that
the Duke of Buckingham paid taxes on 29 hearths for his house in St Mary Bishophill Snr.[20]

From the middle of the seventeenth century onwards York slowly developed into
a major social capital and a centre for leisure. The amount of business such visitors
brought to the city is indicated by the memoirs of Sir John Reresby. In 1667 he
recorded: 'The Summer Assizes were held at Yorke, which lasted 10 days and cost

---

18 Quoted in Palliser and Palliser (1979), p. 37.
19 Palliser (1979), pp. 34, 54, gives the example of a group of Scots in 1583 making a detour from the
    Great North Road 'to see the town and minster'.
20 York City Archives (YCA) M30:26.

me £300'; later, in 1682, he 'removed with my family to Yorke, where I continued some weeks … for the Assizes. I kept a table. The high sherif and most of the gen-tlemen of quality in town dined with me.'[21] Assemblies were recorded in the 1630s and a theatre existed as early as 1609 (Borsay, 1989, p. 349; Richardson and James, 1983, pp. 173–74). The gentry had always visited York, but by the late seventeenth century they were coming in greater numbers, more frequently, and some had even begun to buy houses in the city. The evolution of York as a social centre is also illus-trated by the small but wealthy Catholic community:

> Some 35 families of Catholic gentry invaded York between 1660 and 1688 … Others came briefly to enjoy the increasing genteel society of the city, the races and the political excitements of the 1670s and 1680s … Many … only stayed for a season, others seem to have paid a retainer to keep lodgings over a long period … others leased rooms or whole houses in succession, almost continuously (bringing with them plate, linen and servants for their stays) and others … lived in York continuously for years (Aveling, 1970, pp. 96–97).

With more affluent people coming to the city, the economy began to adapt to meet the needs of an increasingly wealthy population. The range of crafts to which Freemen were admitted increased from 101 between 1625 and 1649, to 130 between 1675 and 1699.[22] Most manufactured specialized goods, but they included chemists and dancing masters while the number of barber-surgeons rapidly increased in the second half of the seventeenth century. One measure reflecting the growth of wealthy residences was that in 1662 the city was assessed on the same number of hearths as Norwich – a town with almost twice the population of York (Slack, 1977, p. 100). In Norwich up to 60 per cent of families were exempt from the Hearth Tax, and while some inhabitants were undoubtedly rich, many were employed in the poorly paid manufacture of cloth (Pound, 1988, pp. 105–14). York's Hearth Tax ranking put it second only to London, and reveals that by the 1670s a considerable number of wealthy families must have been resident in the city. It is difficult to measure this pre-cisely, but it is known that those who styled themselves gentlemen were increasingly being married in the city, whether they lived there or not, and in some of the inner parishes up to 20 per cent of householders were headed by people of 'independent means' (Hibberd, 1981, p. 114).

York's position as the north's administrative and social capital remained unchal-lenged throughout the sixteenth and seventeenth centuries. Much of its economy nevertheless depended on trade both at home and abroad and this economic base remained largely unaltered, making York in essence a large market town. The main change to York's economy occurred following the disruption of the 1640s and the

---

21 Quoted in Corfield (1977), p. 55. When Marmaduke Rawden visited the city in 1664 he also indulged in a constant round of dining and socializing; see Davies (1863), pp. 75–77, 83–84.

22 See Appendix 1. The numbers for each period are as follows: 1500–24, 160; 1525–49, 123; 1550–74, 114; 1575–99, 101; 1600–24, 103; 1625–49, 101; 1650–74, 108; 1675–99, 130. The large numbers of trades in the sixteenth century reflect differences in terminology rather than greater occupational diver-sity.

abolition of the two national courts. This loss was offset by an increasing role as a centre for the social elite. In 1700 York's economy could be described as successful. Its population as a whole was relatively wealthy even though many lived in abject poverty. However, the lack of any substantial industrial base ensured that economic and, hence, population expansion did not occur until after 1750. During the eighteenth century England's second city did not share in the many fundamental changes wrought by the Industrial Revolution. Instead, it gradually became something of an economic backwater, a place instead where the rich gathered to amuse themselves.

YORK AND ITS REGION

Much of York's success during the early modern period was due to the absence of any local rivals. Being one of a small number of regional capitals York prospered, and while a network of much smaller towns existed throughout Yorkshire, only Hull could be classified as large, with a population of about 5,000 in 1600 (Forster, 1969, p. 157) (Fig. 2.2). Even important market towns such as Beverley and Ripon had populations of only 3,000 and 1,500, respectively, at the end of the seventeenth

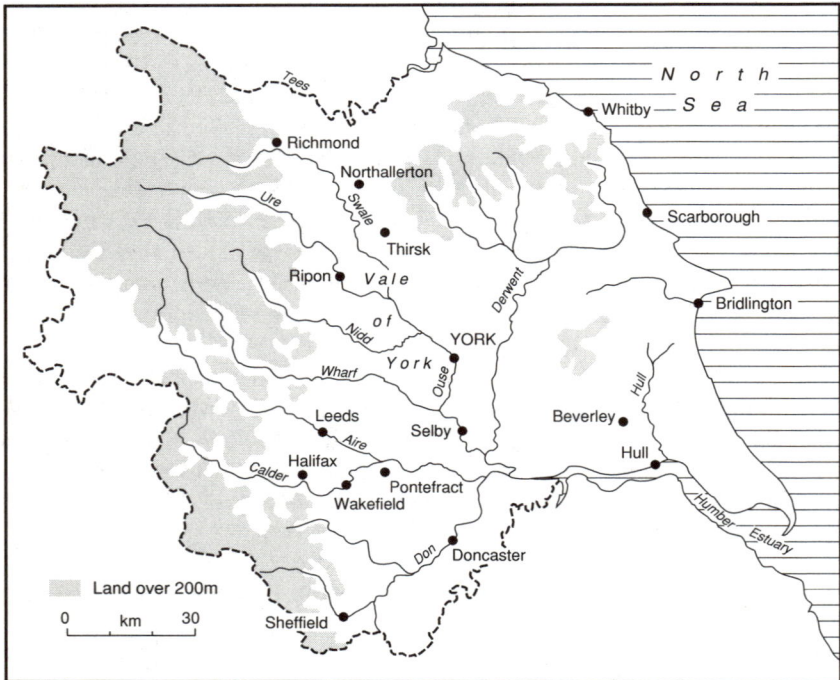

Figure 2.2: The major towns of early modern Yorkshire

century (Clark et al., 1987, pp. 207–09). York's dominant position within the urban hierarchy ensured its economic success, but by 1700 change was beginning to occur as Hull's population had grown to nearly 8,000, and more importantly, Leeds' population had reached about 6,000, double that of its mid-sixteenth-century base (Forster, 1969, p. 158; Hey, 1986, pp. 139, 181). The West Riding experienced considerable population growth during the seventeenth century as industrial development spread through the region. This whole area benefited from a number of natural features, such as rivers which could be easily exploited for water power, which encouraged industrial manufacturing. The existence of scattered settlements, largely free from guild control, also meant that many families were able to combine manufacture with farming, thus ensuring economic prosperity. Much of the growth in the West Riding occurred in rural areas, although at the onset of industrialisation many villages quickly developed urban characteristics. Some West Riding towns also grew; most notably Leeds, which developed after the finishing of broadcloths became concentrated in the town, and Wakefield, which became a centre for the distribution of cloth. In the south of the Riding metal working flourished and the location of cutlery trades near to Sheffield guaranteed that town's prosperity (Hey, 1991). While Yorkshire's population as a whole probably increased during the seventeenth century, outside the West Riding there was little urban growth, the only exception being the port of Hull where trade increased substantially during the second half of the seventeenth century. Traditionally York had few trading connections with the West Riding, and while the relocation of its woollen industry to this area had affected the medieval city, by 1700 any competition was only slight. The beginnings of industrial manufacture and the resultant increase in trade created conditions whereby spectacular urban growth became possible. In Yorkshire this occurred towards the end of the eighteenth century and by 1801 York, with a population of about 17,000, had become dwarfed by Leeds (53,000), Sheffield (46,000) and even Hull (28,000) (de Vries, 1984, pp. 270–71). York was effectively bypassed by many of the changes associated with the Industrial Revolution until the advent of the railways. Instead, with little potential for expansion in its manufacturing capacity, York's economic success, like most early modern cities, was determined by its ability to trade with other areas and its role as an administrative and social centre.

Five spheres of influence have been identified for York's commercial activities: (1) the immediate rural hinterland; (2) the Vale of York; (3) northern England; (4) England, south of the Humber; (5) Europe (Palliser, 1979, p. 185). Within each of these areas York's role was similar: that of a market place and a centre of distribution. Villages near to York were dominated by the city. With no accessible market town, villagers sold the majority of their produce in York's weekly markets; in return they bought provisions in the city and used its services. York also had jurisdiction over the Ainsty, an area of land granted to the city in 1212 which stretched as far as Tadcaster and encompassed around 20 villages to the west of the city, and this further encouraged close contact between the city and its immediate rural hinterland. Throughout the rest of the Vale everyday trade was less dependent on York. A network of much smaller market towns existed; nevertheless, York acted as a centre of distribution for these towns, and its markets, fairs and specialist traders were in great demand.[23] Goods were often transported overland, although this was both difficult and expensive, especially for bulk cargoes. Since river transport was usually cheaper and quicker, longer-distance trade took place along the Ouse and York's trading relations outside Yorkshire were effectively determined by the geography of the river, with both coastal and overseas trade making important contributions towards the city's overall commercial activities. Goods to and from York were often transferred onto smaller vessels in Hull, although lead was loaded directly onto sea-going craft in York. In return, fish came from Bridlington or even Scandinavia, coal from Newcastle, and iron, pitch and flax from the Baltic.[24] Throughout the sixteenth and seventeenth centuries York was at the heart of a complex trading network stretching throughout the country and into Europe. Branches of the Merchant Adventurers and the Eastland Company, groups of overseas merchants trading mainly in the Baltic, were established in York early in the seventeenth century. Some of these merchants became very rich:

> The available evidence shows York merchants of the two companies importing hemp, flax, potash, iron, and timber from Europe, and exporting lead, skins, and, above all, cloth. In 1640 four of seven leading merchants, all aldermen, were each trading in goods worth more than £4,000. Moreover, the city's merchants participated in the coastal trade, importing diverse commodities, amongst them a variety of luxury goods, for local consumption or distribution; the well-stocked markets excited favourable comments from travellers to the city (Forster, 1961, p. 169).

Individual merchants prospered, yet it is difficult to determine the contribution that national or international trade made towards York's economy. During the seventeenth century levels of long-distance trade show no signs of increase and may even have fallen. Towards the end of the seventeenth century the number of enfranchised merchants declined and in 1696 the residence of the Eastland Company was wound up. A number of factors affected York's ability to trade and the position of York merchants was weakened 'by the interruption of continental markets, lack of adequate shipping, piracy and the rivalry of London and local markets' (Forster, 1961, p. 168). The concentration of trade into the capital affected most places, although Hull still managed to prosper and this further diverted trade away from York. Early in the sixteenth century Hull was described as 'port town to the said City of York', but 'by the late 17th century Hull's own merchants were coming to dominate the town's trade' (Forster, 1969, p. 146). The biggest exporter from Hull in 1609 was a York man and as closer relations between Hull and the West Riding wool traders developed, York's share of overall trade diminished (Forster, 1969, p. 143). Competition from London

---

23 By the end of the seventeenth century only four of these market towns, Doncaster, Ripon, Pontefract and Selby, had populations greater than 1,000; Unwin (1981), p. 75; Clark *et al.* (1989), pp. 207–9.

24 Large quantities of lead were transported down the river from Boroughbridge to York and then either along the coast, mainly to London, or sometimes for export; Forster (1961), p. 169; Palliser (1979), pp. 189–92.

and Hull coupled with growth in the West Riding had effectively ensured that York's commercial activities were not able to expand, and may even have contracted; nevertheless, merchants continued to be enfranchised, some became very wealthy and 'the river continued to play an important part in the city's economy' (Forster, 1961, p. 169).

Throughout the early modern period York remained a city of national importance with trading relations that encompassed the whole country and beyond. The city was a centre of distribution for a large part of Yorkshire, but it was pre-eminent only within its immediate rural hinterland. Unlike London or Hull, York did not experience a substantial increase in its commercial activities. Its trading capacity was ultimately limited by its markets and these did not grow. Thus, while York had established trading relations throughout Yorkshire, along the coast from Scotland to London and beyond to northern Europe, the amount of trade carried out in the city remained roughly constant and was ultimately determined by the numbers both buying and selling in the city. By 1700 York was just about managing to hold its own. During the eighteenth century it was bypassed by industrial expansion in the West Riding and was rapidly left behind.

THE POPULATION HISTORY OF YORK, 1500–1800

In 1801 the first national census revealed that 16,846 people lived in York. The lack of any earlier complete enumeration means that it is possible only to provide estimates of the population before this date (Table 2.3). Each of these estimates is based

Table 2.3: Some published estimates of York's population, 1066–1760

Date	Population	Source
1066	9,000	Domesday Book[1]
1377	10,872	Poll Tax[2]
1524	8,000	Assuming same taxable population as Coventry[3]
1548	8,000	Chantry Count (4,131 communicants in 17 parishes)[4]
1600	10,000	Rickman's parish register returns[5]
1601–10	11,000	Parish registers[4]
1630	12,000	Rickman[5]
1671	8,318–11,401	Hearth Tax[6]
1672	9,275–12,712	Hearth Tax[6]
1676	10–12,000	Compton Census[5]
1700	12,400	Rickman[5]
1760	12,400	Parish registers[5]

Sources:
1. Palliser (1990), 13.
2. Russell (1948), p. 142.
3. Hoskins (1976), p. 93.
4. Palliser (1979), pp. 111–12.
5. Forster (1961), pp. 162–3.
6. Hibberd (1981), p. 256.

on parish registers or sources that enumerate only a fraction of the overall population. In addition to problems caused by the partial survival of these sources, the resulting estimates will be reliable only if suitable multipliers can be discovered that convert baptisms, households or communicants into the total population. Unfortunately, independent checks on these multipliers, which often have to be based on national averages, are not possible since no complete listing has survived and all the estimates in Table 2.3 need to be subjected to a considerable margin of error. Despite these problems a broad outline of York's population history can be given. Following its foundation as a legionary fortress in c.71–74 AD, York provided a home to some 6,000 soldiers, and this would suggest an overall population in the region of 10,000 (Hutchinson and Palliser, 1980, p. 6). Throughout Anglian, Viking and Norman settlement York's position as the north's most important city was not challenged, and while periods of growth and decline occurred, its population remained near to the Roman level even though population estimation remains a hazardous process during these periods. Domesday York probably contained in excess of 9,000 people and in the medieval period economic indicators suggest that the city reached a peak in population of more than 12,000 in the early fifteenth century (Bartlett, 1959, p. 33; Sakata, 1988). After a long period of recession, York's population fell to perhaps 8,000 by 1550 when the city was subjected to a succession of severe epidemics which disrupted parochial registration and makes population estimation especially difficult. From 1560 recovery occurred. By 1600 the population was again in excess of 10,000, and by 1640 it was probably greater than 12,000. Following a period of disruption caused by the Civil War, York's population then changed little and for much of the seventeenth and the first half of the eighteenth century it remained near to 12,000. Modest levels of growth occurred after 1760, although by this date York was no longer one of England's great cities.

While the contours of York's population history can be sketched relatively easily, providing accurate estimates or determining the extent of change over a given period proves to be a more difficult matter. When comparisons are made between population estimates based on different sources, discrepancies arise. For instance, during the 1670s three sources have survived that enable the population to be estimated – Hearth Tax returns, the Compton Ecclesiastical Census and parish registers – with each presenting a different set of interpretative problems. Analysis of the 1671 and 1672 Hearth Tax returns reveals considerable population change within a short period and implies a population in the range 8,300–12,700 depending upon which estimate of mean household size is used. In addition to the 1671 and 1672 returns, others exist for some parishes in 1665, 1670 and 1674 (Table 2.4). Considerable variation between returns is evident in some parishes, but rather than reflecting real population change, these are mainly a consequence of differential recording practices which could have been caused by poor administration, or more probably those exempt from paying the tax were simply omitted from some returns.[25] The 11 per

25 Galley (1991), p. 35. In St Margaret Walmgate 35 households were listed in 1670. In 1674 this figure
    had increased to 39 with another 25 given as not liable. Since the purpose of these documents was for
    tax collection, it was often the case that those not liable were simply omitted.

Table 2.4: Hearth Tax returns and the Compton Census, York 1665–76

Parish	Hearth Tax (Households)					Max	Compton Census 1676[6]	Census to Tax Ratio
	1665[1]	1670[2]	1671[3]	1672[4]	1674[5]			
All Saints North Street	54	60	52	61	64	**64**	61	0.95
All Saints Pavement	93	145	158	157	133	**158**	531	3.36
Holy Trinity Goodramgate	107	82	79	104	–	**107**	393	3.67
Holy Trinity Kings Court	110	120	113	115	107	**120**	329	2.74
Holy Trinity Micklegate	74	61	53	70	–	**74**	387	5.23
St Crux	138	114	132	128	127	**138**	416	3.01
St Cuthbert	61	42	65	61	–	**65**	224	3.45
St Denys with St George	46	57	70	73	67	**73**	309	4.23
St Helen Stonegate	71	106	92	107	98	**107**	154	1.44
St John Ousebridge	73	69	84	93	84	**93**	–	–
St Lawrence	8	15	13	14	17	**17**	–	–
St Margaret Walmgate	43	35	59	76	64	**76**	· 203	2.67
St Martin Coney Street	71	74	75	78	–	**78**	–	–
St Martin cum Gregory	20	50	51	51	–	**51**	78	1.53
St Mary Bishophill Jnr	9	58	46	53	63	**63**	–	–
St Mary Bishophill Snr	42	24	47	44	45	**47**	156	3.32
St Mary Castlegate	119	94	84	123	–	**123**	158	1.28
St Maurice	27	31	44	37	–	**44**	–	–
St Michael le Belfrey	109	188	183	185	–	**188**	–	–
St Michael Spurriergate	81	110	106	113	113	**113**	184	1.63
St Olave	34	26	26	34	–	**34**	101	2.97
St Sampson	92	103	93	109	96	**109**	–	–
St Saviour	108	65	71	116	–	**116**	216	1.86
Minster Yard	–	–	73	82	–	**82**	–	–
Totals			*1,869*	*2,084*		*2,140*		

Sources: 1. YCA M30:22.
2. YCA M30:24.
3. Hibberd (1981), p. 256.
4. YCA M30:26.
5. Whiteman (1986), p. 590.

cent increase in population indicated by the 1671 and 1672 returns is therefore likely to be a consequence of administrative differences and by taking the maximum number of householders from each return a closer approximation to the true number of households in York should be forthcoming. This procedure yields 2,140 households, a figure which is probably still an underestimate since consistently low numbers of households were recorded in St Lawrence.[26] The only comparable count of house-

26 During the 1670s an average of 11 baptisms per year were recorded in the parish register of St Lawrence, a figure that is too high from only 17 households; Borthwick Institute of Historical Research (BIHR) PR Y/L1. Since new Hearth Tax lists were often compiled from previous ones, some omissions may simply have been compounded and consequently figures from other parishes may also be underestimates.

holds occurred in 1743, by which time there appears to have been little change in York's population. Archbishop Herring's census of papists recorded 2,289 households in York, although the parish of St Michael le Belfrey has no surviving returns.[27] Correcting for this loss would suggest a figure of about 2,500 households for the city as a whole.[28] If the figure from the Hearth Tax returns and Archbishop Herring's census are correct, then between the 1670s and 1743 there was a 17 per cent increase in the number of households at a time when the average annual number of baptisms actually fell from 398 to 390.[29] There would therefore appear to be problems of consistency between apparently accurate listings of households. Whatever the true number of householders in York it is still necessary to find an appropriate value for the mean household size in order to estimate the total population. Arkell has suggested values in the region of 4.5 or even lower, although a multiplier of 6.1 was appropriate for seven London parishes (Arkell, 1982, p. 54; Laslett, 1972). Since York was a wealthy city it is likely that its mean household size would have been high; however, it is difficult to be certain. At best, population estimates based on the Hearth Tax show that during the 1670s York's population was probably between 9,630 (2,140 x 4.5) and 13,054 (2,140 x 6.1). With omissions from the extra-mural parish of St Lawrence and possibly St Olave, a figure towards the upper end of this range may seem likely. Furthermore, if the figure of 2,500 households from the 1743 count is acceptable, the range would extend from 11,125 (2,500 x 4.5) to 15,250 (2,500 x 6.1). Clearly then, in order to obtain anything other than a broad population estimate using these types of sources requires a series of assumptions, all of which are subject to doubt. Direct comparison between the Hearth Tax and the Compton Census reveals even more problems. The Compton Census was supposed to count the number of persons in each parish, indicating those who were 'Popish Recusants' or 'other Dissenters' (Whiteman, 1992, p. 81) Unfortunately, the question was posed in such a way that it was open to different interpretation by the parish clerks. Consequently, in some parishes the whole population was enumerated and in others households, communicants (those aged over 15) or adult males were counted. No indication is given in the individual returns as to which of the above alternatives has been

27 Aveling (1970), p. 271; Ollard and Walker (1927–31). Aveling gives a false impression of the accuracy of this census. Ollard and Walker, who transcribed the original documents, revealed that in six parishes – Holy Trinity Goodramgate, St Martin Coney Street, St Mary Bishophill Jnr, St Mary Bishophill Snr, St Maurice, St Sampson – only approximate figures were recorded. For instance, in St Martin Coney Street the number of families is given as 'About Fourscore. More in Winter; Fewer in Summer'; (Ollard and Walker, 1929, p. 172).
28 Substituting the Hearth Tax figure of 188 households for St Michael le Belfrey gives a total of 2,477.
29 In 1743, 121 and 59 households were listed in St Olave and St Lawrence respectively compared with a maximum of only 34 and 17 in the Hearth Tax; Ollard and Walker (1929), pp. 139, 207. An earlier count of houses, not households of which only the totals survive, showed that there were 2,156 in 1639 which compares with 2,407 from the 1801 census; Palliser (1979), p. 113. If the ratio of the number of persons per house did not change between these dates, then this would suggest a population of c.15,000 in 1639. However, it is difficult to determine the accuracy of the 1639 count, especially since what constituted a house may have changed between these dates.

counted, although this should be possible to infer by dividing the numbers given in the Compton Census by the Hearth Tax (Table 2.4). Arkell indicates that if this ratio is 1, households must have been counted; if it is 1–1.9 adult males, 2.2–3.7 adults and 3.7–5.2 individuals (Arkell, 1992, p. 104). The wide range of ratios revealed by Table 2.4 shows there was no consistency in recording practices across York, and any population estimate that uses a single multiplier will give a misleading picture. If Arkell's ratios are valid then York's population can be estimated by assuming that the proportion of adults and children in York's population was the same as in Lichfield and using the Hearth Tax figures to correct for the missing parishes.[30] This procedure yields an overall figure of 10,368 for the population in 1676. Its accuracy is dependent upon the accuracy of both returns, estimates of the mean household size and knowledge of the age-structure of the population, all of which are subject to a considerable degree of uncertainty. While population estimates based on household listings are relatively easy to provide, their accuracy is open to question, especially in cities where the mean household size may be subject to variation.[31] The often contradictory evidence from York suggests that if no complete enumeration has taken place, the lack of knowledge about household size and the limitations of contemporary numeracy ensure that providing any figure for the population of an early modern town must involve a considerable amount of guesswork and be subjected to a wide margin of error.

Problems also arise with population estimates based on parish register evidence since their accuracy is dependent on knowledge of the crude birth rate, or more correctly, the crude baptismal rate. Unfortunately, different assumptions are sometimes made in order to convert baptisms into population totals. In Table 2.3 Palliser assumes that the population is 30 times the average number of baptisms (a crude baptismal rate of 33.33 per 1,000), while the estimate for 1760 takes the crude baptismal rate to be 30.[32] Changing levels of nonconformity will obviously affect the crude baptismal rate and furthermore, there is no evidence to indicate that birth rates, especially in cities, remained constant over long periods.[33] Despite these drawbacks, of all the sources parish registers probably give the best indication of the dynamics of population change for early modern towns (Table 2.5). Baptism rates outside the range 30 to 35 may have occurred and annual variations will be masked by these decadal averages. York's parish registers confirm that the population was increasing

---

30 Variations in infant and childhood mortality coupled with differing patterns of migration mean that it is likely that the ratio of children to adults was not the same in Lichfield and York; however, they should have been similar; see Table 1.3.

31 In periods of population increase, subdivision of properties was common and it is difficult to know precisely how households were identified; Woodward (1995), p. 66.

32 This is based on Cox (1910) who assumed that the total population was about 30 times the annual number of baptisms. Also, see Tate (1969), p. 81. Estimates based on the number of burials or marriages can also be made, but these are likely to be even less accurate.

33 The crude birth rate for quinquinnea from 1541 to 1700 in England varied between 26.78 and 39.84; Wrigley and Schofield (1981), p. 529. Variations in cities are likely to have been even more pronounced, see Woods (1989), p. 87.

Table 2.5: Estimates of York's population using parish registers, 1561–1700

Decade	Average annual baptisms	Population given baptismal rate (per 1,000)		
		35	33.33	30
1561–70	234	6,686	7,020	7,800
1571–80	264	7,543	7,920	8,800
1581–90	317	9,057	9,510	10,567
1591–1600	321	9,171	9,630	10,700
1601–10	(329)	9,400	9,870	10,967
1611–20	354	10,114	10,620	11,800
1621–30	358	10,229	10,740	11,933
1631–40	409	11,686	12,270	13,633
1641–50	(409)	11,686	12,270	13,633
1651–60	353	10,086	10,590	11,767
1661–70	390	11,143	11,700	13,000
1671–80	398	11,371	11,940	13,267
1681–90	425	12,143	12,750	14,167
1691–1700	398	11,371	11,940	13,267

Source: original parish registers.
Note: annual baptisms for the years 1601–10 and 1641–50 are placed in brackets because the presence of mortality crises in these decades may mean that the figures are slightly unrepresentative.

until c.1620. Between 1620 and 1660 a period of stability gave way to one of renewed growth immediately before the Civil War when, after some disruption, the population then remained constant. It is clear that York's population did not change dramatically during the seventeenth century and a figure in the region of 12,000 may appear to be a reasonable estimate for the 1670s.[34] York maintained this population level until c.1760. Difficulties inherent in analysing York's census-type data coupled with the likelihood that baptism rates were subject to change ensure that it would be unwise to provide anything other than rough estimates of York's population before 1800. After this date such problems do not occur and, following the introduction of new industries, the city expanded from 16,846 in 1801 to 21,711 in 1821, 28,842 in 1841, 40,433 in 1861, 49,530 in 1881 and 77,914 in 1901.

ECONOMY, SOCIETY AND POPULATION

The size and composition of an early modern urban population was directly linked to its economic function, and in order to survive, towns needed sufficient customers for the products that were manufactured or traded in the city. Put simply, the number of bakers or shoemakers who were able to maintain a business in a city was determined by the numbers wanting to buy the products they made. The population therefore responded to the demands of the urban economy and any change to that

34 Taking all the evidence together, a figure within the range 10–14,000 would be a safer estimate.

economy would cause comparable changes to the population. This relationship was dependent on the availability of a regular stream of potential migrants who were willing to move to cities providing that job opportunities were available. Throughout the early modern period few towns appear to have had problems recruiting migrants (witness how quickly most towns recovered from outbreaks of plague); indeed, the reverse appears to have been the case since the existence of guild restrictions may have mitigated some forces for economic change to the short-term benefit of urban traders, and at certain times poor migrants were removed from cities. Towns were often the focus of economic change and when urban economies grew, their populations usually did likewise. In most cases however, change only occurred slowly. The reasons for this were relatively straightforward. In an age when communications and travel were difficult, most markets needed to be close to the areas they served and only a few places were able to develop wider trading relations. Consequently, the majority of early modern towns were small, and while a large proportion of any pre-industrial urban population was employed in maintaining the town itself, the rest of the economy was influenced by external demand which was limited by the size of the rural hinterland. Even regional capitals were relatively small since the demand for their specialized services was also limited. Some cities did grow rapidly. The expansion of its commercial activities throughout the seventeenth century created population increase in Bristol, and during the same period the concentration of cloth manufacturing in Norwich enabled it to double in population. London experienced truly spectacular growth as administration, trade and commerce became concentrated in the capital. By comparison, the economies of most early modern towns hardly changed and most remained little more than market towns. Substantial growth only occurred in exceptional circumstances and this almost always necessitated the concentration of manufacture or distribution in the city. Therefore, in order to expand, a city needed a population within its sphere of influence that was increasing or a means by which new markets could be exploited. Before the middle of the eighteenth century, when rapid economic and population growth occurred throughout the country, only a few towns were able to take advantage of any changing economic circumstances.

With a few exceptions, the livelihood of most early modern towns depended on their ability to act as markets and centres for distribution. With no economic specialization, the size of most towns was therefore determined by the extent of their rural hinterlands, although in some cases national and even international markets were important. Figure 2.3 provides a simple model of how early modern economies influenced urban populations.[35] Expanding economies, for whatever reasons, create opportunities for some to marry and start families while at the same time more people are able to move into the city. The possibility of economic advancement also outweighed any perceived threat to life since a vibrant economy caused population increase irrespective of prevailing levels of mortality.[36] Early modern urban

35 This figure is based on Wrigley and Schofield (1981), Figure 11.5, p. 465.
36 London grew despite repeated outbreaks of plague and periods of extremely high mortality; see Landers (1993).

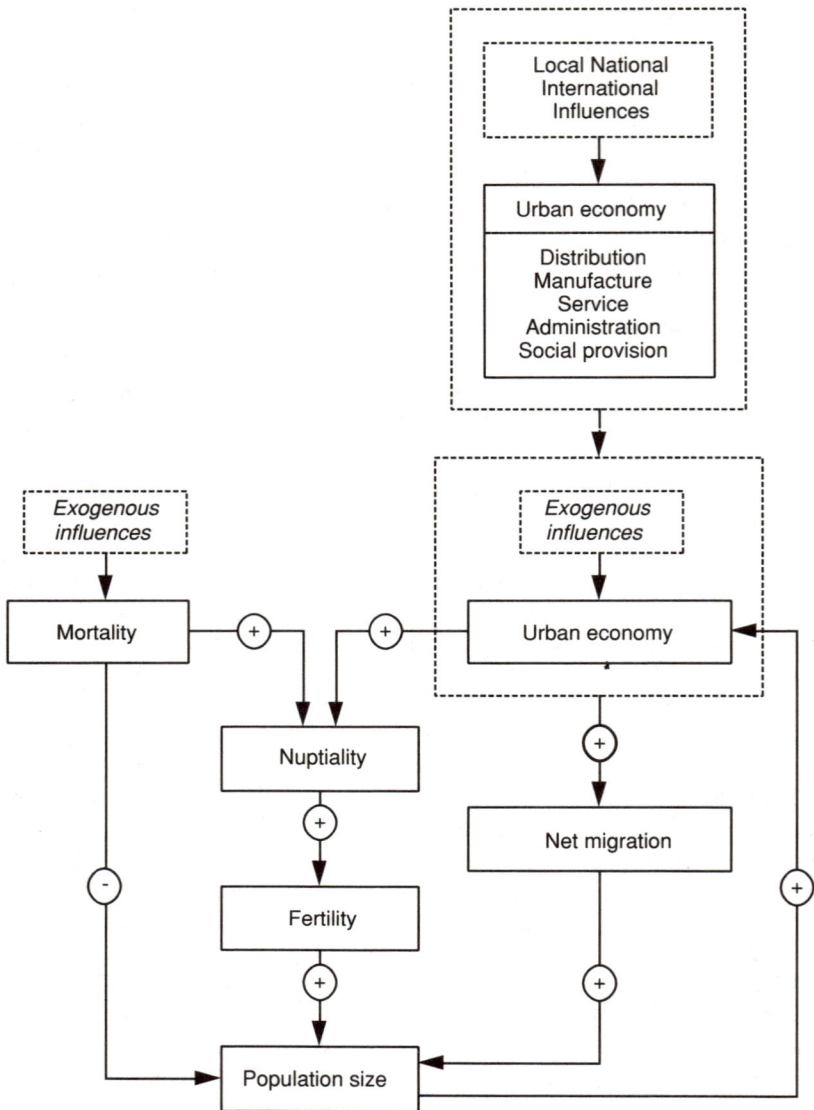

Figure 2.3: The relationship between population size and the urban economy in an early modern society

economies can be considered to be composed of a number of sectors, although such divisions necessarily oversimplify matters since there was significant overlap. The extent and importance of each sector depended on a variety of differing factors. Service and market provision was determined by the size of the immediate rural hinterland. The administrative and social sectors influenced wider areas, yet outside the capital their effects on urban growth were limited by the relatively small numbers wishing to use these services and the location of rival attractions. To a certain extent, levels of urban manufacture and distribution were also dependent on the size of the city's hinterland, but given appropriate conditions both were capable of growth if markets beyond the bounds of a city's natural influence could be exploited. Substantial population growth for early modern towns was therefore feasible only if conditions existed in which manufacture or distribution could be increased, and in the majority of cases growth was caused by influences exogenous to the city. The economy also influenced the composition of the urban population. The core of all early modern towns was likely to have been similar since this was composed of those who were employed in feeding and clothing the urban population and in providing the usual range of services. The composition of the rest of the population will have been affected by alternative employment opportunities. For instance, most of those working in the cloth industry may typically have been poor while towns with substantial leisure facilities were likely to have attracted richer households employing large numbers of servants, even though some may have stayed only on a seasonal basis. To what extent such variations yielded distinct population structures is as yet unknown, although in London the central more wealthy parishes had higher mean household sizes than the poorer suburbs (Glass, 1965, pp. 174–75). The composition of the population, in particular the sex-ratio, would also have affected the ability to marry of some sections of the population, as would the general state of the economy. More importantly, a vibrant expanding economy could bypass all internal demographic factors and create conditions in which migrants were attracted to the city and sustained population growth was possible.

Figure 2.3 can also help to explain how changes to York's economy and population were linked. Throughout the early modern period, the livelihood of most of York's population was geared towards maintaining the city's traditional role as a commercial and market centre. York was also the north's most important administrative centre and by the second half of the seventeenth century it was still one of only a handful of regional capitals. It could therefore be described as a successful city at the local, national and even international levels. However, with little manufacturing capacity and no sign of commercial expansion, by 1600 it was entering a period of population stagnation which lasted until the 1750s. Some of its administrative duties were removed as a consequence of the Civil War, exports may have declined and while it slowly evolved into a major social capital after 1650, this change by itself could not create substantial population growth. Even when York was at its height as a social centre in the middle of the eighteenth century, its population had not increased from seventeenth-century levels since there were simply not enough wealthy individuals within York's sphere of influence to create substantial economic and population growth. Most of York's economy was geared to serving a local market and this also showed little sign of growth, especially after 1650. Population estimates for the rural parishes close to York are not available, but the pattern in a sample of 38 Yorkshire parishes was almost identical to the national trend (Fig.

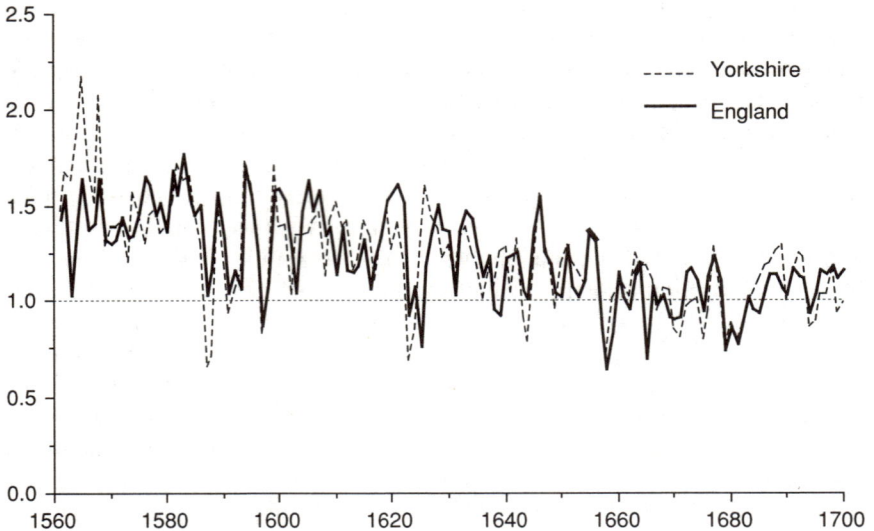

Figure 2.4: Baptism/burial ratios for England and a sample of 38 Yorkshire parishes, 1561–1700
Source: see text.

2.4).[37] Whilst it is not altogether surprising that a subset of the parishes that were selected to model national trends should follow similar patterns, this evidence does seem to indicate that regional population trends in Yorkshire were very similar to those in the rest of the country. If this is true then the population of Yorkshire will have increased until 1660, after which a period of stagnation occurred (Wrigley and Schofield, 1981, p. 531). While there was probably disproportionate growth in the West Riding caused by substantial expansion of the region's economy, throughout the Vale of York any population increase was more likely to have reflected national trends.[38] With no immediate rival, York's markets were maintained, but these could not increase substantially without comparable increases in its rural hinterland, and this did not occur, especially during the second half of the seventeenth century. Many businesses were able to flourish in York and its Hearth Tax assessments show the city to be affluent even if many lived in poverty. The number of households contributing towards poor relief increased during the seventeenth century, and while the number of families in receipt of relief may also have increased, this is probably indicative of

37 The sample of 38 parishes form the Yorkshire subset of the 404 used in Wrigley and Schofield (1981), p. 489. I am grateful to the Cambridge Group for the History of Population and Social Structure for allowing me access to these data. A similar pattern is also revealed by a sample of 29 seventeenth-century Yorkshire parishes in Woods (1982), p. 97.

38 Pickles (1996) shows that many parishes even lost population.

a general increase in prosperity.[39] York was therefore maintaining its markets and increasingly it attracted wealthy visitors. York's economy was crucial in determining both the composition of its population and the extent of any changes. The importance of York's market and service sectors meant that a natural ceiling for its population appears to have been between 12,000 and 14,000, which it reached by the middle of the seventeenth century. With no fundamental change to its economy, York's population remained at this level for the next 100 years, and while minor changes occurred to overseas trade and its administrative and social sectors, these could not cause significant changes in the overall population, even though they did affect the composition of the population (see pp. 141–49). The core of York's economy changed relatively little during the sixteenth and seventeenth centuries; it was never seriously challenged in its immediate hinterland and throughout it retained its function as the north's major distributive centre.

The lack of good quality economic indicators for York means that the relationship between economy and population cannot be described fully. Short-term trends are impossible to discern without the appropriate economic statistics, and contemporary descriptions of the city can be misleading. For instance, the minutes of the Corporation c.1660 record that:

> The shoes of our predecessors are too big for our feet ... The inhabitants [of York] have many of them forsaken it, and those who have not, she cannot maintain ... Trade is decayed (quoted in Palliser, 1979, p. 288)

while Blome, a visitor in 1673, described the city as:

> a fair, large and beautiful City, adorned with splendid buildings, both publicke and private, is very populous, much resorted unto, and well inhabited by Gentry, and wealthy Tradesmen (quoted in Palliser and Palliser, 1979, p. 23)

Despite such anomalies, the link between population and economy is clear, even if its exact nature is complex and difficult to determine. Short-term variations in both variables no doubt occurred even though they cannot be measured. However, over the longer term, York's economy underwent a series of subtle changes and these had an important impact on the city's population history.

---

39 Slack (1988), pp. 176–77, Tables 6–7. In order to estimate the proportion of the population in receipt of poor relief, an estimate of 12,000 for the city's population in the period 1630–1760 was used. If the estimates from Table 2.5 are substituted, slight modifications to Slack's conclusions will therefore be forthcoming.

THE DEMOGRAPHY OF YORK

Chapter 3

THE FLOW OF VITAL EVENTS

Given the difficulties of providing population estimates for most early modern towns, the best way of examining the dynamics of population change is by an analysis of vital events. Little evidence concerning births and deaths exists prior to the introduction of Civil Registration in 1837; however, York's parish registers provide a rich alternative source and it is a relatively straightforward, if time-consuming procedure to construct time series of baptisms, burials and marriages for the city as a whole. Levels of mortality and fertility cannot be calculated directly from these series, but they will reflect population change, show levels of natural change and thereby indicate the changing relationship between mortality and fertility throughout the period.[1] Before discussing the results of this procedure, it is necessary to show that York's parish registers are sufficiently accurate to warrant analysis and that the recorded number of baptisms, burials and marriages provide a true reflection of the number of births, deaths and marriages in the whole population.

THE ACCURACY OF YORK'S PARISH REGISTERS

In 1700 York had 23 parishes, a considerable reduction from its medieval total of about 40 (Fig. 3.1). Depopulation and economic recession meant that by 1547 many churches had fallen into disuse and unions between parishes became necessary.[2] This process was protracted, but by 1586 all the unions had been ratified and York's parishes numbered 24. A final reduction occurred when, following the destruction of its church during the siege of 1644, the small extra-mural parish of St Nicholas was united with its neighbour St Lawrence. All of York's 23 parishes have extant registers covering at least part of the period 1538–1700. Unfortunately, most contain gaps and only those for St Olave begin in 1538. The quality of the early registers is poor, partly because a succession of severe epidemics during the 1550s disrupted registration, and it is only from 1561 that a representative sample of six good quality registers survive. No registers from any of the united parishes exist, yet given that most of these churches fell out of use well before 1586, it is unlikely that separate registers were ever kept.[3]

The register of St Nicholas was presumably lost when the church was destroyed during the Civil War, and while three Bishop's transcripts from this parish have sur-

---

1 Wrigley and Schofield (1981) demonstrate what can be done when such data are assembled at the national level.

2 Palliser (1974). Some of the united parishes survived as administrative units into the nineteenth century.

3 Palliser (1974) shows that most of the united churches were no longer in use by 1538. The only exception was St Maurice which was formally united with Holy Trinity Goodramgate, although both churches maintained independent registers: BIHR PR; Y/HTG, Y/M.

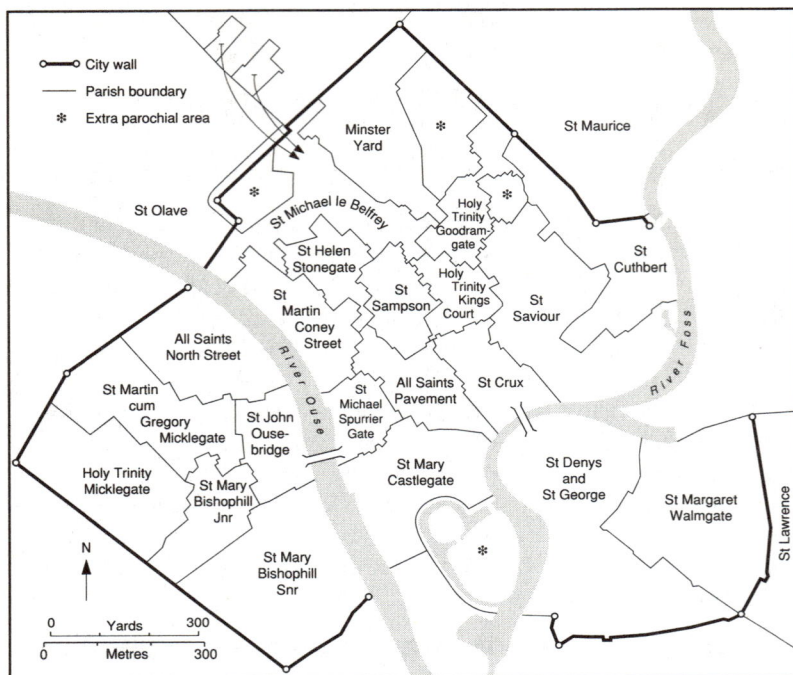

Figure 3.1: York's parish boundaries

vived, they record very few events.[4] A separate register, mainly of marriages, was
kept by the Minster and a register of baptisms from the extra-parochial Bedern
Chapel has also survived. It is therefore a simple task to go through each register and
count the number of baptisms, burials and marriages occurring in each year. Gaps,
often caused by missing sections of registers, are easy to identify since in the majority of cases registration ceased abruptly. Occasionally the quality of a register dete-
riorates to such an extent that suspicions are aroused. This often followed the death
of the parish clerk and can usually be identified by a change of handwriting. Once all
obvious signs of deficient registration have been eliminated there are three main reasons why the aggregate number of events recorded in the registers may not accurately represent the true level in the city. First, a section of the population may have
consciously opted out of the Anglican registration system. Secondly, and more difficult to detect, even though a register appears to be complete it may still have been
badly kept and an unknown and possibly varying number of events may be missing
from it. Thirdly, any infants who died unbaptized will obviously be missing from the

4 In 1597 annual transcripts of parish registers (usually referred to as Bishop's transcripts) had to be sent
   to the local diocese. The numbers of baptisms, burials and marriages respectively recorded in St
   Nicholas were as follows: 1600 (1, 2, 0), 1601 (2, 0, 0), 1604 (2, 42, 1); BIHR PRT 540. The large number of burials in 1604 was due to plague.

baptism register, but they may also be missing from the burial register since it is uncertain whether unbaptized infant burials were consistently recorded. In each case the probable extent of under-registration can be determined and this will then allow the number of births and deaths in the population to be estimated.[5]

Throughout the period 1561–1700 the vast majority of York's population used the Anglican registration system. While York was a centre for northern Catholicism, as late as 1676 the Compton Census revealed that in 17 parishes the communicant population was 3,699, the number of 'popish recusants' 86 and 'other dissenters' 145.[6] Thus, six per cent of the population at most might have been excluded from Anglican registers for this reason by the late seventeenth century. The actual numbers who escaped registration remained well below this level, however. According to Scott, 'Many non-churchgoers … continued to rely upon the officers of their own or an amenable parish minister whenever a baptism, marriage or burial was in order'.[7] A Presbyterian chapel was opened in St Saviours Gate in 1692 and a Catholic register was started at the Bar Convent in 1680. These early registers are now lost, although it is likely that only a few events would have been recorded before 1700.[8] Furthermore, the lack of alternative burial sites ensured that most under-registration would have been confined to baptisms.[9] Before the Civil War, pressure to conform meant that registration loss would have been minimal and the Quakers, who established a sizeable community in York and often refused to baptize their children, were responsible for most of any loss after 1650 (Royle, 1985, pp. 3–5). A seventeenth-century Quaker register was kept and a burial site was opened in Bishophill in 1667. These early registers have also been lost, but the Quaker cemetery was small and few burials occurred there during the seventeenth century.[10] It is possible to estimate the extent of Quaker under-registration in the early eighteenth century since between 1702 and 1706 the parish register of All Saints Pavement contains a list of births of

---

5 It is not possible to be completely confident about the accuracy of a particular register; however, sufficient studies have been undertaken that demonstrate the reliability of parochial registration in general, the most important being Wrigley and Schofield (1981). In York occasional instances of 'traffic in corpses' and baptisms outside the parish of residence can be discovered, but virtually all events took place within the city itself and will therefore not affect aggregative analysis; Schofield (1984).

6 Whiteman (1986), p. 590; ([86 + 145]/3,699 = 0.062).

7 Scott (1990), p. 192. Parish registers occasionally recorded the burials of non-Anglicans, for instance 'Sarah ye wife of George Gilman died October ye 3 1700 and was buried October ye 5 1700 Amongst ye Quakers'; BIHR Y/SAM 1.

8 Registers survive from the eighteenth century: four baptisms were recorded at St Saviours Gate during the decade 1721–30 and six baptisms were recorded at the Bar Convent in 1771: PRO R4 3780; 'Miscellanea IV Catholic Register of the Bar Convent', *Catholic Record Society* (1907), p. 374.

9 There was no burial ground at the Bar Convent and the first recorded burial at St Saviours Gate occurred in 1794. Instead, burials would usually have taken place in the parish of residence, for example, 'Mr Asquith a roman Catholick (February, 1708)'; BIHR PR Y/OL. Aveling (1970), pp. 244–46 gives further examples of known Catholics who recorded their baptisms, burials and marriages in the Anglican registers. This list is by no means complete and in most instances no indication is given that the individual was a Catholic.

10 Allott (1978), p. 24. The extant register begins in 1776 when an average of only five burials took place each year. A few burials of non-York residents also occurred there; Brotherton Library I 2.1–2.3.

infants who were not subsequently baptized.[11] Only 10 children from six families were recorded, nine per cent of the total baptized. All Saints Pavement contained about 20 per cent of all Quaker families and if this level of under-registration was representative of the city as a whole, at most only three per cent of baptisms would be missing from the registers by 1700.[12] Whatever the actual level of under-registration was, it is likely that more baptisms than burials were lost through nonconformity; however, it seems safe to conclude that by 1700 nonconformity had little impact on the accuracy of York's parish registers and virtually none before 1650.

It is possible to infer whether a register is obviously defective using a technique,

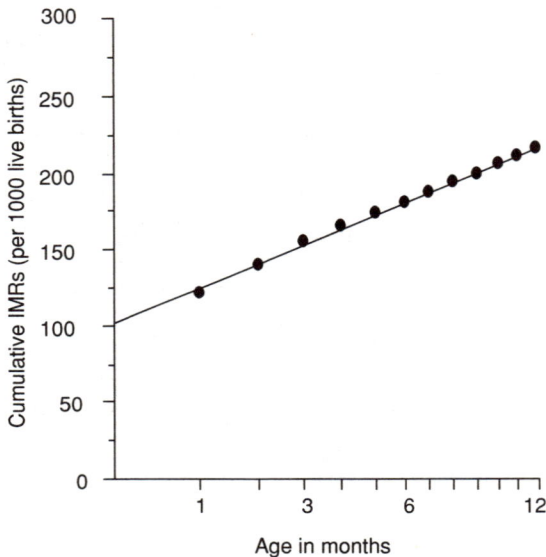

Figure 3.2: The biometric analysis of infant mortality for 13 York parishes, 1561–1700. Source: original parish registers.

the biometric analysis of infant mortality, which was devised by Bourgeois-Pichat and has been used on English parish registers by Wrigley.[13] When registration is poor it is likely that infant burials will be affected most, and if it can be shown that this vulnerable section of the population has been accurately recorded it should then follow that the rest of the burial record is also reliable. Accordingly, if a graph of the

11 BIHR PR Y/ASP 2.
12 Scott (1990), Map 1. An average of two non-baptized births occurred between 1702 and 1706. If all these were Quakers, only ten would have occurred throughout the whole of York, and since c.350 baptisms occurred each year, the level of under-registration would be almost three per cent (10/350 = 0.028).
13 Bourgeois-Pichat (1952); Wrigley (1977). The technique is discussed in Pressat and Wilson (1985), p. 17.

cumulative infant mortality rate (IMR) is plotted against age at death, scaled to $\log^3(n+1)$ where n is age at death in days, the line summarizing the relationship should be approximately straight and intercept the vertical axis, indicating a positive level of endogenous mortality (those deaths associated with congenital malformations and birth trauma). When calculations of infant mortality were made from 13 of York's registers and subjected to this 'test', it is therefore reassuring to discover that these conditions were met (Fig. 3.2).[14] Endogenous mortality rates varied considerably in early modern England, as did IMRs, and rates over 100 are high in comparison with others calculated for English parishes.[15] Most under-registration occurred in the first month and can only be detected if rates of endogenous mortality were sufficiently low for suspicions to be aroused. This did not occur in the York parishes, and whilst it would be naive to assume that any register which appears to pass this 'test' is guaranteed to be accurate, no obvious deficiencies in registration in York can be detected.[16]

Table 3.1: Unbaptized burials, York 1563–1700

Parish	Period	Unbaptized burials	Baptisms	Ratio unbaptized to baptized
All Saints Pavement	1563–73	11	120	9.2
	1601–10	8	157	5.1
	1646–73	39	528	7.4
Holy Trinity Goodramgate	1693–1700	25	163	15.3
Holy Trinity Micklegate	(1607–23)	25	385	6.5
	1630–43	25	314	8.0
St Crux	1663–74	16	284	5.6
St Martin Coney Street	1602–19	24	213	11.3
	1654–67	17	217	7.8
St Mary Bishophill Jnr	(1615–28)	16	107	15.0
St Michael le Belfrey	(1572–88)	59	650	9.1
	1613–22	20	497	4.0
	1644–63	40	973	4.1
	Overall	*325*	*4,608*	*7.1*

Note: the years in brackets denote that unbaptized burials were specifically mentioned in the registers.
Source: original parish registers.

14 The equation of least squares regression is $Y = 101.96 + 6.7952x$ where $x = \log^3(n+1)$ ($R^2 = 0.998$, based on 5,298 burials). See pp. 95–100 for a discussion of how these rates have been calculated and which registers were used. IMRs were also calculated for the parishes of St Martin Coney Street and St Michael le Belfrey by the more rigorous method of family reconstitution, and again no sign of defective registration was revealed: $Y = 116.74 + 8.1302x$ ($R^2 = 0.995$, 351 burials), $Y = 124.00 + 6.4029x$ ($R^2 = 0.992$, 192 burials), respectively; see Galley (1994), pp. 31–32.

15 Schofield and Wrigley (1979), p. 78 give endogenous rates between 1550 and 1649 as high as 138 and 93 for the market towns of Gainsborough and Banbury, although the mean of the seven parishes studied was only 71. Landers (1990), p. 42 found rates near to 80 for seventeenth-century London Quakers. The variability of endogenous mortality is as yet unexplained.

16 See the discussion in Galley, *et al.* (1995).

Table 3.2: Birth-baptism intervals, York 1653–1812

Parish	Period	Interval in days by which stated per cent of births were baptized				Number of observations	Per cent incomplete
		25	50	75	90		
Holy Trinity Goodramgate[a]	1653–63	4	5	6	8	201	7
Holy Trinity Kings Court[c]	1654–56	4	6	7	9	49	12
St John Ousebridge[a]	1653–61	4	6	8	10	113	4
St Martin cum Gregory[c]	1653–63	4	7	8	10	129	17
St Maurice[a]	1654–63	4	5	7	8	42	4
St Michael le Belfrey[a]	1653–57	4	6	8	9	171	2
St Olave[c]	1653–58	3	4	7	9	30	36
Bedern[c]	1682–1719	8	14	22	28	118	20
St Martin[b]	1774–80	2	8	29			8
	1804–20	3	12	23			4
St Michael le Belfrey[c]	1803–12	3	7	25	57	585	0

Sources: a. Woodward (1975), pp. 30–31.
          b. Berry and Schofield (1971), p. 457.
          c. original parish registers.

Table 3.3: Birth-baptism intervals for infants dying within one year of baptism, York 1653–63

Period	Interval in days by which stated per cent of births were baptized				Number of observations
	25	50	75	90	
1653–63	3	5	6	8	136

Source: original parish registers of Holy Trinity Goodramgate, St Martin cum Gregory, St John Ouse-bridge and St Michael le Belfrey.

The final problem is more serious. It is a consequence of high levels of infant mortality and may have affected both baptismal and burial registration. If an infant died before it could be baptized in the parish church, it was likely that all reference to that child will be absent from the baptism register. Moreover, there is also the possibility that in some cases the child's burial may not have been recorded either, since it is uncertain the extent to which unbaptized infants were denied Christian burial. During the period 1571–86 the register of St Michael le Belfrey was exceptionally well-kept and details of many infants who died without being baptized in church were given. For example in 1580:

John Franklande, sonne to Mr Richard Frankeland, Register, about one hower oulde, buryed the
xxviij day of June; baptized at home becawse of weakness.[17]

This entry is taken from the burial register, not the baptism register. In exceptional
circumstances church law allowed anyone to perform the rite of baptism, but with no
formal ceremony having taken place it is very unusual to find the parish clerk recording the event. Some registers occasionally identify unbaptized infant burials, for
instance 'A man child of Nycholas Banyels unbaptized (16 October 1607)'.[18] On
other occasions entries refer to 'a child of' and, if the quality of registration is good,
it is likely that these also refer to unbaptized infant burials. Table 3.1 shows the proportion of burials identified in this way. Up to seven per cent of infants may have died
unbaptized and were therefore absent from the baptism register. In some instances
the child may have been named, perhaps in an informal ceremony, and its burial may
have been recorded even though no indication was given that the infant was indeed
unbaptized. Evidence from the reconstitution of St Martin Coney Street and St
Michael le Belfrey shows that on many occasions burials occurred to families without evidence of that infant having been baptized. In these cases so-called 'dummy
births' are created and the infant is assumed to have died shortly after birth. In St
Martin Coney Street these amounted to 5.1 per cent of all baptisms and in St Michael
le Belfrey 3.3 per cent.[19] It would therefore seem safe to conclude that most unbaptized infant burials were not labelled as such, and while the level of under-registration throughout York will obviously have varied from parish to parish depending on
the diligence of the clerks, baptismal under-registration was substantial – at least five
per cent and perhaps as high as seven per cent.[20]

Burial under-registration was much lower; some unbaptized burials were not
recorded, although the majority appear to have been, even though most were not
labelled as such.[21] This type of under-registration was a consequence of the delay
between birth and baptism and high infant mortality rates. During the mid-seventeenth century, when for a short period both birth and baptism dates were recorded
in some parishes, birth-baptism intervals were usually short, with over 75 per cent of
infants having been baptized within a week of their birth (Table 3.2). By the eighteenth century, some but not all infants were being baptized later in life, although it

---

17 BIHR Y/MB.
18 BIHR Y/HTM 1.
19 Galley (1991), p. 109. In 1604 canon law was changed so that all baptisms had to be conducted by a
    priest. Midwife and lay baptisms were outlawed and consequently from this date unbaptized infant
    burials should be excluded from the registers; see Collinson (1983), p. 46; Babbage (1962), pp. 65–67.
    Table 3.1 shows that in practice this did not happen; furthermore, in St Martin Coney Street there was
    no difference in the level of 'dummy births' before and after 1604.
20 The level of 'dummy births' in St Martin Coney Street is probably more representative of the rate
    throughout the city since the quality of St Michael le Belfrey's register is so good that a large propor-
    tion of unbaptized burials were identified.
21 Burial under-registration was probably the difference between baptism under-registration and the
    level of 'dummy births'. This would suggest a level of about two per cent, but given the paucity of
    information it is difficult to be certain.

is unlikely that birth-baptism intervals had increased much by 1700.[22] The greatest risk to infants occurred during the first few days of life, and given the theological consequences of dying unbaptized, there may have been a tendency for parents to seek to baptize weak infants at the earliest opportunity. There are few recorded examples of this, but one from the eighteenth century illustrates the panic which must have surrounded such events:

> Rebecca, daughter of Charles Copeland, Paver by Ruth his wife, was baptized Privately Febr 13, 1747 N.B. That child last mentioned, being born long before due time, & extremely like to dye, was baptized as soon as possible. In their Hurry on which Occassion, they mistook its sex; for afterwards it manifestly appeared to be a Boy. It died soon; & was buried ye second day after its Birth, ie Febr 15 1747.[23]

It is difficult to determine the extent to which all weak children were baptized early. Birth-baptism intervals of infants dying within one year were not significantly different from those who survived, whereas if the majority of weak infants had been baptized early these intervals should have been shorter (Table 3.3). Of course, any infants who died unbaptized will be missing from this table, but given the very high levels of mortality during the first few hours and days, it seems more likely that if a baptism had taken place it would have been an informal one.[24] Unbaptized infant burials may also have been confused with stillbirths (Table 3.4).[25] The stillbirth rate in York was high, but comparable with the few others that have been discovered for early modern England.[26] It is rare to find stillbirths recorded consistently and it is reassuring that on three occasions unbaptized burials were also specifically identified in the registers. Thus, from what little evidence that has survived it appears that there was little confusion between unbaptized burials and stillbirths in sixteenth- and seventeenth-century York.

22 Berry and Schofield (1971) p. 457. The Bedern register may be unrepresentative as to birth-baptism delay since many infants had previously been baptized in a private ceremony prior to receiving the public rite in the chapel.
23 BIHR Y/MAUR 2.
24 In Sheffield during the 1870s when precise ages at death data are available, 2.4 per cent of infant deaths were aged less than two hours, five per cent less than one day and 12 per cent less than one week; Galley et al. (1995), Table 5. There would be obvious difficulties in finding a priest if a death occurred close to birth and in Sheffield many infant deaths were not recorded in either the ecclesiastical or cemetery register. Thus, while these infants were buried, no ceremony took place and consequently no entry was made in the corresponding register.
25 Finlay (1980), pp. 26–41 discovered some confusion between stillbirths and unbaptized infant burials in the parish of Hawkshead.
26 Finlay (1981c), p. 37 found stillbirth rates between three and five per cent for early seventeenth-century London. Forbes (1971), p. 65 gives a rate of over seven per cent for the London parish of St Botolph without Aldgate, 1584–1623. The relative rareness with which stillbirths were recorded does suggest the possibility that omissions could have occurred.

Table 3.4: Burials of stillbirths, York 1614–1700

Parish	Period	Stillbirths	Baptisms	Ratio of stillbirths to baptisms
All Saints Pavement	1614–24	8	145	5.5
	1651–64	12	226	5.3
Holy Trinity Goodramgate	1662–98	39	775	5.0
St Michael le Belfrey	1633–46	47	816	5.8
	1650–1700	95	2,398	4.0
St Olave	1631–40	19	264	7.2
	Overall	*220*	*4,624*	*4.8*

Source: original parish registers.

In total the evidence suggests that while some systematic under-registration occurred, York's parish registers are sufficiently accurate to warrant demographic exploitation and that once an aggregate series of baptisms, burials and marriages has been constructed, it is capable of accurately reflecting trends throughout the city. The quality of the parish registers is good and the biometric analysis of infant mortality revealed no glaring deficiencies in registration. The Quakers were responsible for a small amount of under-registration during the second half of the seventeenth century, but the major source was a consequence of the delay between birth and baptism. Baptisms were mainly affected and a large proportion of unbaptized burials appear to have been recorded in the registers. More importantly, there is little evidence to suggest that levels of under-registration varied significantly over time, at least until 1700. Thus, by using York's parish registers carefully it will be possible to provide a range of demographic measures for the city and demographic analysis in an early modern English city therefore becomes a practical possibility.

BAPTISMS, BURIALS AND MARRIAGES IN YORK

After each register had been checked for signs of poor registration, annual series of baptisms, burials and marriages were compiled and these were then combined to produce an aggregate series for the whole of York. Wrigley and Schofield were faced with a similar problem when constructing their national series based on a sample of 404 registers. Their solution was to start from a fixed point in time, then working backwards for each year, add together annual totals from each register, and if a gap occurred, assume that the contribution of that parish to the overall series remained constant.[27] This method was applicable to the York data since there is no evidence to show that disproportionate growth occurred in any of its parishes. Wrigley and Schofield's sample of registers was chosen because they were complete between 1662 and 1811, and if a gap occurred before 1662, that register no longer contributed

---

27 Wrigley and Schofield (1981), p. 61 assume that each register contributed the same proportion of events that it did in the ten years immediately before passing out of observation.

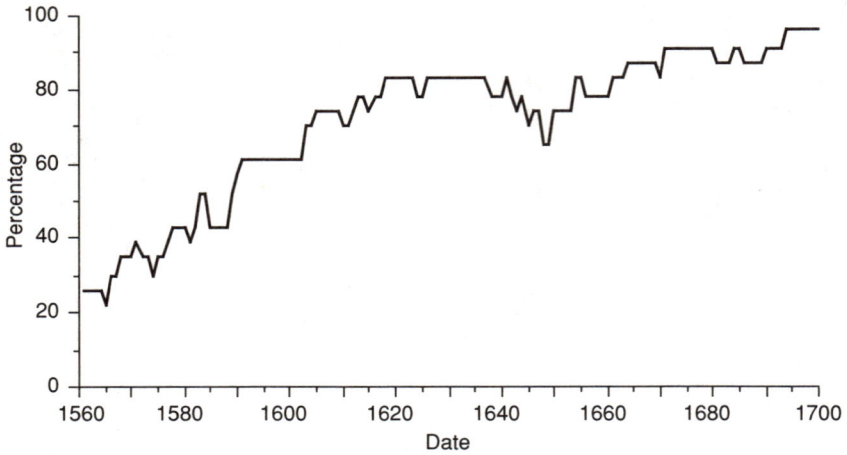

Figure 3.3: Percentage of parishes contibuting to the York series of baptisms

to the overall series. Most of York's registers contained gaps and few would pass Wrigley and Schofield's strict criteria; but by allowing the York registers to move both in and out of observation when registration appeared to be good, all available data could be incorporated into the series. Starting in 1700 the numbers of baptisms, burials and marriages from each parish were aggregated, with allowance being made for St John Ousebridge which lacked burial and marriage records at this date.[28] Working backwards, annual totals for the extant, accurate registers were aggregated and a proportion for the missing registers calculated. Finally, events from the extra-parochial areas of Minster Yard and Bedern were added to produce a total for the whole city.[29] It proved impossible to proceed beyond 1561 due to the poor quality of the early registers. Figure 3.3 shows the percentage contribution of the individual registers towards the aggregate series of baptisms. For most of the period, over 50 per cent of registers contributed towards the series and at no point does this fall below 20 per cent.[30] Coverage during the seventeenth century is good, although problems caused by the Civil War created some disruption to registration. Therefore, unless there were considerable inter-parish variations in demographic rates, suffi-

---

28 The number of burials and marriages in St Ousebridge was assumed to be in the same proportion as that parish's contribution to the 1671 Hearth Tax.

29 An attempt was also made to incorporate the three surviving Bishop Transcripts for St Nicholas into the series, but with few events being recorded in two of these years this was not possible. The 42 burials recorded in 1604 were added to the total for that year; see footnote 4, p. 58. Appendix 2 gives details of when each parish contributed to the overall series.

30 The graphs for burials and marriages are very similar. These figures are comparable with Wrigley and Schofield (1981), Figure 2.4, p. 61. Some of the earlier registers are from parishes with large populations, so in 1565 only 30 per cent of registers contributed to the series, but these contributed 42 per cent of all baptisms.

cient registers have been used for the aggregate series to accurately represent York's changing demographic fortunes.[31]

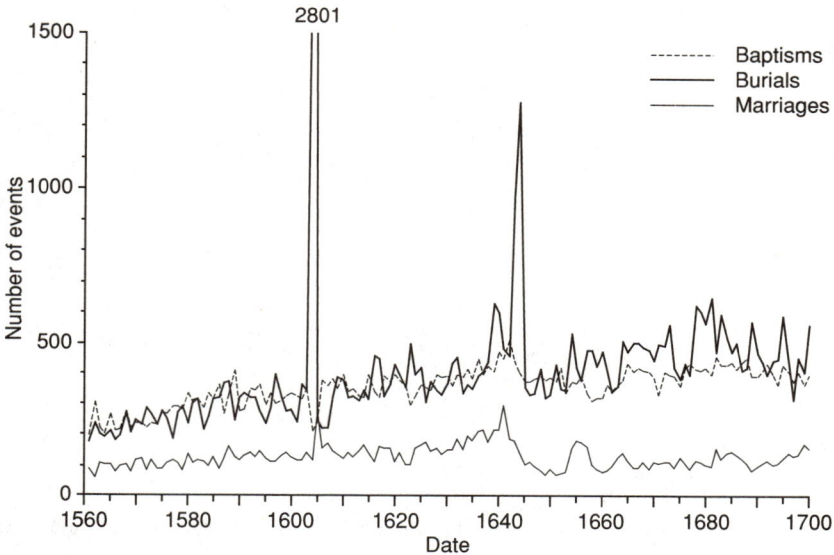

Figure 3.4: York aggregate series of baptisms, burials, and marriages, 1561–1700
Source: original parish registers.

The aggregate series of baptisms, burials and marriages is shown in Figure 3.4. It is dominated by two spectacular peaks in mortality. The first in 1604 was caused by an outbreak of bubonic plague which killed up to a third of York's population within the space of a few months. The second crisis was less intense and was spread throughout 1643 and 1644. It had no single cause, although it was associated with the Civil War. Few military deaths were recorded in York during these years and a temporary increase in population, caused in part by the billeting of troops through-out the city, probably created conditions in which diseases such as typhus could spread easily throughout the whole population. Following both crises, recovery was quick as in-migration made up much of the loss and the demographic consequences of crisis mortality were confined to the years immediately following, with any longer-term effects being slight. In the aftermath of each crisis, marriage rates increased substantially, fertility did likewise, and large amounts of in-migration probably created a younger age-structure; but since rates of mortality, fertility and, more importantly, migration were high at all times, the population would have quickly reverted to its pre-crisis structure. Figure 3.4 reveals three phases in York's demographic history which appear to be framed by the two periods of crisis mortal-

31 Tables 3.7 and 4.6 show that inter-parish variations were at most only small.

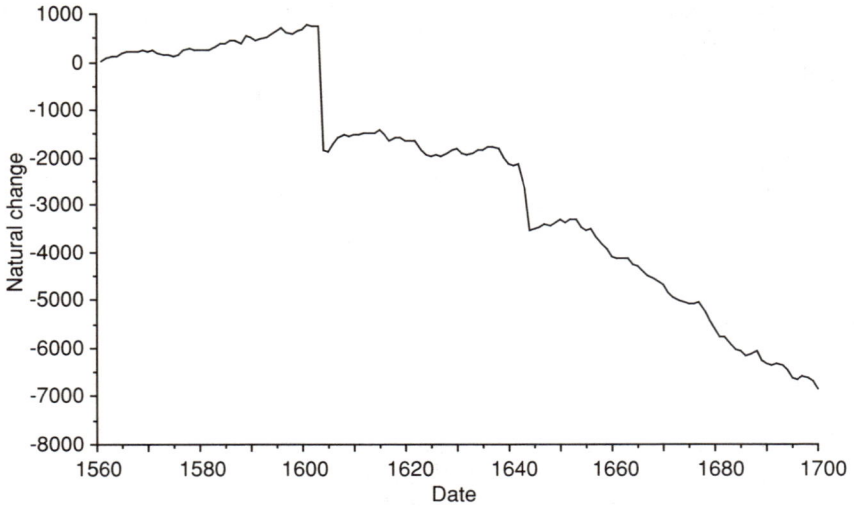

Figure 3.5: Cumulative natural change, York 1561–1700 (1561 = 0)
Source: original parish registers.

ity: the period from 1561–1600 is characterised by natural increase, between 1610 and 1640 a more balanced regime emerges and after 1650 natural decrease becomes almost universal. These three phases become clearer if cumulative natural change is graphed separately (Fig. 3.5). It is apparent that York's demographic regime changed during the period as natural increase gave way to natural decrease at some point during the seventeenth century. Taking each period in turn and excluding the crises, burial/baptism ratios were 0.94 (1561–1602), 1.02 (1605–1640), and 1.19 (1651–1700).[32]

Table 3.5: Possible levels of under-registration, York 1561–1700

Period	Baptisms (per cent)			Burials (per cent)		
	Max	Min	National	Max	Min	National
1561–1602	7	5	2.0	2	0	0
1605–40	7	5	3.2	2	0	0
1650–1700	10	5	7.2	5	0	1.9

Source: the national figures are taken from Wrigley and Schofield (1981), Table A4.2, p. 561.

32 Annual averages were (baptisms, burials, natural increase): 1561–1602 (285, 268, 17); 1605–40 (370, 377, –7); 1651–1700 (393, 467, –74).

Table 3.6: The effect of under-registration on death/birth ratios, York 1561–1700

Period	Burial/baptism ratio	Possible death/birth ratio
1561–1602	0.94	0.88–0.91
1605–40	1.02	0.95–0.99
1651–1700	1.19	1.08–1.19

It is possible to speculate on whether the varying pattern of natural change revealed by Figure 3.5 is a consequence of differential under-registration by using estimates from the previous section.[33] Since the absolute level of under-registration is not known, it is appropriate to give maximum and minimum estimates. Before 1650 registration loss due to nonconformity was negligible while during the second half of the seventeenth century at most three per cent would be missing from both baptism and burial registers.[34] By contrast, most loss was due to baptismal delay and levels from this source did not change significantly throughout the period. At most an additional seven per cent may have died unbaptized, although the evidence from reconstitution suggests a figure nearer to five per cent, with the difference probably representing the extent of burial loss. Maximum and minimum estimates of registration loss can now be given (Table 3.5). Wrigley and Schofield suggest that nationally, under-registration rates were low until the middle of the seventeenth century, although this does not preclude higher rates in some places, especially when IMRs were high and concentrations of nonconformists occurred. By applying correction factors to the baptism/burial ratios it is possible to give a range of death/birth ratios (Table 3.6). Since baptismal under-registration was always greater than burial under-registration, the death/birth ratio is lower than the burial/baptism ratio at all times. Furthermore, with little variation apparent throughout the period, the pattern revealed by Figure 3.5 is confirmed and the evidence for natural increase is strengthened. Indeed, in order for this pattern to be entirely caused by deteriorating registration, baptismal under-registration would need to have been in the order of 25 per cent during the second half of the seventeenth century, a figure that is clearly too high.

Finally, it is necessary to comment on the marriage series, which is probably less accurate than those for baptisms and burials. There are three reasons for this. First, small numbers of events occurred and since, couples had some choice over where they married, each parish series exhibits greater variability. Secondly, unlike bap-

---

33 Since it is obvious if a marriage took place there is no need to attempt to correct the marriage series. However, it is likely that some clandestine marriages (those undertaken in the absence of a priest) occurred and these will obviously have affected levels of nuptiality in York; see Wrigley (1973); Boulton (1993); Outhwaite (1995).

34 Most of the registration loss was due to the Quakers, so it is likely that actual levels were probably lower in 1650 and higher in 1700. It is difficult to determine how these levels changed throughout the period, but it is unlikely that levels would have been much greater than three per cent in the whole of this period.

tisms and burials, the proportion of marriages occurring within each parish did not remain constant. During the Commonwealth period, between 1653 and 1660, only certain churches were licensed to perform marriages. In some registers, the number of marriages recorded increased dramatically, while in others recording became erratic and it is difficult to determine whether this was because no marriages occurred or there is a gap in the register. Thirdly, when assessing nuptiality it is necessary to have some measure of the number of York couples who married and then remained in the city. Unfortunately, such information was not recorded and it is not known if those who married in York also remained there. York was a fashionable place to marry and many couples from outside the city chose to do so there. The possibility of clandestine marriages further complicates these issues. Nevertheless, with the exception of the period 1640–60 the overall stability of the marriage series suggests that it does give a broad indication of levels of nuptiality in York, with the marriage rate during the seventeenth century being lower than in the sixteenth century.

York's demography was therefore characterized by natural increase during the second half of the sixteenth century which gave way to natural decrease at some point during the seventeenth century. There are clearly a number of possible explanations for York's changing pattern of natural change since mortality, fertility and nuptiality could all be subject to change; however, before proceeding to examine the implications of these results in greater detail it is necessary to consider if inter-parish variations occurred.

INTER-PARISH VARIATIONS

Substantial variations in natural change among any of the 23 individual parish series could cause the aggregate series to simply reflect compositional rather than real changes as the various registers moved in and out of observation. Some variability is likely to occur when the components of any aggregate series are examined and it is also unreasonable to expect that the demography of any early modern city was entirely homogeneous. Nevertheless, a number of consistencies are immediately apparent when inter-parish variations are examined (Table 3.7). With the exception of St Martin cum Gregory, where burials matched baptisms exactly, every parish experienced natural decrease in the period 1650–1700. Burial/baptism ratios in the nine parishes, grouped together at the top of Table 3.7, increased at levels broadly similar to the overall series. In another seven, grouped in the middle, this pattern also appears to be evident, although it cannot be confirmed due to gaps in registration. Of the other seven: the ratio in St Michael le Belfrey almost matches the overall series; in St Denys with St George, St Margaret Walmgate and St Martin cum Gregory there is little variation between periods, and it is only in Holy Trinity Micklegate, St Mary Bishophill Jnr and St Mary Castlegate that significant differences occurred. These three parishes, together with St Saviour, St Cuthbert and St Maurice, recorded high burial/baptism ratios for at least part of the period. With the possible exception of these six parishes, little variation occurred across the other parishes which accounted for over 75 per cent of York's baptisms and burials during the 1690s.[35] It is unfortu-

Table 3.7: Burial/baptism ratios by parish, York 1561–1700

Parish	Period 1561–1602	1605–40	1650–1700	Percentage contribution to overall series 1691–1700 Baptisms	Burials
All Saints North Street	0.82	0.95	1.10	2.6	3.4
All Saints Pavement	0.78	0.95	1.19	5.7	5.2
Holy Trinity Goodramgate	0.93	1.07	1.24	5.1	5.9
St Crux	0.78	0.88	1.07	6.7	6.3
St Helen Stonegate	0.73	0.97	1.07	4.8	4.6
St John Ousebridge	0.72	1.06	1.16	3.0	4.3
St Martin Coney Street	0.83	1.02	1.13	3.4	3.3
St Olave	0.87	1.05	1.23	5.4	4.3
St Saviour	1.01	1.08	1.53	2.8	4.3
			Sub-total	*39.5*	*41.6*
Holy Trinity Kings Court	–	0.50	1.12	6.0	4.3
St Cuthbert	–	–	1.43	3.4	3.3
St Lawrence	–	1.10	1.23	1.6	1.6
St Mary Bishophill Snr	–	–	1.08	2.3	2.1
St Maurice	–	–	1.92	1.4	2.3
St Michael Spurriergate	–	1.03	1.10	5.4	5.9
St Sampson	–	–	1.15	4.5	4.2
			Sub-total	*24.6*	*23.7*
Holy Trinity Micklegate	1.35	0.98	1.15	4.4	4.8
St Denys with St George	1.10	0.99	1.15	3.4	3.3
St Margaret Walmgate	1.07	1.02	1.08	2.2	2.4
St Martin cum Gregory	1.10	1.03	1.00	3.4	2.4
St Mary Bishophill Jnr	–	1.92	1.14	4.9	4.2
St Mary Castlegate	–	1.46	1.42	5.3	6.6
St Michael le Belfrey	0.92	0.85	1.09	11.8	10.8
			Sub-total	*35.4*	*34.5*
Overall	*0.94*	*1.02*	*1.19*	*99.5*	*99.8*

Note: the percentages do not add up to 100 due to the small number of events recorded in Bedern Chapel and the Minster.
Source: original parish registers.

nate that of the parishes recording high burial/baptism ratios only St Saviour has a surviving sixteenth-century register, and to what extent the discovery of these missing registers might affect the overall ratio is of course impossible to tell. But by assuming that the proportion of events remained constant after a register passed out of observation, the high burial/baptism ratios in these parishes are also assumed to have occurred in the earlier period. Thus, the small parish of St Maurice contributed

35 Similar proportions occurred in other decades.

1.4 per cent of York's baptisms and 2.3 per cent of its burials in the 1690s, with similar proportions, based on the decade before it passed out of observation, being assumed to have occurred before 1650 when the register begins. Consequently, if the pattern of decreasing ratios in St Saviour had been replicated in these parishes, then the amount of natural increase during the sixteenth century would have been greater than that indicated by the aggregate series. Indeed, burial/baptism ratios for each decade from 1561, without inflating for the missing registers, were 0.84, 0.85, 0.91 and 0.92, respectively. Thus, compositional changes within the aggregate series do not explain York's changing demographic regime. A few parishes did experience large amounts of natural decrease; nevertheless, demographic patterns in most of early modern York, at least with respect to natural change, were remarkably uniform.

Table 3.8: York parishes ranked by wealth, 1671–72

Parish	% exempt from Hearth Tax (1672)		Mean number of hearths per household (1671)		% receiving poor relief (1671)	
All Saints North Street	6.5	(3)	2.8	(19=)	2.7	(5)
All Saints Pavement	26.1	(15)	2.9	(17=)	3.7	(9)
Holy Trinity Goodramgate	27.8	(17)	3.1	(10=)	5.9	(14=)
Holy Trinity Kings Court	7.8	(4)	3.1	(10=)	6.4	(18)
Holy Trinity Micklegate	17.1	(11)	3.4	(7)	5.6	(13)
St Crux	12.5	(8)	2.9	(17=)	3.7	(9)
St Cuthbert	42.5	(21)	2.2	(23)	8.6	(18)
St Denys with St George	24.6	(14)	2.8	(19=)	2.9	(7)
St Helen Stonegate	17.7	(12)	3.9	(5)	4.3	(12)
St John Ousebridge	16.1	(10)	3.2	(8=)	1.6	(2)
St Lawrence	–	–	3.6	(6)	–	–
St Margaret Walmgate	36.8	(19)	2.3	(21=)	6.2	(17)
St Martin Coney Street	10.2	(7)	6.2	(1)	3.2	(8)
St Martin cum Gregory	3.9	(1)	4.3	(4)	0.8	(1)
St Mary Bishophill Jnr	35.8	(18)	1.9	(24)	5.9	(14=)
St Mary Bishophill Snr	45.4	(22)	3.0	(14=)	2.4	(4)
St Mary Castlegate	38.2	(20)	3.1	(10=)	9.7	(19)
St Maurice	27.0	(16)	2.3	(21=)	1.8	(3)
St Michael le Belfrey	4.8	(2)	4.5	(3)	5.9	(14=)
St Michael Spurriergate	13.0	(9)	3.2	(8=)	2.7	(5)
St Olave	20.5	(13)	3.1	(10=)	–	–
St Sampson	9.1	(6)	3.0	(14=)	3.7	(9)
St Saviour	50.8	(23)	3.0	(14=)	11.3	(20)
Minster Yard	8.5	(5)	5.1	(2)	–	–

Source: Hibberd (1981), pp. 148, 180, 256.

It is difficult to explain why high burial ratios occurred in some parishes.[36] The
ratio in St Cuthbert may have been influenced by the small sample size (only 216
burials) and the location of the city's largest gaol in St Mary Castlegate explains
some, but not all, of that parish's excess mortality. Frequent executions were carried
out at the Castle, but a prisoner was more likely to contract some fatal disease in this
unhealthy institution than be executed. No single reason can be given for the high
burial/baptism ratios in the other parishes. The parishes where the highest rates
occurred, St Saviour, St Cuthbert, St Maurice, St Mary Bishophill Jnr and St Mary
Castlegate, are all located towards the south-east edge of the city (Fig. 3.1). There
was a tendency for the rich to live in the centre of the pre-industrial city, with the
poor and more transient elements within the population located in the outer parishes
and suburbs. The high ratios could therefore be explained if a correlation between
poverty and differential demographic rates can be established (Sjoberg, 1960). Such
a relationship is by no means obvious and is difficult to test. Studies of the early modern city have demonstrated that while the rich were indeed more likely to live in the
central parishes where many of the best houses were located, the poor often lived
alongside their richer neighbours, albeit in overcrowded courts away from the main
thoroughfares (Boulton, 1987a, pp. 166–205; Slack, 1985, pp. 123–26). There were
undoubted concentrations of rich and poor in certain parts of York, but it would be
misleading to classify parishes simply as 'rich' or 'poor' given the diversity within
parishes. Methodological problems also arise when attempts are made to determine
the wealth profile of individual parishes. During the 1670s a variety of information
is available from which inferences about the wealth of York's parishes can be made.
Table 3.8 ranks parishes according to the three best surviving data sources: the mean
number of hearths, the percentage exempt from the Hearth Tax and the percentage
receiving poor relief. Each source suggests that there were great variations in wealth
between parishes, with exemptions from paying the Hearth Tax varying from 4.8 to
50.8 per cent. St Martin cum Gregory scores high on each list, while St Cuthbert, St
Margaret and St Saviour appear near the bottom using every criteria. By comparison,
St Maurice had large numbers exempt from the Hearth Tax and only a small number
in receipt of poor relief. In St Michael le Belfrey few were exempt from paying the
Hearth Tax, the mean number of hearths per households was high, yet a large proportion of the parish were still in receipt of poor relief. Indeed, given that St Michael
le Belfrey contained about ten per cent of York's population, there was probably a
greater number of poor here than in any other parish. There may also have been a
greater likelihood of receiving poor relief for those living near the rich who could
easily afford to pay; however, transfers of payments between parishes did occur.[37]
Examining Table 3.8 as a whole, only a small correlation between the three indicators of wealth used emerges.[38] Some differences may have been caused by the qual-

36 There is little to suggest that graveyards were full or parishes accepted burials from elsewhere in the
city.
37 Slack (1988), pp. 173–82 discusses proportions contributing towards and in receipt of poor relief.
38 Using Spearman's rank correlation coefficient to compare columns 1, 2 and 3, $r_s = +0.544$ (1, 2); $r_s =
+0.431$ (1, 3); $r_s = +0.172$ (2, 3).

ity of the source material, yet this cannot explain all the variation, and clearly over-reliance on a single source when assessing wealth will create problems, especially if the structure of the parishes was more diverse than is often assumed. Consequently, labelling parishes 'rich' or 'poor' is likely to prove misleading. A better way of approaching this topic would be to examine the experiences of individual families. This would involve linking family reconstitution data with additional sources that indicate wealth such as the Hearth Tax. Unfortunately, such studies are extremely time-consuming, limited by the survival of sources, often restricted to small periods of time and consequently end up with a very small and possibly unrepresentative sample.[39] Despite these considerable reservations, Table 3.8 has indicated that there is a group of parishes, St Cuthbert, St Margaret Walmgate, St Mary Bishophill Jnr, St Mary Castlegate and St Saviour, where concentrations of poverty occurred, and these were also the ones that recorded the highest levels of natural decrease.[40] It is often assumed that the poor suffered higher levels of mortality than the rich, but before the twentieth century this relationship is far from universal and difficult to establish.[41] Many variables influenced mortality, and since wealth may also have affected household composition and the ability to marry, which in turn influenced overall levels of fertility, it is not necessarily surprising that at the parish level it is difficult to find more than a slight correlation between natural change and a variety of indicators of poverty.[42] Overall, York appears to have been remarkably homogeneous with respect to natural change. A small group of poorer parishes exhibited above average burial/baptism ratios, yet these provided only a quarter of York's total baptisms and burials.

YORK'S DEMOGRAPHIC REGIME

Two important conclusions can be drawn from the analysis of natural change in early modern York: (1) the city was affected by crisis mortality relatively rarely; (2) York's underlying demographic regime changed from one of natural increase to natural decrease at some point during the seventeenth century. In the short term, crisis mortality had a devastating impact on the city's population; however, longer-term effects were slight and recovery occurred quickly, especially after the 1604 plague. This was

39 Hibberd (1983) managed to link only 65 families to the 1671 Hearth Tax.
40 Other parishes such as St Lawrence, St Mary Bishophill Snr and St Denys with St George were located in the same part of the city and experienced different patterns of natural change.
41 Slack (1985), pp. 113–43 associates variations in plague mortality with the spatial distribution of wealth. The most effective measure against plague was to leave infected areas, and this course of action may have been more readily available to the rich. To what extent other diseases disproportionately affected the poor is difficult to determine. Woods and Williams (1995) suggest that this subject is complex, with few variations being apparent before 1850. Also, see Woods *et al.* (1993), pp. 36–41.
42 Most who qualified for poor relief at the end of the seventeenth century were listed under a single name and presumably many would have been old and/or sick and consequently have experienced high rates of mortality. On 3 May 1676, 399 payments for poor relief were made: 98 to men, 224 to women, 23 to men and children, 34 to women and children, 11 to couples and 9 to children; YCA E74.

fortunate since, unlike Norwich which was affected by repeated outbreaks of plague, York's underlying demographic regime clearly emerges. Between 1561 and 1603 baptisms exceeded burials as York's population steadily increased. By the second half of the seventeenth century burials exceeded baptisms and the population had entered a period of stagnation. Clearly, between these two periods there was an increase in mortality relative to fertility, and the early seventeenth century can therefore be viewed as one of transition, with baptisms matching burials and population increase being only slight. Analysis of the aggregate series cannot determine what caused this change, and most of Chapters 4 and 5 will be devoted to analysing patterns of mortality and fertility in the city with emphasis being placed on finding when and how changes occurred.

Much of the literature concerning the demography of early modern towns has sought to explain the causes and consequences of natural decrease. The analysis of York's parish registers has shown that natural decrease was not a universal phenomenon and it is likely that York was not exceptional in this respect. The underlying trend within York's demographic regime was undoubtedly natural increase, yet this needs to be set alongside what happened when plague struck. Any accumulated natural increase was wiped away within months and it is unlikely that any large city would have escaped its effects entirely. This means that even though cities may have experienced natural increase at other times, they would still be an overall drain on national population resources and their survival be dependent on rural immigration. Nevertheless, at other times the York evidence clearly shows that under certain circumstances, and these have yet to be determined, cities were not always 'urban graveyards' – they could and indeed did experience natural increase for long periods.

Chapter 4

BRIEF LIVES

The threat of death was ever present in early modern York and the suddenness with which it could strike is apparent from the events of 1604, when over 3,000 died of bubonic plague, most within the space of a few months. Such 'crises' were rare and when a further outbreak of plague occurred in 1631 the disease was brought under control following the introduction of appropriate public health measures. Isolated instances of crisis mortality had relatively little impact on the urban demographic regime since a large influx of migrants caused the population to recover quickly; of greater importance was the general 'background' level of mortality throughout the city. While York's parish registers occasionally hint that this was extremely high (for instance, 'Margaret Metcalf had twelve children of whom eleven died before she was buried [23 October 1579]'), such examples are far from typical and not representative.[1] Much of this chapter will therefore be devoted to establishing accurate estimates of mortality for early modern York. In 1600 about 300 burials took place; half were infants and young children, the rest were spread fairly evenly amongst the other age groups. Many were able to live into comparative old age, but since little accurate data concerning age at death exists it is only by linking together baptisms and burials from the parish registers that levels of mortality can be assessed. Before proceeding to estimate mortality rates for early modern York it is nevertheless important to examine the frequency of crisis mortality since these incidents had such devastating short-term consequences for early modern society.

MORTALITY CRISES

Dramatic surges in mortality were a common feature of early modern demography and Figure 3.4 has already shown that mortality was exceptionally high in 1604 and 1643–44. There are a number of ways of measuring these increases, the simplest being the crisis mortality ratio – the number of burials in a year compared with the average of the previous decade.[2] A doubling of mortality is usually taken to indicate that a crisis has occurred, but in order not to miss any periods of high mortality Table 4.1 indicates all years with crisis mortality ratios of at least 1.5. For most of the period 1561–1700 levels of mortality in York remained relatively stable. The increases in 1616, 1639 and 1654 can be associated with high childhood mortality rates, while the crisis in 1643–44 coincided with a period of considerable turmoil caused by the Civil War. The truly spectacular increase in mortality occurred when

---

1 BIHR PR Y/J. A later example gives an equally horrendous picture: 'John the new born Son of Absalom Bluitt, dancing Master, being the 27th Child he has buried, all in Infancy, by two wives (11 September 1783)'; PR Y/MCS.

Table 4.1: Crisis mortality ratios, York 1561-1700

Year	Crisis mortality ratio
1604	10.1
1616	1.6
1639	1.6
1643	2.6
1644	3.3
1654	1.5

Source: original parish registers.

the city was infected with plague in 1604. York was fortunate that it was not affected by this disease as much as many provincial cities, although this favourable picture is distorted by the survival of few parish registers from the 1550s, a decade of exceptionally high mortality, especially during 1550–52 and 1557–58 (Slack, 1988, Tables 3.3–3.4, pp. 61–62). In both cases it is difficult to be certain what caused these crises; both periods coincided with national crises and it is likely that the city was infected with plague in 1550.[3] After the 1550s, while York was under almost constant threat from epidemic disease, it succumbed on only two further occasions.

When plague was reported to be in the vicinity of York during 1563–64 and 1579–80, the city Council attempted to prevent trade with infected areas, thereby hoping to avert a crisis and ensure the city's economic prosperity.[4] In both periods the threat passed quickly and in 1603–04 when plague approached the city similar measures were implemented. This time they proved inadequate. As early as July 1603 restrictions on trading with infected areas were introduced.[5] These were then extended to include Hull when plague broke out there; the bars (entrances through the city walls) were locked at night, watches were set and efforts were made to place a *cordon sanitaire* around the city.[6] It was clearly impossible to isolate York completely since a number of traders flouted these regulations. William Morton was even caught transporting his goods over the walls at night in an effort to escape detection.[7] By October 1603 plague had reached parts of the Ainsty, yet prosecutions for trading with infected areas still continued.[8] Throughout the winter there is little mention of plague in the Council's minutes. This is not surprising given that the aetiology of plague depends on the complex interaction between rat, flea and man and the rat flea is less active during the winter months. On 14 February 1604 trading restrictions with London were lifted providing that wares were not bought directly from houses

2 See Wrigley and Schofield (1981), pp. 646–49 for a more sophisticated approach.

3 Wrigley and Schofield (1981), pp. 670–71. Palliser (1973), pp. 49–52 discusses possible causes.

4 YCA BXXIII fols 106a–45a; BXXVII fols 170a–222b.

5 YCA B XXXII fol. 279a. Extracts from the Council's minutes (House Books) concerning the 1604 plague have been published in Sakata (1982a); also, see Davies (1873).

6 YCA B XXXII fol. 282a.

7 *Ibid.*, fol. 290a; others were also prosecuted for the same offence, see fol. 292b.

8 *Ibid.*, fol. 291a.

known to be infected.[9] Any optimism was short-lived, however, since in March the threat of infection reappeared. Watches were set to ensure that vagrants did not enter the city and the poor were prohibited from begging.[10] How effectively these measures were enforced is not known, but in April it was noted that there was 'great abuse in the watchmen & wardes at the barres & posterns of the Cittie'.[11] By early May, plague had entered the city. A 'viewer and clenser' was sought from Newcastle, plague lodges were erected outside the walls and a number of other public health measures, including the killing of cats and dogs, were enacted.[12] How the disease entered the city is not known, yet once it had breached the city walls the Council were unable to control its spread. An assessment was made of those suspected to be infected, further plague lodges were erected, but still disease continued to slowly spread throughout the city.[13] On 1 June the mayor sent a letter to Members of Parliament in London listing 17 households 'that are infected within this Cittie to my knowledge'.[14] During June and July the Council met only occasionally; it made no attempt to control the disease, but instead made further assessments for poor relief and tried to prevent councillors from fleeing the city:

> it hath pleased Almightye God to visite this Cittye with a greivous infection which doth dailye increase more and more in diverse stretes and places in this Cittye, and for that we that are the Magistrates of this Cittye are nowe to bestirr ourselves, and to advise and governe carefullye in this time of visitacon and not to care for ourselves onlie and lett the poore and visited here be unprovided for and not governed, therefore for the better governinge of this Cittye in this time of visitacon, it is agreed by me and the Aldermen my Bretheren that none of the Aldermen should go forthe of this Cittye duringe this time of visitacon.[15]

Many did not listen to this plea. Between 16 July to 21 September, no doubt overcome by the enormity of the situation, the council failed to meet and when it finally reconvened the main topic of business was the fining of absent councillors.[16]

The demographic impact of the disease was indeed severe. The city annals compiled in 1639 reveal that there 'dyed in York 3,512 persons', although it is not possible to give such a precise figure since the parish register of St Olave recorded that 'Thes months followinge viz August September October november & December people dyed so fast that they could not be well nombred'.[17] In most parishes registration remained good throughout the epidemic and analysis of the surviving

---

9 *Ibid.*, fol. 316a.
10 *Ibid.*
11 *Ibid.*
12 *Ibid.*, fols 325b, 329b. It was believed that plague miasmas would stick to the coats of cats and dogs. Similar measures were taken in other cities; see Slack (1985), pp. 199–226.
13 YCA B XXXII, fols 329b, 332b.
14 *Ibid.*, fol. 332b.
15 *Ibid.*, fol. 339b.
16 *Ibid.*, fol. 341b.
17 Palliser (1973), p.54; BIHR PR Y/OL 1.

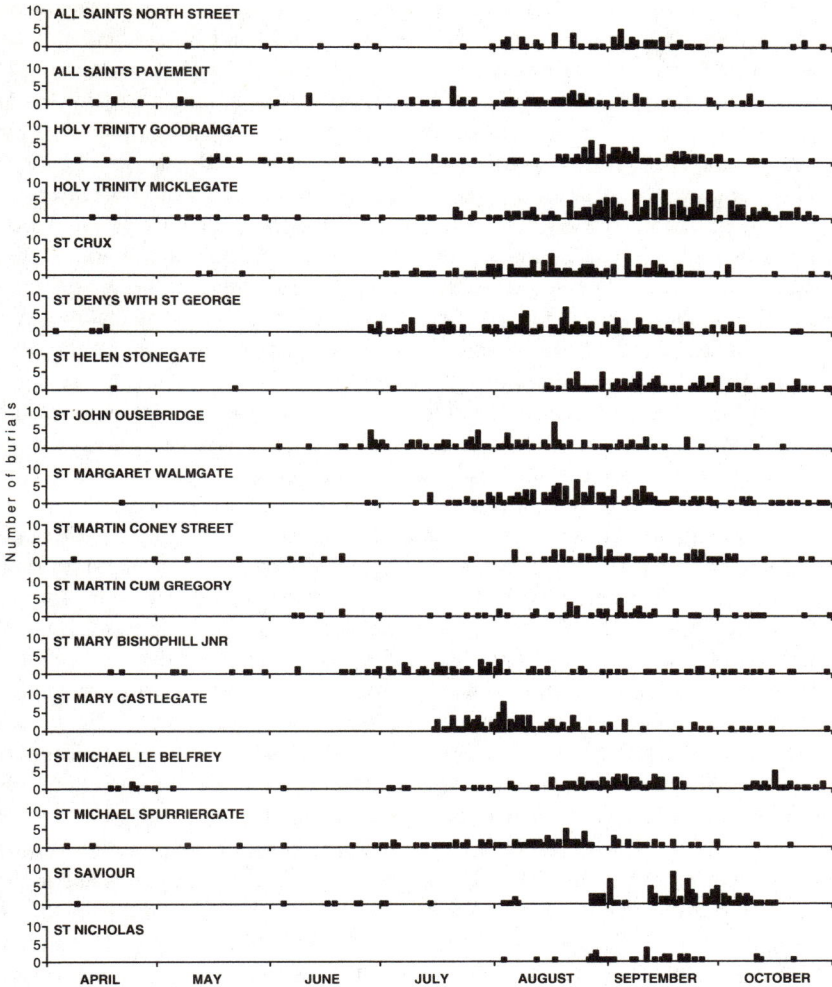

Figure 4.1: Daily burials, York 1604
Source: original parish registers.

registers reveals the full impact of the disease (Fig. 4.1).[18] The Council reported that on 5 May houses had been infected in the parishes of Holy Trinity Goodramgate, St Martin Coney Street, St Mary Bishophill Jnr, St Michael Spurriergate and St Olave,

18 This graphical presentation of the course of an urban epidemic was used by Paul Laxton, Department of Geography, University of Liverpool, in an unpublished paper on Norwich. I am grateful to him for allowing me to read his work.

yet in each case substantial increases in mortality only took place some months later.[19] In All Saints Pavement plague burials were specifically identified; the first occurred on 19 April, followed by a group of four between 7 and 10 May, one on 2 June, three on 11 June and it was only from 6 July that plague burials began to occur on an almost daily basis.[20] Plague therefore took time to become established and a few isolated cases did not necessarily spark an immediate epidemic. It is probable that following these first cases an epizootic amongst the rat population occurred and it was only then that plague could spread quickly throughout the human population. Substantial increases in burials first occurred in St Mary Bishophill Jnr and St John Ousebridge, and as the disease diffused from these foci other centres of infection erupted simultaneously throughout the city. It is likely therefore that by inadvertently transporting infected rats or fleas, human intervention was responsible for the complex way in which plague spread throughout the city.

The 1604 York plague epidemic exhibits all the classic characteristics of the disease.[21] Eighty-two per cent of all burials in 1604 occurred between July and October. All households were not affected equally since 47 per cent of all burials came from households recording three or more burials. In many ways the distribution of burials matched the population as a whole since the sex-ratio of plague burials was 96 males per 100 females and at least 40 per cent of deaths were of children. The number of baptisms decreased substantially once the epidemic had started, but more surprisingly the IMRs (284 per 1,000 live births) remained similar to non-crisis levels. All parishes were affected and only St Michael le Belfrey experienced the relatively low crisis mortality ratio of 4.1 compared with a range from 7.6 to 15.9 from the others.[22] While registration appears to have remained good, some burials must not have been recorded and what is not known of course is the number who fled the city during the epidemic. By October the disease was beginning to run out of victims, both rat and human, although colder weather may also have slowed down its progress. Nevertheless, mortality remained high in Holy Trinity Micklegate throughout November and December, in part because burials from the plague lodges were recorded in this register. By the end of the year the number of burials had returned to pre-crisis levels in all parishes even though in both All Saints North Street and All Saints Pavement four plague burials were recorded in 1605, the last being on 30 April.[23] Further cases did not occur and by this date up to a third of York's population had died from the disease.

---

19 YCA BXXXII fol. 332b.
20 BIHR PR Y/ASP 1. In St Michael Spurriergate on 23 April a burial 'supposed to be of the plague' occurred. This was followed by the first plague burial on 4 June; the next was on 23 June and from 29 June burials occurred almost daily with the last on 20 October; PR Y/MS 1.
21 See Slack (1985), pp. 111–43. The epidemic is discussed in detail in Galley (1991), 204–16.
22 No correlation between parochial wealth profiles and crisis mortality ratios could be discovered. The recording of burials from the plague lodges erected outside the city walls in certain registers was responsible for the highest ratios.
23 BIHR PR Y/ASN 1; Y/ASP 1.

York recovered from the epidemic remarkably quickly. Those who left the city to escape the disease soon returned, the marriage rate more than doubled, baptisms were higher between 1605 and 1610 than in 1603 and even burials had reached pre-plague levels by 1608. Much of this upsurge was due to those having survived the plague being in a favourable economic position to marry, but migrants must have flocked to York after 1604 and entries to the Freedom more than doubled in 1605. Evidence about population size is of course not available. In March 1604, 39 households contributed to a rating assessment in the parish of Holy Trinity Goodramgate, and when the next assessment took place a year later, the same number of households made contributions.[24] While some of the richer households may have fled the city during the epidemic, the turnover rate between these assessments was 36 per cent, well over twice the normal level. Within a few years the city had achieved complete demographic recovery – it was almost as though the epidemic had never taken place.

Some of the social repercussions of plague cannot be revealed by the bare demographic facts. One extract from the Council minutes, which has survived by chance, indicates that not everyone suffered quietly. It describes a riot outside Bootham Bar:

> in the tyme of the late visitacon at diverse tymes the said inhabitantes in St Mariegate were verie disorderous and wold not be kepte in by the watchmen when the same strete was sore infected, whereupon the watchmen, constable and other inhabitantes in Bowthome were by then greatlie trobled & putt in great feare and did compleyne to my Lord Maior.[25]

The crowd were objecting to their richer neighbours inside the walls denying them access to food. They were finally dispersed only after a gun had been fired which left at least one person wounded. The Council did make special provision for poor relief, yet it would appear that such measures were insufficient. How typical this incident was is difficult to say. Records for the worst period of the epidemic are missing and evidence of this incident has survived only because the person who was wounded applied for relief at a later date. Plague brought untold misery to a population and even those who were fortunate to survive the disease itself still suffered.

In 1610, 1624–26 and 1636–37 the threat of plague reappeared; some households were quarantined and in 1645 there was even a suspected case of plague.[26] On each occasion the threat never materialized and York was infected only once more, in 1631. This time the disease was effectively controlled and confined almost entirely to one parish. In May the possibility of infection spreading from London had been reported to the Council and in June plague was said to be prevalent in several small towns near to York.[27] In August, watch was set throughout the Ainsty and by the 29th the Council minutes record that 'it hath pleased Almighty God to visit some persons

---

24 BIHR Y/HTG 12.

25 YCA B XXXII fol. 372b; Slack (1985), p. 288.

26 YCA B XXXIII fols 46b–47b; B XXXIV fols 197b–298a; B XXXV fols 334a–35b; B XXXVI fol. 7b; fols 149a–50a. What happened to the plague suspect is not known, the register of St Martin Micklegate is missing during 1645.

27 YCA B XXXV, fols 105a, 107a.

in St Lawrence churchyard with the infection of the plague'.[28] Six watchmen were set to keep people away from the churchyard, all beggars and wanderers were removed from the city, a plague lodge was erected and the parish was effectively isolated from the rest of the city. By 31 August there were '16 dead thereof in St Lawrence and one in St Margaret's parish';[29] ominously it appeared that the events of 1604 were to be repeated. On the same day the Council received a letter from Sir Thomas Wentworth, the President of the Council in the North, which instructed the city to adopt a series of public health measures against the plague. These included restrictions on movement, and more importantly, the rigorous isolation of the sick, those suspected to be sick and all who came into contact with the sick. Similar measures had been implemented in 1604, the difference being that in 1631 Wentworth's orders were accompanied with threats:

> I am sorie to hear that the sicknesse hath sett foote within the walles of this cittie, and conceiving the danger to be verie great ... and that it maie be the easilie prevented in the beginning than hearafter ... I do repeat that you punctually observe theise orders followinge withall I must tell you plainelie I will informe myself very dilegentlie how they are observed and executed, and shall proceed sevearly to punich your negligence and others disobediense of them ... if anie disorderlie p'sons shall not obey your dyrections hearin ... if they be men of substance you doe acquaint me & the Council therewith, who you shall see will make their doeings exemplarie, if they be poore & meane people you are to appoynt your officers to see them to be soundly whipped severall days after if there be cause to the terror of such desperate people.[30]

Wentworth's instructions appear to have been enforced vigorously. All those suspected of being infected along with any contacts were immediately quarantined. Special attention was given to ensure that St Lawrence remained isolated and watch was 'sett at the end of St Nicholas forthwith to keepe out strangers and to keepe in the inhabitants without Walmgate Bar'.[31] Throughout September there are frequent references to those falling sick or coming into contact with the sick.[32] In every case the individuals concerned were quarantined and their houses shut up. As the plague abated in St Lawrence, some houses were cleansed, although even after being allowed back into their houses these individuals were still kept under tight quarantine, 'the inhabitants on without walmgate be all shutt up in their own several houses and their back doors lock upp or nayled upp and their fore doors also lock upp on the day'.[33] On 9 November the worst of the plague had passed 'in regard the infection of the plague (god be thanked) is well abated and that there is now any one sick within

28 *Ibid.*, fol. 113b.
29 *Ibid.*, fol. 114b. Only 11 burials had been recorded in St Lawrence's parish register by the end of August, although a plague burial is specifically mentioned in St Margaret Walmgate; BIHR Y/L 1; PR Y/MARG 1.
30 YCA B XXV 115b–17a. This has been published in Sellars (1913), pp. 456–57.
31 *Ibid.*, fol. 122a.
32 *Ibid.*, fols 122a–27a.
33 *bid.*, fols 130a–33b.

the walls of the citty therof'.[34] The orders were still not suspended, however, and later in the same month several people within the walls were isolated:

> it is ordered that Thomas Walker dyer his house in Conistreete be forthw[th] shutt up for that his daughter Rebecca a convicted recusant is dead this morning and feared to be of the infection and a watch sett at the doore and the corps viewed before she be buried & be buryed at ix of the clocke this night but neither in the church nor church yard but on toft Greene and there the clenser to view her and bury her.[35]

Indeed, individuals and families continued to be isolated until the end of March 1632, well after any threat had disappeared. Such measures were extreme, but they proved to be effective. Within the city walls few plague deaths were recorded – five from one household in St Denys with St George and in the adjoining parish of St Margaret Walmgate three burials from one household together with four others.[36] As in 1604, isolated cases of plague did not spark an immediate epidemic and in 1631 a large-scale epizootic amongst the city's rat population must have been prevented. The black rat is a sedentary creature and in the absence of human intervention plague is likely to spread only slowly, especially if suspected households were quarantined immediately. Only the small extra-mural parish of St Lawrence was badly affected by plague. The crisis mortality ratio for this parish was 4.2, compared with a figure for the city as a whole of only 0.97. Burials were high throughout September in St Lawrence, with 58 per cent from households recording more than three burials.[37] Whether all those who died had resided in St Lawrence is difficult to say since some falling sick inside the walls may have been removed to the plague lodges which were erected in the churchyard. With plague appearing much later in the year, during 1631 favourable climatic conditions or even simple chance may also have helped to prevent its spread. However, such a conclusion seems unlikely and for possibly the first time in England there is strong evidence to suggest that public health initiatives had managed to avert an epidemic (Slack, 1989).

The extended crisis in 1643–44 had no single cause, although it coincided with intense military activity both in and around the city. During the 1640s royalist York became a military stronghold, and as early as 1639 about 30,000 troops were quartered nearby, together with many in the city itself (Warmington, 1990, p. 17). Charles I moved his court to York in 1642, a permanent garrison was established in the city and during the winter the Earl of Newcastle arrived with some 6,000 men (Newman, 1978). It is not possible to give precise details of the number of troops either visiting or staying in York, but in early 1644 the Royalist garrison numbered around 4,000 and at one point 500 men were billeted at free quarters in one parish containing only 40 households (Wenham, 1970, p. 2; Warmington, 1990, p. 21). Part of the increase in burials in both years can therefore be explained by a greater population at risk.

---

34 *Ibid.*, fol. 139a.
35 *Ibid.*, fols 141b.
36 BIHR PR Y/SDG 1; Y/MARG 1.
37 Galley (1991), pp. 217–20. A total of 73 burials is recorded in St Lawrence's register during 1631.

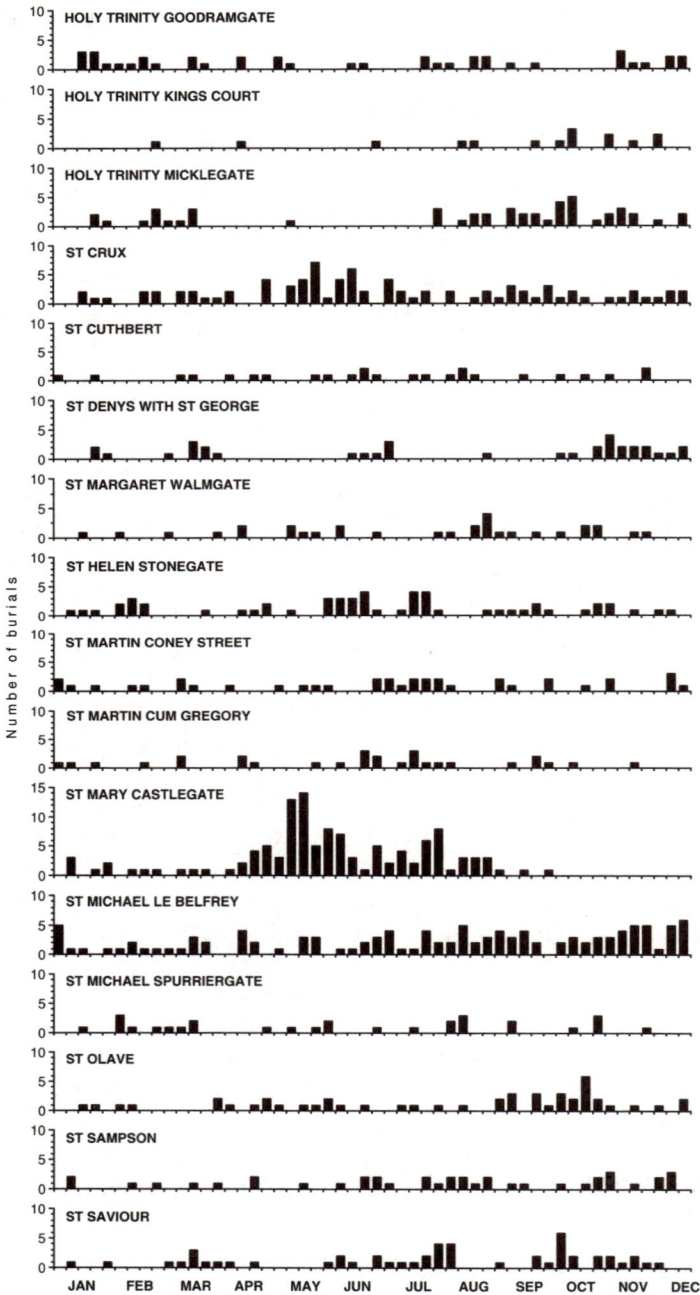

Figure 4.2: Weekly burials, York 1643.
Source: original parish registers.

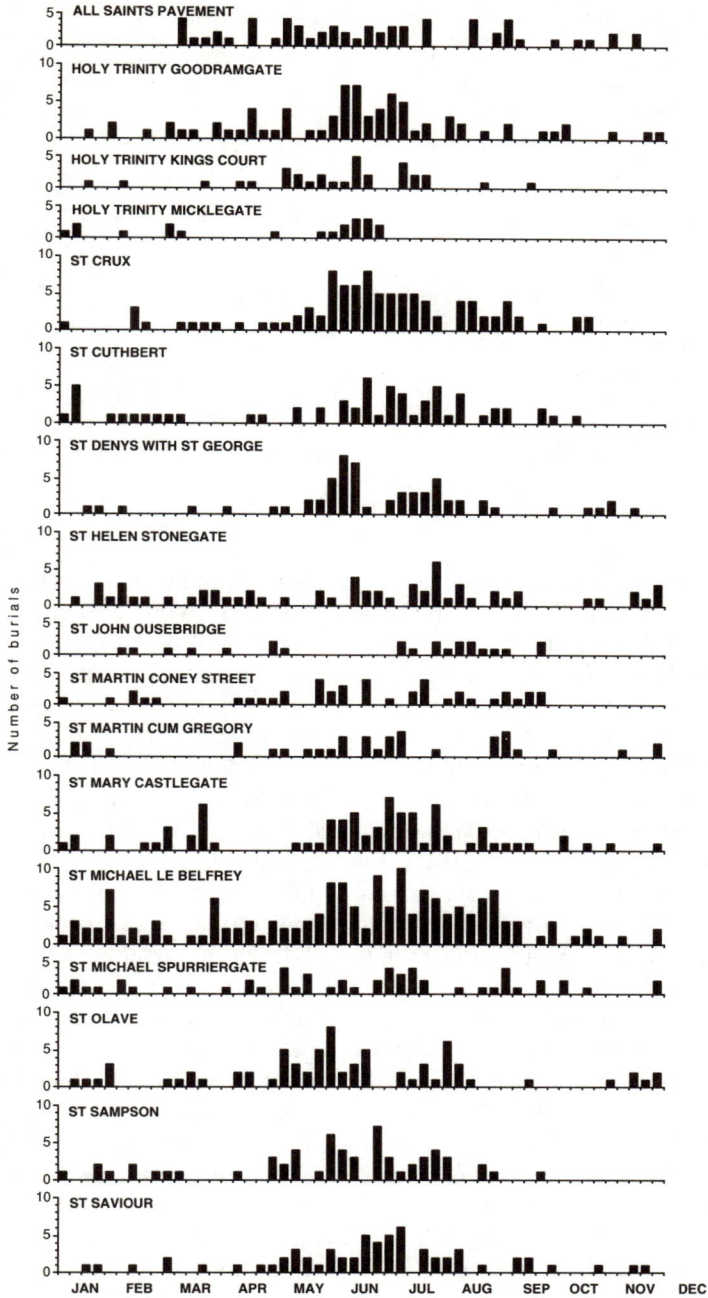

Figure 4.3 Weekly burials, York 1644.
Source: original parish registers.

Table 4.2: Monthly 'prisoner' and/or 'soldier' burials, York 1643

Parish		J	F	M	A	M	J	J	A	S	O	N	D
St Crux	Soldiers/Prisoners				2	11	9	2					
	Others	3	4	6	1	4	7	6	4	9	7	3	5
	Total	3	4	6	3	15	16	8	4	9	7	3	5
St Helen Stonegate	Soldiers/prisoners		1		1		7	3		1			
	Others	3	6	1	2	2	2	6	3	4	2	5	7
	Total	3	7	1	3	2	9	9	3	4	3	5	7
St Mary Castlegate	Soldiers/prisoners				3	30	13	2	3				
	Others	5	3	3	5	6	5	12	14	4	1	6	3
	Total	5	3	3	8	36	18	14	17	4	1	6	3

Source: original parish registers.

Severe problems of overcrowding must have occurred, and with troops being notorious disseminators of disease, it is perhaps surprising that mortality did not increase even more. Figures 4.2 and 4.3 show weekly burials in 1643–44. The distribution of burials in both years follows no simple pattern. The lack of a clear summer peak and the absence of any contemporary references suggests that the increases were not caused by plague. In 1643 most parishes experienced a general increase in mortality throughout the year and there is little evidence of epidemic disease. The exception was St Mary Castlegate where the county gaol was located. Here an epidemic, which later spread to the civilian population, occurred in the Castle, causing many soldier and prisoner burials (Table 4.2). In St Crux and St Helen Stonegate some of the increase in mortality can also be associated with the influx of soldiers. Despite this evidence and the possibility that under-registration affected some parishes, no epidemic occurred throughout the city even though levels of mortality more than doubled. Mortality remained high throughout the winter and, following a series of military reversals, Royalist York was besieged at the beginning of June. On 6 June the suburbs were burned and all troops and inhabitants were withdrawn inside the walls. Throughout the siege no serious food shortages occurred. There was little actual fighting in York, with military activity being mainly confined to an assault on the King's Manor. Overall, few military or civilian casualties were caused directly by the war. The siege was eventually lifted with the arrival of Prince Rupert's army at the end of June. Relief was short-lived, however, and following the defeat of the royalist forces at Marston Moor, York was forced to surrender on 16 July 1644. Figure 4.3 shows that the number of burials increased considerably during the siege period, then they rapidly declined from September. The most likely explanation of this can be related to changes in the population at risk. The suburbs which 'of late amounted to a sixth part of the city ... were wasted to ashes with fire', and this caused a substantial increase in the population inside the walls (Widdington, 1897, p. 5). Others, including the Royalist mayor of Beverley, had also found temporary refuge within the city, and while some may have fled, the population of most parishes would have been substantially higher in 1644 than they were before the war (Wenham, 1970, pp. 125–27). During 1644, eleven per cent of all burials were described as military, and this is certainly an underestimate since not every parish register specifically identified such burials.[38] Sanitary conditions severely worsened and it is therefore not surprising that the highest IMRs of the seventeenth century occurred in 1643 and 1644.[39] The influx of population encouraged the spread of disease as a contemporary description of conditions in the city after the siege records: 'Through the long siege the Town was unhealthful, we found and left many sick of the spotted fever'.[40] The crisis in 1643–44 was therefore caused by a number of factors, and while disease played its part, the major cause was the social dislocation brought by war. This disruption also affected the economy for some years after the war had ended, and this must be seen as the main reason why recovery in York was much slower after 1644 than it had been after 1604.

Table 4.3: Crisis mortality ratios for suspected famine years

Year	Crisis mortality ratio
1586	1.21
1587	1.40
1588	1.41
1596	0.91
1597	1.28
1598	1.03
1622	0.95
1623	1.35
1624	1.07

Source: original parish registers.

Table 4.1 is notable for the absence of three periods when grain shortages can be associated with widespread increases in mortality in parts of the North: 1586–88, 1596–98 and 1623 (Appelby, 1978). In each of these periods concern was expressed about the supply of food to York, and one person is recorded as having starved to death, 'a poore man who was found dead w'thin Roocklif feilds, by famishment, was

38 Wenham, 1970, pp. 148–55 gives a list of military burials in the city's parish registers.
39 Galley (1991), p. 231. IMRs in 1643 and 1644 were 346 and 359 deaths per 1,000 live births.
40 Ash (1644) quoted in Wenham (1970), p. 106. Spotted fever is generally considered to be typhus, which is spread by the body louse.

buried the xxii day of March (1587)'.[41] Fortunately, this individual proved to be exceptional, any increases in mortality were small and there is little demographic evidence that indicates the presence of famine (Table 4.3).[42] In each of these periods there was a threat of famine, but prompt action by the City Council managed to avert crises from developing. In May 1586 a letter was sent to York from the Privy Council concerning:

> the redressings of some disorders touchinge the dearth of corne and victuall ... We are given to understand of great scarcitie and dearthe in divers counties of the realme ... by the unseasonablenes of the last harvest but chiefly by the gredynes of the farmors and others having sufficient provision of corne in their barnes and grayners and yet of purpose to enhance and raise the prices do forbeare to serve and furnishe the markette of such convenient quantities.[43]

Whether the shortages were caused by farmers' greed is uncertain, but immediately York Council sought to maintain a weekly supply of grain at 'a resonable price'.[44] During the summer, prosecutions took place of merchants who purchased grain in Hull and preferred to sell it in Selby rather than at market in York.[45] In February 1587 an order was made 'to see the poore served before anye Cittizens; and then straingers'.[46] Restrictions on the quantities of grain that could be purchased were introduced and corn badgers (merchants) were prevented from trading without a licence. In July, measures were taken to fix the price of grain and stabilize bread prices.[47] Throughout the Council ensured that the poor were always able to buy grain, and in addition to controlling prices, much of its work was concerned with the relief of poverty. As early as February 1586 the Council minutes noted that 'the inhabitantes of the Cittye are sore charged with the relief of a great number of poore people, a great number wherof beinge straingers, and such as have come forthe of the countrye'.[48] Two years later the situation must have deteriorated since a 'generall viewe' of all poor people in the city was made.[49] Those who were not born or who had not lived in York for three years were banished, while the 'aged, lame and impotente and past ther worke' were given better provision.[50] Work was provided for the unemployed and houses of correction and stocks were set up to deal with the problem of 'roges, vagabondes and strange beggers'.[51] The Council sought to prevent famine in two ways: first, by maintaining a supply of grain at prices all could afford,

---

41 BIHR PR Y/MB 1; Palliser (1982), p. 90.
42 Galley (1991), pp.196–204. Burial seasonality during these periods does not suggest famine.
43 YCA B XXIX fol. 116a.
44 *Ibid.*, fol. 117b.
45 *Ibid.*, fols 120a–b. Also, see fols 123b–24a.
46 *Ibid.*, fol. 174b.
47 *Ibid.*, fol. 204b.
48 *Ibid.*, fol. 190b. It is not surprising that subsistence migrants would head for York given its local economic domination.
49 YCA B XXX fols 4a–5b.
50 *Ibid.*
51 *Ibid.*

and secondly, by controlling poverty. Relief was provided for the 'deserving poor' and migrants were dissuaded from flooding into the city seeking food and charity. There was also new legislation regulating brewers, tiplers and innholders.[52] This ensured that too much grain was not diverted from the market place into making ale and also as a means of social control since some of the poor who 'get sufficient to mayntene them may be restrained from the alehouse where they drinke all that should mayntene ther poore wifes and children at home'.[53] Alehouses could be the focus for social unrest and throughout all the Council's efforts there was an underlying desire to maintain order. This it managed to achieve. There were no food riots, widespread starvation did not occur and the small increase in burials can perhaps be explained by the arrival of migrants, temporarily increasing the population at risk and helping to spread disease throughout the population.

Similar successes were repeated in 1596–98 when food shortages were more serious, both nationally and in York (Palliser, 1983, pp. 189–92). In October 1596 the Council regulated that:

> for good order to be kept in the corne markets and for saile of corne in this cittie ... it is ordained that no corne bought or bringinge unto or towards the markets be solde in aine place either by the waye or elles where but onlie in open marketes.[54]

The maintenance of social order by regulating the grain supply was again of primary concern to the Council. The poor were to be served first, 'at a reasonable price'; no one was to buy more corn than they needed for themselves and any unsold corn was 'not to be taken from York'.[55] Restrictions were imposed on corn badgers, millers and brewers, who were only allowed to purchase reasonable quantities of grain. In November 1596 the citizens were 'commanded to abstayne from Wednesday suppers, from eating of the flesh upon fasting days & from making fasts & suppers on Fridays & fastings days at night'.[56] By February 1597 the Council minutes speak of a 'great want of grain in the citie' and letters were sent to both Leicestershire and Nottinghamshire to procure it.[57] In April no malt or barley was allowed to be malted.[58] Throughout the summer no new regulations were introduced, but in September there were still grain shortages and further action was taken to ensure no one made purchases before it came to market.[59] Once again there was great concern over the number of 'rogues, vagabonds and beggars' in the city.[60] Country beggars were 'kept forth of the city' and orders were given to apprehend any found within the

---

52 YCA B XXIX fols 164a–166a; 175b.
53 YCA B XXX fol. 5b.
54 YCA B XXXI, fol. 223a.
55 *Ibid.*
56 *Ibid.*, fol. 242b.
57 *Ibid.*, fol. 254a.
58 *Ibid.*, fol. 266a.
59 *Ibid.*, fols 293a–b.
60 *Ibid.*, fol. 251a.

walls.[61] At the same time there were fears that York would be infected with plague: the bars and posterns in the city walls were locked at night and people from 'Newcastle & other places thereabouts' were refused entry.[62] There was also further legislation concerning drink, with all brewers, tiplers and innholders having to be licensed (Cooper, 1928–29, pp. 292–301). These measures were identical to those a decade earlier and again they proved successful. When faced with a severe dearth, York Council managed to secure sufficient grain, controlled its price and ensured that all had enough to eat. Famine was averted and levels of mortality remained low.

In June 1622 the Mayor of York described the shortage of corn as 'greater than ever known in the memory of man'.[63] In contrast with the earlier periods, the Council minutes are silent as to whether food shortages occurred in the city itself. In November 1622 a letter was received from the national government in London stating that:

> while the present rates of corne throughout the whole kingdom are generally as high we hold it
> fitt to enter into consideracon from the poorer sorte of his majesties subject (who are like to suffer the greatest wante) that they might in some sort be releiued by an abatement of the prices.[64]

The letter goes on to state that vigilant care should be taken over the amount of grain used to make beer and ale. In consequence innholders, tiplers and brewers were once again licensed, but this proved to be the only legislation relating to the possibility of famine. Indeed, the threat of famine may even have been used as an excuse to close down some alehouses, since the moral tone of the legislation emphasized that they were 'lewd & debauched' places.[65] Between 1622 and 1624 there was no legislation concerning grain purchases or increasing levels of poverty and nothing to suggest food shortages actually occurred.

Throughout the period 1561–1700 York Council played an active role in attempting to avert crisis mortality. At all times the Council was keen to ensure that trade could continue uninterrupted, thereby maintaining economic and social stability. They were largely successful in these aims, although part of this success may have been connected with its fortuitous location – it was far away from the south-east coast where the repeated waves of plague epidemics entered the country and in an area less prone to harvest failure than some. When famine threatened, the grain supply was maintained at prices the poor could afford, and while York's privileged position may have exacerbated shortages elsewhere, this policy ensured that its population did not starve. Given the limited knowledge about the causes of plague, the Council was largely successful in averting epidemics and on only one occasion was the city overwhelmed. The Council's active policy culminated when it managed to control the 1631 epidemic even though Wentworth's involvement appears to have

61 *Ibid.*, fol. 242a.
62 *Ibid.*, fol. 276a.
63 Quoted in Long and Pickles (1986), p. 27.
64 YCA B XXXIV fol. 253a.
65 *Ibid.* Also, see fols 254b–55b.

been crucial in ensuring that the plague orders were enforced to the letter. Nevertheless, at all times the city remained vulnerable to crises and in 1643–44 when, overcome by national events, the Council were powerless to prevent the spread of disease. Despite suffering extreme levels of mortality in 1604, the city recovered from this disaster very quickly. Recovery took longer after 1644; the suburbs had been severely damaged and its overall prosperity was also affected, especially after the Council in the North had been abolished. Thus, while crisis mortality, or more correctly the threat of it, permeated many aspects of early modern society, it had less influence on urban demographic regimes – of far greater importance was the underlying level of mortality.

INFANT AND CHILDHOOD MORTALITY

In the absence of data about population structures and age at death, the best way of establishing levels of mortality is by a technique known as family reconstitution which involves linking together entries from parish registers to recreate individual family histories.[66] This process is time-consuming and the number of individuals about whom sufficient information can be determined is small, which means that results often have to be reported in cohorts of at least 25 years. In cities, these problems can be compounded since most parishes were small and moving house could easily involve crossing parish boundaries. Turnover rates were often high and it was rare to discover a register which recorded a female's baptism, her subsequent marriage and finally the baptism of her children.[67] However, by not attempting inter-generational links and performing a partial rather than a full reconstitution, the process is simplified, and while this limits the amount of information that is forthcoming about fertility, the estimation of infant and childhood mortality rates is not affected (Finlay, 1981c, pp. 12–13, 43). Examination of York's registers revealed only two, St Martin Coney Street and St Michael le Belfrey, that appeared to be sufficiently complete during the period 1561–1700 to warrant reconstitution.[68] Child life tables for these two parishes are given in Table 4.4. The small number of burials recorded by the age group 10–14 together with the possibility that by these ages some children may have left their parental home suggests that this rate should be treated with caution.[69] Fewer reservations need be applied to the other figures and three patterns

66 The rules for the application of family reconstitution to English parish registers are given in Wrigley (1966b). Also, see Wrigley (1973b).

67 In reconstituting the register of St Martin Coney Street the age of only one bride could be determined: Jane Middleton, baptized 9 May 1583, married 4 March 1606; she then baptized eight children between 17 April 1606 and 17 April 1618.

68 In addition to the absence of gaps in a register, each entry must contain sufficient details to allow children to be linked to their parents. Hibberd (1981) reconstituted the register of St Michael le Belfrey between 1600 and 1720. To complement this study the reconstitution was extended to the period 1565–1602, the date when the register begins until there is a gap caused by a missing page. Hibberd also reconstituted the register of St Mary Bishophill Jnr; unfortunately, under-registration during the Civil War period makes these results unreliable.

69 Wall (1978), pp. 181–202, using a limited number of places, concluded that despite local variations, the vast majority of children were still living with their parents into their teens. Also, see Wall (1987).

Table 4.4: Child life tables, York 1561-1720

4.4a) By parish

Parish	Period	Age	Deaths	Rate 1,000q_x	Survivors l_x
St Martin Coney Street	1561-1700[a]	0	351	257	1,000
		1-4	157	180	743
		5-9	44	95	609
		10-14	15	58	551
		15			519
St Michael le Belfrey	1565-1602[a]	0	192	234	1,000
		1-4	58	121	766
		5-9	10	65	673
		10			632
	1600-1720[b]	0		233	1,000
		1-4		198	767
		5-9		41	615
		10			590

4.4b) St Martin Coney Street, by period

Parish	Period	Age	Deaths	Rate 1,000q_x	Survivors l_x
St Martin Coney Street	1561-1600[a]	0	61	186	1,000
		1-4	30	125	814
		5-9	12	76	712
		10			658
	1601-1640[a]	0	108	289	1,000
		1-4	37	162	711
		5-9	13	114	596
		10			528
	1641-1700[a]	0	182	274	1,000
		1-4	90	226	726
		5-9	19	105	562
		10			503

Sources: a) original family reconstitutions.
           b) Hibberd (1981), p. 368.

emerge from Table 4.4a. First, infant and childhood mortality rates were high and they fell substantially as children became older. Secondly, there was little variation or change in infant mortality; the evidence from St Michael le Belfrey is striking, especially since that parish contained approximately ten per cent of York's population and its register was of exceptional quality. Thirdly, the only significant change occurred to early childhood mortality (1–4) which increased in the seventeenth century. When the results from St Martin Coney Street are distinguished by period

(Table 4.4b), the increase in early childhood mortality becomes more evident and is shown to have occurred mainly after 1640. Older children (5–9) experienced a much smaller increase after 1600 and none after 1640. Major differences emerge with respect to infant mortality, however. In St Martin Coney Street IMRs were stable during the seventeenth century, but these were much higher than the sixteenth-century rate. This earlier figure is based on only 61 deaths, and since infant mortality was often concentrated within certain families, its accuracy needs to be subject to further scrutiny. Consequently, before conclusions may be drawn about changes in infant mortality, the extent of temporal and spatial variations throughout the city needs to be determined. Despite this apparent anomaly, the reconstitutions have confirmed that mortality rates in early modern York were high, with up to half of all infants born in the city not surviving to reach their fifteenth birthday.

Table 4.5: English age-specific mortality rates $(1,000q_x)$

Parish	Birth cohort	Age		
		0	*1–4*	*5–9*
Hartland[a]	1550–99	92	38	21
	1600–49	87	48	29
	1650–99	83	50	25
	1700–49	85	93	34
Colyton[a]	1550–99	129	72	24
	1600–49	93	85	39
	1650–99	109	112	64
	1700–49	106	73	32
Gainsborough[a]	1550–99	166	102	28
	1600–49	254	134	65
	1650–99	254	174	61
	1700–49	272	181	69
Banbury[a]	1550–99	154	81	56
	1600–49	172	105	48
	1650–99	169	121	35
	1700–49	239	122	29
London: St Peter Cornhill[b] St Michael Cornhill[b] St Mary Somerset[b] Allhallows[b] Quakers[c]				
	1580–1650	105	148	46
	1580–1650	139	156	83
	1605–53	265	246	93
	1570–1636	184	178	104
	1650–99	260	244	67
	1700–49	342	298	95

Sources: a) 1550–99 – Smith (1978), pp. 210–11 (mean of male and female given); 1600–1749 – Wrigley and Schofield (1983), pp. 177–79.
   b) Finlay (1981c), p. 85.
   c) Landers (1990a), p. 39.

Comparable age-specific mortality rates, all calculated via reconstitution and chosen to encompass the extent of spatial variations in mortality throughout early modern England, are given in Table 4.5. An infant born in London was up to four times more likely to die in its first year than one born in the Devon parishes of Hartland and Colyton. London was exceptional and most places in England would have experienced mortality rates between those of Hartland and Gainsborough.[70] Indeed, mortality rates in the remote rural parish of Hartland were amongst the lowest yet discovered for an English early modern population and its IMR hardly changed between 1550 and 1900.[71] By comparison, the market town of Gainsborough, with a population of only c.4,000 at the end of the seventeenth century, experienced a considerable urban mortality penalty (Clark *et al.*, 1989; p. 107; Kearns, 1988). Mortality in Colyton and Banbury, as in most places, lay between these extremes. Explaining these variations is difficult. The poor quality of the physical environment, especially in towns, was probably responsible for most differentials; however, there was no simple correlation between population size and infant mortality since Gainsborough's mortality profile was very similar to York's.[72] A definite gradient is evident with respect to early childhood mortality rates (ECMRs). Since many deaths in early childhood were caused by infectious diseases, the likelihood of being exposed to these diseases was probably the most important factor influencing ECMRs.[73] Hence, differences between parishes were determined by factors such as population size and density, coupled with the degree of isolation from possible sources of infection. London's sheer size ensured that there, many infectious diseases were endemic and ECMRs were very high in comparison with the rest of the country. They also increased substantially during the seventeenth and eighteenth centuries. IMRs in the capital soared during the early eighteenth century, but before 1700 they are more difficult to determine.[74] Landers' work on the London Quakers revealed IMRs during the second half of the seventeenth century similar to those in Gainsborough.[75] A range of rates has also been derived from parish registers, yet their interpretation remains difficult. Spatial variations no doubt occurred, but IMRs near to 100, which otherwise occurred only in rural areas, do not appear tenable especially given the far higher eighteenth-century rates. Finlay argues that such variations were caused by a combination of infants being sent out to rural wet nurses and the high wealth profile

70 Woods and Williams (1995) p. 116, Figure 5. Some rural areas such as the Fen parishes of Leake and Wrangle also experienced very high rates; see West (1974).
71 Woods and Williams (1995) p. 116. The 'best rural' line on Figure 5 is based on Hartland's mortality experience. Also, see Figures 7.6, 7.7.
72 Dobson (1992) discusses spatial variations in mortality. For the nineteenth century see Williams and Galley (1995).
73 See Landers (1993), pp. 7–39 for a discussion of mortality theories.
74 Laxton and Williams (1989), p. 126, Figure 7 suggests that IMRs could have been in the region of 400 during the early eighteenth century; also, see Landers (1992), p. 56.
75 Vann and Eversley (1992), p. 194 give a different pattern of mortality with IMRs of 342 (1650–99, based on 330 deaths) and 263 (1700–49, 519 deaths).

of some parishes.[76] Another interpretation of these low rates would be that some parishes were affected by the severe under-registration of infant burials and estimates from another London parish appear to provide some confirmation of this. Between 1584 and 1598 the register of St Botolph without Aldgate was maintained in great detail (even stillbirths were recorded), and here IMRs were in the region of 400 per 1,000 live births.[77] Whatever the true level of infant mortality in sixteenth- and seventeenth-century London may have been, the extent of spatial variations and the pattern of change in the capital made it unique, in England at least. The York reconstitution data are therefore consistent with what is already known about early modern England. Mortality rates in York were much higher than in most rural areas and lower than in London. More surprisingly, York's mortality profile was almost identical to Gainsborough's.

In order to test the reliability of the reconstitution results and examine spatial variations, it is necessary to investigate a wider sample of registers. Since the other registers were unsuitable for reconstitution, a simpler method was employed which involved linking baptisms directly to entries in the burial register in order to determine the proportion buried within one year.[78] This method has the advantage of including illegitimates who as a group often experienced very high IMRs and necessarily have to be excluded from family reconstitution studies; however, the true rate will be underestimated since unless unbaptized infant burials were specifically identified, there is no way of linking these to the baptism register.[79] Decadal IMRs for 14 parishes are presented in Table 4.6, with all periods having been excluded from analysis if there was doubt as to a register's accuracy or insufficient detail was included.[80] An indication that these results merit serious consideration is the high level of neonatal mortality (those infants buried within one month of baptism) in each parish. These rates are comparable with the endogenous mortality rates of 117 in St Martin Coney Street and 124 in St Michael le Belfrey calculated by reconstitution (see page 61). Some infants will have died from exogenous causes during the first month and these measures should not be considered identical; nevertheless, they are within a similar margin of error and suggest that IMRs calculated by this method should give a broad indication of the extent of variations in infant mortality throughout the city.

---

76 Finlay (1981c), pp. 146–49. IMRs amongst wet-nursed infants were high and those who died in the countryside would be absent from the London registers. The unreliability of London's parish registers led to their exclusion from Wrigley and Schofield's reconstruction of England's population history; Wrigley and Schofield (1981), pp. 77–83.
77 Forbes (1971), Table 2, p. 65: Forbes records 2,850 baptisms, 873 infant burials and 462 chrisoms (unbaptized burials); IMR = 403 [(873 + 462)/(2,850 + 462)].
78 Wrigley (1977), pp. 292–96. Time is saved by reversing the procedure and linking infant burials to the baptism register.
79 Reconstitution overcomes this problem by inventing dummy births if burials occur to a family and there is no record of the infant having been baptized.
80 The 14 parishes were chosen because their registers had been published or a transcript was available. This speeded up the linking process.

In the parishes of All Saints Pavement, Holy Trinity Goodramgate and St Olave, some rates are sufficiently low, near to or below 100, for suspicions to be aroused about the accuracy of these registers in a few decades. In the vast majority of cases, however, the decadal IMRs are in excess of 200 and only one register, St Lawrence, recorded an exceptionally high rate.[81] Throughout Table 4.6 there is an impressive degree of consistency. Excluding St Lawrence, little variation occurred between parishes: only St Olave and St Michael le Belfrey, parishes which both included rural areas, together with St Mary Bishophill Jnr which probably suffered some degree of under-registration during the mid-seventeenth century, had overall IMRs less than 200. Despite these minor variations the majority of rates in most parishes were similar to each other. The quality of registration is obviously an important factor influencing the accuracy of these rates. In St Michael le Belfrey during the 1580s, when registration was exceptional, the IMR was 249, but during the 1590s when the register included fewer details it fell to 142. Similar variations in other parishes coincided with differences in recording practices, although since each decadal rate is based on a relatively small number of baptisms, some degree of variation is to be expected.[82] By assuming that most parishes did not identify unbaptized burials and levels remained constant throughout the period, it is possible to provide corrected IMRs for these parishes. The rates in Table 4.6 were therefore corrected using the assumption that seven per cent of infants died unbaptized.[83] To check whether this method provides plausible estimates of infant mortality, the rates for St Martin Coney Street and St Michael le Belfrey can be compared with those calculated by reconstitution (Table 4.7). The uncorrected rates are lower than the reconstituted rates by a considerable amount. After correction there is much greater agreement and these corrected rates should therefore provide a closer approximation to the true rate.

---

81 This was based on only 119 baptisms.
82 Comparison with Table 3.1 reveals that increases in All Saints Pavement (1640–60s), Holy Trinity Goodramgate (1690s), Holy Trinity Micklegate (1610s), St Martin Coney Street (1650–60s) and St Michael le Belfrey (1610s) coincided with periods when unbaptized burials were recorded.
83 See Table 3.1. IMRs were corrected only if the proportion of unbaptized burials fell below seven per cent for each decade. Minor differences occur between Table 4.8 and Galley (1994), Tables 5 and 8. In an effort to check for defective registration, especially in the period before 1600, each register was rechecked and some periods were excluded from the analysis. This had the effect of increasing the weighted mean from 225 to 228.

Table 4.6: Infant mortality rates (per 1,000 live births) for 14 York parishes, 1561–1700

Parish	Decadal infant mortality rates														Overall		
	1561–	1571–	1581–	1591–	1601–	1611–	1621–	1631–	1641–	1651–	1661–	1671–	1681–	1691–	Total	Neonatal	Per cent
All Saints Pavement	180	120	–	–	255	235	179	175	237	293	279	167	245	203	219	119	54
Holy Trinity Goodramgate	–	–	86	117	127	218	278	239	248	215	250	233	218	262	220	117	53
Holy Trinity Kings Court	–	–	–	–	–	–	–	–	–	–	–	–	283	235	251	113	45
Holy Trinity Micklegate	–	–	–	–	174	278	224	223	213	321	160	223	232	183	222	142	64
St Crux	–	–	205	189	230	200	194	227	280	187	244	264	242	235	227	126	56
St John Ousebridge	–	–	–	209	218	291	235	193	238	220	227	234	250	–	231	118	51
St Lawrence	–	–	–	–	–	–	–	–	–	–	–	370	–	–	370	176	48
St Martin Coney Street	178	184	191	241	287	214	182	236	200	266	302	229	173	200	223	122	55
St Martin cum Gregory	–	–	–	272	225	237	171	239	281	275	125	296	206	153	223	109	49
St Mary Bishophill Jnr	–	–	–	–	260	302	272	–	98	143	139	184	243	161	197	100	51
St Mary Castlegate	–	–	–	–	271	247	274	262	180	214	250	265	267	261	247	138	56
St Maurice	–	–	–	–	–	–	–	–	–	270	152	260	333	271	267	100	37
St Michael le Belfrey	192	231	249	142	155	202	194	220	223	195	230	183	186	125	198	119	60
St Olave	131	231	152	97	204	171	173	246	–	–	–	–	–	–	182	91	50

Source: original parish registers.

Table 4.7: Comparison between infant mortality rates (per 1,000 live births) calculated by family reconstitution and simple linking methods in two York parishes

Parish	Family reconstitution	Simple linking uncorrected	corrected	Difference	
St Martin Coney Street[a]					
1561–1700	257	223	252	–34	–5
St Michael le Belfrey					
1565–1602[a]	234	208	231	–26	–3
1600–1720[b]	233	197	236	–36	+3

Source: a) original family reconstitutions.
          b) Hibberd (1981), p. 368.

Table 4.8: Corrected infant mortality rates by parish and period, York 1561–1700

Parish	1561–1600	1601–40	1641–1700
All Saints Pavement	180	252	270
	(175)	(725)	(1,365)
Holy Trinity Goodramgate	169	280	284
	(230)	(770)	(1,306)
Holy Trinity Kings Court	–	–	304
			(324)
Holy Trinity Micklegate	–	248	255
		(769)	(821)
St Crux	245	270	287
	(400)	(893)	(1,567)
St John Ousebridge	267	286	271
	(139)	(464)	(686)
St Lawrence	–	–	370
			(119)
St Maurice	–	–	267
			(270)
St Martin Coney Street	234	248	270
	(478)	(520)	(960)
St Martin cum Gregory	276	262	269
	(124)	(412)	(745)
St Mary Bishophill Jnr	–	299	230
		(245)	(923)
St Mary Castlegate	–	310	284
		(577)	(1,266)
St Michael le Belfrey	231	243	237
	(1,280)	(1,933)	(2,962)
St Olave	217	256	–
	(589)	(821)	–
Weighted mean	228	261	266
	(3,415)	(8,129)	(13,314)

Source: original parish registers.
Note: figures in brackets refer to the number of baptisms on which the calculations were based.

Corrected IMRs for three periods are given in Table 4.8. Little change is apparent during the seventeenth century when about one in every four infants died before reaching their first birthday. Only St Lawrence experienced an exceptionally high IMR; the rate in the other two extramural parishes, St Maurice and St Olave, being similar to the mean of the sample. Excluding St Lawrence little variation occurred between parishes and none stand out as having especially high or low IMRs during the seventeenth century. Furthermore, there is no obvious correlation with the wealth profile of individual parishes (see Table 3.8). Three parishes – St Maurice, St Mary Bishophill Jnr and St Mary Castlegate – which were ranked low on all criteria did not experience especially high IMRs; indeed, the rate in St Mary Bishophill Jnr was the lowest of all the parishes between 1640 and 1700. Likewise, the 'richer' parish of St Martin cum Gregory recorded rates almost identical with the mean for the city. Only St Michael le Belfrey had a high wealth profile and experienced lower rates.

Table 4.9: Infant mortality rates (per 1,000 live births) for 14 York parishes combined, 1601–1700

Period	Rate	Corrected rate
1601–10	204	236
1611–20	225	262
1621–30	213	264
1631–40	229	277
1641–50	226	268
1651–60	223	252
1661–70	229	267
1671–80	226	280
1681–90	228	279
1691–1700	199	250

Source: original parish registers.

The stable seventeenth-century rates represent an increase of about 40 deaths per 1,000 live births from the sixteenth-century level. However, the figure of 228 needs to be treated as an absolute minimum. This rate includes a number of decades in All Saints Pavement, Holy Trinity Goodramgate and St Olave when the IMRs were suspiciously low, and while inspection of these registers reveals no obvious deficiencies in registration, it is possible that some details may have been lost when the registers were transcribed at the end of the seventeenth century.[84] In St Crux, St John Ousebridge, St Martin Coney Street and St Martin cum Gregory, any increase between the sixteenth and seventeenth century was only slight. More importantly, rates in St Michael le Belfrey remained stable and these were consistently lower than the mean

84 Finlay (1981b), p. 7. Even if registers are accurate, details of at least the infants' father are required in order to make definite links.

– this parish recorded the lowest rate in the period 1601–40 and the second lowest rate between 1641 and 1700. The size of St Michael le Belfrey dominates the sample to such an extent that the weighted mean is probably not representative of the whole city in the period 1561–1600. The evidence from St Martin Coney Street is particularly interesting since the corrected rate, based on a larger sample than the reconstituted rate, is much higher. Many registers were in observation for only part of the period 1561–1600, and since spatial variations in infant mortality throughout early modern York were not significant, it is probable that if the true sixteenth-century rate could be calculated, it would only be slightly lower than the seventeenth-century rate. The IMRs presented in Table 4.8 are sufficiently close to each other to infer that the weighted mean provides a good indication of the overall IMR for the city during the seventeenth century (Table 4.9).[85] Given St Michael le Belfrey's role in reducing the overall mean, it is probable that if this exercise was undertaken on the other registers, the mean would be increased slightly. However, the relatively crude way in which the rates were corrected ensures that all the rates must be taken as approximations. Little change is apparent throughout Table 4.9, with the uncorrected rates almost identical between 1631 and 1690. The corrected rates are substantially higher, between 29 and 54, than the uncorrected rates and must therefore be viewed merely as indicating the likely levels of infant mortality throughout the city; nevertheless, they do confirm the general stability of infant mortality in early modern York. Furthermore, with most of the correction being caused by the deaths of very young infants, they show the important contribution of neonatal and endogenous mortality in explaining these high urban rates.

The evidence from seventeenth-century York shows that IMRs were high and changed very little either across space or through time. Less evidence is available for the sixteenth century, but sufficient exists to indicate that similar patterns also occurred. Throughout the whole of the period 1561–1700, IMRs in York remained remarkably stable.

VARIATIONS IN INFANT AND CHILDHOOD MORTALITY

While the overall IMR changed little, annual rates, which were influenced partly by the climate, fluctuated considerably – during the seventeenth century the uncorrected annual IMR varied from 145 (1633) to 359 (1644). Every infant did not have the same chance of survival and special groups suffered additional risks. In part attributable to low birth weight, IMRs amongst twin and multiple births were extremely high, in the region of 600 per 1,000 live births (Galley, 1993). Illegitimates also suffered very high rates, probably well in excess of 300.[86] An infant's chances of sur-

85 In the 1690s the 13 parishes contributing towards the weighted mean accounted for 68 per cent of York's baptisms. The arithmetic means and standard deviations for the parishes are: 1601–40 – 268.5, 22.48; 1641–1700 – 276.8, 34.4 or 269, 20.8 if St Lawrence is excluded.
86 Of the 59 illegitimate baptisms in Table 5.1 seventeen were buried within one year (IMR = 288). This evidence is slight, but under-registration of illegitimates was probably high and, with many dying shortly after birth, an illegitimate IMR greater than 300 seems likely. Similar high levels were found in the small Swedish town of Linköping; see Sundin (1995).

vival depended on a multiplicity of factors, many of which were related to conditions within the family, and two examples from the reconstitution of St Martin Coney Street reveal the extent of such differences. Matthew Batchelour married Emot Harrison on 21 April 1629; between 28 February 1630 and 21 July 1641 they baptized seven children. Four died in infancy, two died aged one and four, while the other appears to have survived. By contrast Bernard Ellis married Marie Darley on 1 May 1597; between 9 November 1597 and 15 October 1615 they baptized 14 children. Only one died in infancy. Another two died aged six and eight and the rest survived. Why these families had such different experiences cannot be known, of course. Generally, infant survival chances were governed by two sets of factors. One relates to conditions within the city – the provision of clean water, levels of sanitation, climate, the disease environment – which taken together represent the threat to the infant posed by the environment in which they lived. The second relates to conditions within the family – method of infant feeding, quality of child care, housing conditions, and biological status of the parents – and these factors determine the effectiveness with which individual families were able counter the environment threats.[87] Often lack of data at the family level ensures that explanations for variations in infant mortality have to focus on intermediate factors such as wealth, class or geography, and consequently in the early modern city many influences on child survival cannot be addressed directly.[88]

Due to poor sanitary conditions and lack of knowledge, mortality was likely to be very high amongst those infants who were not breastfed (Sundin, 1995, pp. 119–22). The stability of the overall IMR suggests that there were no significant changes in either the extent or length of breastfeeding during the period. This does not, however, mean that breastfeeding was universal, and given York's role as an important social centre, some better-off families may have sent their children out to wet nurse, as frequently happened amongst London's rich (Finlay, 1981c, pp. 146–48; Fildes, 1985, pp. 79–82; Clark, 1987). There is little evidence about this subject in York. Few references to wetnursed infants exist – there are none in the rural parishes immediately surrounding York and only two in the city itself.[89] It is possible however to infer something about breastfeeding by examining the seasonality of infant burials (Fig. 4.4). Baptismal seasonality, which since birth-baptism intervals were small can be taken as a surrogate for birth seasonality, was very similar to that in the country as a whole (Wrigley and Schofield, 1981, p. 288; Dyer, 1981). The pattern of neonatal and post-neonatal burials is more intriguing. During the nineteenth century the high urban IMRs can partly be explained by the incidence of diarrhoeal-type infections which particularly affected infants aged between one and eleven months during the

---

87 This idea is based on Mosley and Chen (1984). Both lists are by no means exhaustive. For a similar analysis in nineteenth-century cities see Williams and Galley (1995).

88 The problems of examining trends in infant mortality are discussed in Woods *et al.*

89 BIHR PR Y/MG (St Martin cum Gregory, September 1658); BIHR PR Y/HTM (Holy Trinity Micklegate, February 1699).

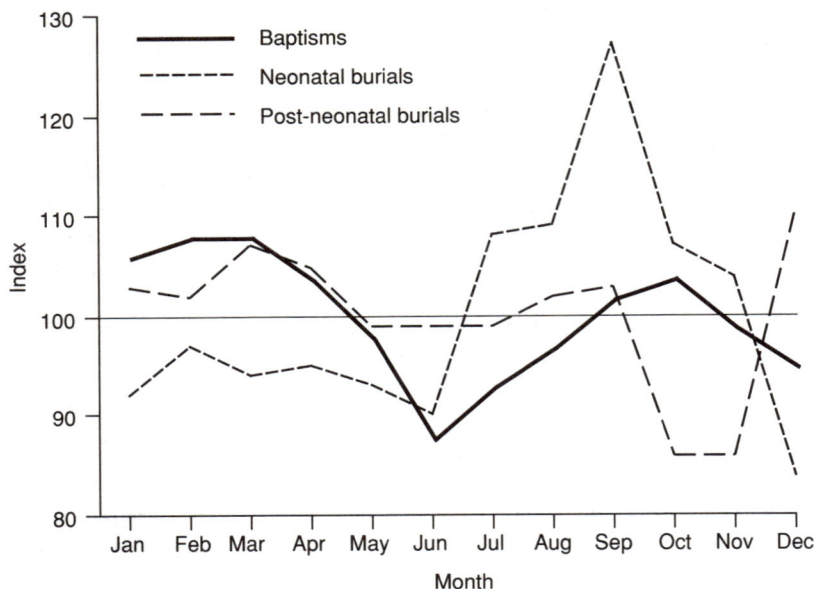

Figure 4.4: Seasonality of baptisms, neonatal and post-neonatal burials, York 1561–1700
Source: original parish registers.

summer months.[90] In York no summer peak in post-neonatal infant burials is evident, but summer neonatal burials are much higher than expected.[91] Endogenous deaths should not be subject to seasonal variations and the most likely explanation for this pattern is that neonatal infections occurred more often during the summer. Breast-feeding should minimise these risks and therefore it is possible, as Fildes has suggested, that *some* infants were denied colostrum in the mistaken belief that it was harmful.[92] Instead they may have been fed artificially for a short period after birth; some may even have been given purges. Such life-threatening, unhealthy feeding practices would also help to explain the very high rates of neonatal mortality. Alternative explanations are also possible. If in addition to being breastfed some infants

90 Woods *et al.* (1988), p. 360. Urban IMRs could increase substantially during periods of hot weather; Williams (1992).
91 The post-neonatal line is only a crude measure of burial seasonality since, in order to examine the seasonality of infant burials properly, it is necessary to relate the proportion of infant deaths by age to the month of their birth. Hence, the post-neonatal line does not take into account baptismal seasonality; however, baptismal seasonality was not sufficient to suggest that a substantial summer peak in post-neonatal burials was likely. Neonatal burials are dependent only on the seasonality of baptisms in the month of burial and the previous one; therefore an excess can be considered to have occurred when the index of neonatal burials is greater than that of baptisms.
92 Fildes (1980). Landers (1993), pp. 143–46 found similar patterns amongst the London Quakers.

were given water, a practice that is common today, gastro-intestinal infections could easily have occurred and these would have been exacerbated during hot weather. Whatever method of infant feeding was employed, protecting infants, especially new born ones, from the unhealthy urban environment clearly proved difficult.

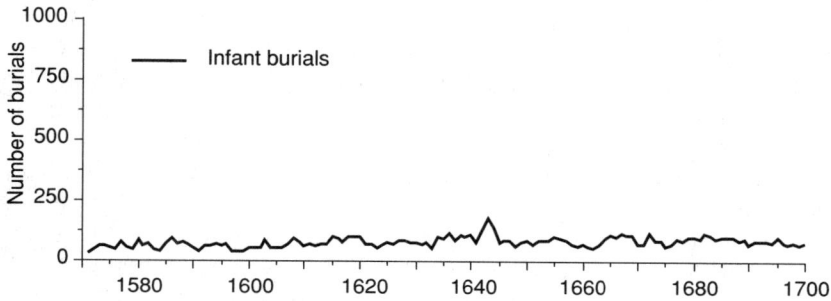

Figure 4.5: Annual infant burials, York 1571–1700
Source: original parish registers.

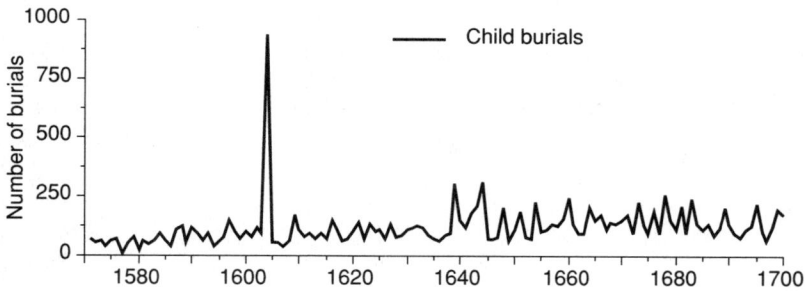

Figure 4.6: Annual child burials, York 1571–1700
Source: original parish registers.

Despite substantial individual, seasonal and annual variations in infant mortality Table 4.9 reveals considerable long-term stability and this is further reflected in the annual series of infant burials calculated using the annual IMR and the number of baptisms (Fig. 4.5). IMRs would have to have changed dramatically to alter the over-all proportion of infant burials.[93] This did not happen and infants contributed about 22 per cent of all burials in early modern York. The number of child burials can also

93 Given an average of 300 baptisms per year, an increase in infant mortality of 100 would result in only an extra 30 infant deaths.

be estimated from the aggregate series using the number of infant burials and the proportion of individuals listed as 'son' or 'daughter' in the burial register (Fig. 4.6). This method is crude and assumes that the deaths of any adults still residing in their parental home were not recorded as though they were still children.[94] A few adults may be included in these figures, but the vast majority were children and Figure 4.6 shows that the annual number of child burials was subject to considerable variation. Large numbers died during the two crisis periods and from 1639 children were subjected to a succession of epidemics.[95] The increase in ECMRs revealed by the reconstitutions can therefore be associated with epidemics which affected the city every three to four years. There is no direct evidence about the cause of these epidemics since, with the notable exception of plague, cause of death is almost entirely absent from the sixteenth- and seventeenth-century registers. The pattern is, however, consistent with the action of a viral disease or diseases. Successive epidemics would infect a large proportion of the susceptible population (those not having been exposed to the disease) and since large numbers of susceptibles were required in order to sustain an outbreak, epidemics could occur only every three or four years. In a city as large as York, almost the entire population would at some stage in their lives be exposed to these diseases. Infants who were being breastfed would inherit short-term immunity from their mothers and the peaks in the child series were not replicated in the infant series. Many older children would already have been exposed to the disease, hence as Tables 4.4a and b have already shown most of the increases in mortality were confined to young children.

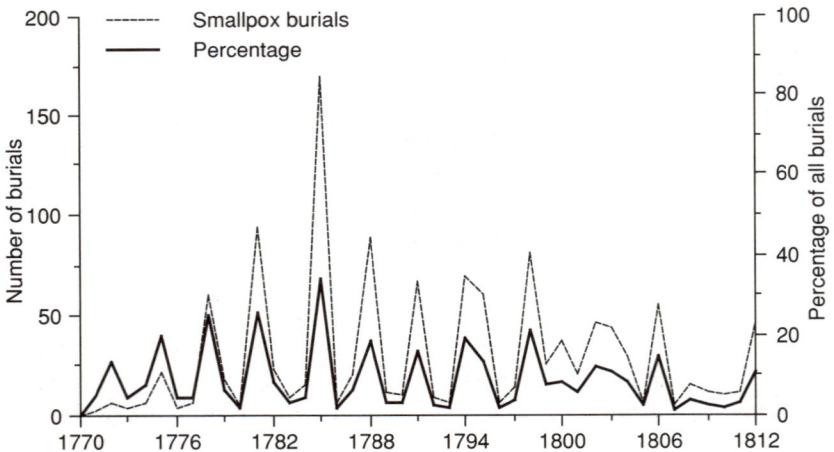

Figure 4.7: Annual smallpox burials, York 1770–1812
Source: original parish registers.

94 When ages were given in the register of St Michael le Belfrey only children were described as 'son' or 'daughter'; see Table 4.11.

Table 4.10: Age distribution of smallpox burials, York 1770–1812

Age	Number	Per cent	Cumulative per cent
Infants	30	2.4	2.4
0–3 months	15	1.2	3.6
3–6 months	34	2.7	6.3
6–9 months	79	6.4	12.7
9–12 months	84	6.8	19.5
0–	242	19.5	19.5
1–	283	22.8	42.3
2–	277	22.3	64.6
3–	195	15.7	80.3
4–	99	8.0	88.3
5–9	100	8.0	96.3
Over 10	33	2.7	99.0
None given	14	1.1	100.1

Source: original parish registers.

By reference to eighteenth-century evidence it is possible to infer that smallpox was responsible for most of these epidemics. Dr Clifton Wintringham published a study of the weather and epidemics in York which showed that 'smallpox appeared at three or four intervals during the 20 years over which his observations extend (1715–35)'.[96] From 1770, cause of death gradually appears in York's registers, although following Rose's Act of 1812, burials had to be entered on special forms and there was no space for cause of death (Finlay, 1981b, pp. 7–10). Unlike many of the causes of death included in the registers, such as 'decline' or 'teeth' which were descriptive of the deceased's symptoms, smallpox was a relatively easy disease for contemporaries to identify directly (Fig. 4.7).[97] The dotted line shows the number of smallpox burials and this increases as more registers recorded cause of death. Between 1770 and 1812 there were at least 12 occasions when epidemics of small-pox affected the city, although in every year after 1771 at least one smallpox burial was recorded.[98] In epidemic years about 20 per cent of all deaths were caused by

95 In 1639 the crisis mortality ratio for children was 2.2. Ignoring 1604 and 1643–44, the next highest ratios occurred in 1616 and 1654 (both 1.7). During the second half of the seventeenth century there was so much variability that it is difficult to determine the underlying pattern and crisis mortality ratios are an unreliable measure of increases in childhood mortality.
96 Quoted in Laycock (1844), p. 127. Wintringham also mentioned epidemics of measles and influenza during the same period. Wrigley and Schofield (1981), p. 668 note that 'smallpox epidemics are often referred to in contemporary literature, especially in the late sixteenth and seventeenth century, both in towns and the countryside'. See also Mercer (1990), pp. 8, 46–73; Duncan et al. (1994).
97 Certain less common forms of smallpox can occur without skin eruptions and these would have been very difficult to identify.
98 London was large enough for a different pattern to emerge. While epidemics still occurred, the disease was endemic and large numbers of smallpox burials occurred in each year throughout the eighteenth century; see Creighton (1965), pp. 531, 535.

smallpox and in 1785 one in three deaths were caused by the disease. When epidemics occurred, burials were concentrated into particular months, but since smallpox could attack throughout the year there was little overall seasonality. In 1782
White reported that inoculation had helped to reduce levels of mortality in York.[99]
The truth of this statement is difficult to verify; clearly inoculation could by no
means have been universal as the frequency and intensity of smallpox epidemics
remained undiminished. At the end of the eighteenth century vaccinations were first
carried out, and while local evidence is lacking, from 1800 the epidemics appear to
have become less severe, although the series ends too soon to determine whether this
was mere coincidence. Age at burial was given for most smallpox victims and the
age distribution is typical for a virulent viral disease (Table 4.10). Nearly 90 per cent
of victims were aged under five and the small numbers dying aged between five and
nine years had probably escaped infection during previous outbreaks. There were
very few deaths over ten, which suggests that by this age virtually the whole population had been exposed to the disease. The few older deaths were confined to young
adults, mainly aged 15–24, and most were probably recent migrants.[100] Those who
were fortunate to survive the disease gained life-long immunity, even though their
pock-marked faces may have borne witness to their earlier illness.[101] Of the large
numbers of infants dying from smallpox, 77 per cent were aged over six months and
40 per cent over nine months. The small number of infant deaths under six months
reinforces the view that many infants were protected from infection because they
were being breastfed by a mother who herself had acquired immunity to the disease.
If similar patterns occurred in the seventeenth century, this distribution of smallpox
burials would have the effect of raising the IMR by only 13 per 1,000 live births, a
figure that is consistent with the evidence.[102] It is possible that other diseases may
have caused the epidemics and the cause of death data also allow two other common
diseases to be examined, measles and whooping cough (Figs. 4.8 and 4.9). Burials
from these diseases were often clustered together with most again occurring in early
childhood; yet epidemics were less frequent and caused fewer deaths. There may
have been greater difficulty in identifying these diseases and even the most severe
epidemic of measles, in 1810, was responsible for only ten per cent of all deaths. The

99   White (1782), 179. White did not calculate mortality rates and his conclusions are based only on pat-
     terns of natural change.
100 In London over 20 per cent of smallpox deaths were aged over 20; see Landers(1993), p. 153.
101 Smallpox remained a very visible disease since it often left its victims disfigured as Mrs Hardcastle
     implies in Goldsmith's *She Stoops to Conquer* (1771): 'I vow that since inoculation began there is no
     such thing to be seen as a plain women; so one must dress particular or one may escape in the crowd'
     (Act II Scene 1, lines 686–89). While inoculation may have been common amongst some sections of
     society, its use throughout the whole of the population is more difficult to determine.
102 Assuming 20 per cent of all deaths during epidemic years were caused by smallpox; with epidemics
     occurring every four years and 20 per cent of smallpox victims being infants, only 1.25 per cent of
     all deaths would be infants dying from smallpox. Assuming that 370 baptisms and 377 burials
     occurred between 1601 and 1640 (p. 68, footnote 32), an increase in burials of 1.25 per cent is 4.7
     additional burials. This represents an increase in infant mortality of 12.7 per 1,000 live births,
     (4.7/370) x 1,000.

pattern revealed by Figures 4.8 and 4.9 is very similar to that of smallpox, with the differences in mortality probably being accounted for by lower case fatalities rates.[103] It is likely that every child would also have been exposed to these diseases, and while they could have been responsible for some of the epidemics noted by Figure 4.6, the most likely culprit remains smallpox.

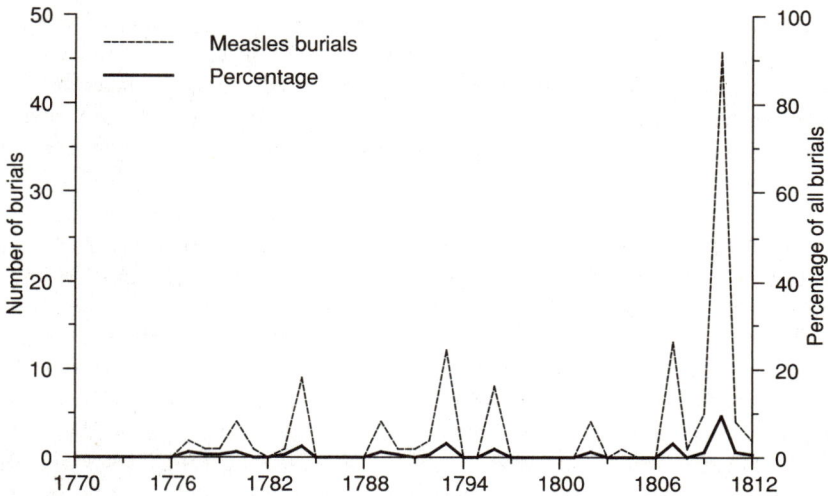

Figure 4.8: Annual measles burials, York 1770–1812
Source: original parish registers.

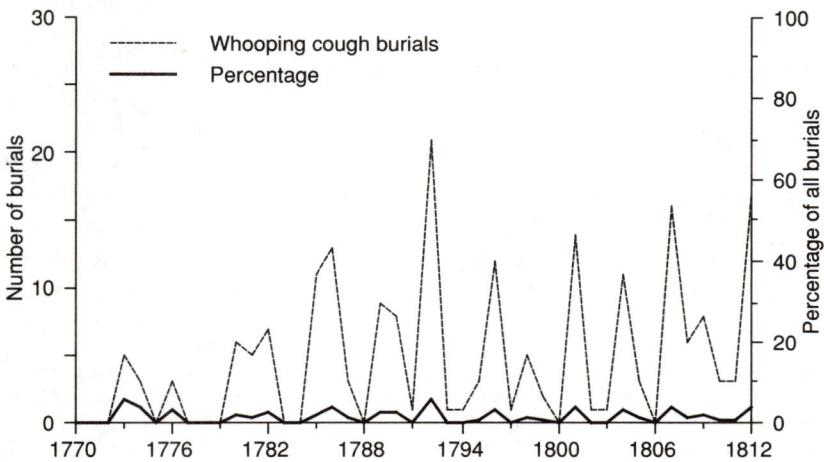

Figure 4.9: Annual whooping cough burials, York 1770–1812
Source: original parish registers.

103 Creighton (1965), p. 655 gives comparable numbers of deaths from smallpox, measles and whooping cough in London and Glasgow 1783–1812 and reveals similar patterns. Also, see Dyer (1985).

108 THE DEMOGRAPHY OF EARLY MODERN TOWNS

The analysis of variations in infant mortality has revealed an apparent anomaly: individual infants were subject to great differences in their survival chances, yet overall IMRs remained relatively stable. This stability implies that environmental conditions remained largely unaltered and there were no significant changes in chil- drearing practices during the period. The disease environment does, however, appear to have changed following the introduction or increased virulence of a variety of dis- eases.[104] Young children were affected by repeated epidemics, mainly of smallpox, and while ECMRs increased substantially, older children were less affected. York was sufficiently large for almost the whole population to have come into contact with these diseases, although new epidemics occurred only every three to four years once there were sufficient susceptible young children in the population to sustain them.

ADULT MORTALITY

The only direct evidence about levels of adult mortality in early modern York is con- tained in the register of St Michael le Belfrey, where between 1571 and 1586 age at death was reported for most burials. While the ages of infants and children were given in great detail, the adult data are disappointing. Many ages were rounded to the nearest ten and a few were reported in multiples of twelve. The accuracy of these data must therefore be open to question; nevertheless, they do provide a broad indi- cation of the overall distribution of burials (Table 4.11). Infants accounted for 29 per cent of all burials, children (1–14) 18 per cent and the remaining 53 per cent were aged over 15.[105] The distribution of burials in St Michael le Belfrey was similar to West level 7 of the Princeton model life tables, which means that expectation of life at birth (e_0) was about 33 years and at 20 (e_{20}), a better measure of adult mortality, about 35.[106] Once the perils of infancy and childhood had been overcome, the chances of living into moderate old age were good and 15 per cent of adults buried in St Michael le Belfrey were aged over 60 years. Comparative figures show that, not sur- prisingly, e_0 in Gainsborough was also about 30 years; it may have been 50 or more in Hartland and less than 30 in London (Wrigley and Schofield, 1983, pp. 178–89; Landers, 1990a, p. 57). It is not possible to estimate adult mortality directly from the reconstitutions.[107] In urban parishes which were subjected to high rates of turnover and the ages at death of very few adults are known, the only way that adult mortal- ity can be estimated is by inference from model life tables using the IMRs and ECMRs. Estimates of e_0 based on the York parish reconstitutions are given in Table

104 During the nineteenth century scarlet fever underwent similar changes; see Woods *et al.* (1997).
105 The proportion of infant burials is lower than in some early modern populations; see Friedrichs (1995), pp. 124–25.
106 Coale and Demeny (1983), p. 111 (males) assuming an annual growth rate of five per 1,000. The best fit is between model West levels 6 and 7. Fitting model life tables to historical populations is an imprecise art and it is necessary to assume that the population was closed which, of course, was not true. The results are therefore merely illustrative and subject to some margin of error. Model West levels 4, 5 and 6 will all give similar distributions for stable populations.
107 Estimates of adult mortality are usually obtained by making assumptions about the distribution of deaths of those whose ages are unknown. The method is described in Wrigley (1972), pp. 247–53.

Table 4.11: Distribution of burials, St Michael le Belfrey, York 1571–86

Age at burial	Number	Per cent	Cumulative per cent	Cumulative per cent West level 7
0–	135	29	29	29
1–	58	12	41	41
5–	10	2	43	44
10–	15	3	47	47
15–	9	2	49	49
20–	34	7	56	55
30–	35	7	63	63
40–	64	14	77	71
50–	36	8	85	80
60–	72	15	100	100

Source: BIHR Y/MB 1.

Table 4.12: Expectation of life at birth (e_0) in two York parishes, 1561–1720

Parish	Date	Age	Rate	Model life table West	North	East	South
St Martin Coney St	1561–1700	0	257	31(6)	26(4)	36(8)	27(4)
		1–4	180	29(5)	34(7)	26(4)	37(8)
		5–9	95	19(1)	26(4)	19(1)	20(1)
		10–14	58	19(1)	21(2)	19(1)	20(1)
St Michael le Belfrey	1565–1602	0	234	34(7)	29(5)	39(9)	30(5)
		1–4	121	39(9)	41(10)	36(8)	46(12)
		5–9	65	21(2)	36(8)	21(20)	27(4)
	1600–1720	0	233	34(7)	29(5)	39(9)	30(5)
		1–4	198	26(4)	31(6)	24(3)	34(7)
		5–9	41	34(7)	46(12)	34(7)	37(8)

Note: the level is given in brackets.
Source: original parish registers; Coale and Demeny (1983).

4.12. Clearly there are considerable differences depending on which family of models is used. West, between levels five and seven, would appear to provide the best fit and this reassuringly supports the evidence of the distribution of burials in St Michael le Belfrey. West, level 6 predicts that e_{20} was 34 years, which means that about a quarter of those aged 20 would be likely to die before their fortieth birthday (Coale and Demeny, 1983, p. 44). These ages are precisely those when most people married and raised families. So, if a couple married on their respective twentieth birthdays, their marriage would have had only about a 50 per cent chance of surviving for 20 years.[108] Consequently, remarriage and widowhood must have been important facets of life in early modern towns. Despite agreement in these estimates of adult mortality in York, the application of model life tables, calculated mainly from nineteenth- and early twentieth-century national populations, to small populations

108 Assuming that the probability that each partner is independent, then the probability of both surviving from the age of 20 to 40 is 0.75 x 0.75=0.5625, or just over half.

subject to large and possibly changing patterns of migration is likely to yield considerable inaccuracies. Furthermore, it is also necessary to assume that a constant relationship between infant, child and adult mortality was maintained (Woods, 1993). This clearly did not happen since child mortality increased independently of infant mortality during the seventeenth century, and similar changes also occurred during the nineteenth century (Woods *et al.* 1993). Model life tables which are based on the mortality experiences of populations from the recent past when applied to earlier populations may therefore distort the mortality profile of that population. Estimates from model life tables also do not take into account the likelihood of crisis mortality decimating a population. At best they can only provide a broad indication of the prevailing levels of adult mortality. However, the evidence from St Michael le Belfrey together with the reconstitutions indicates that, despite what appears to be very high levels of mortality, many could and did enjoy more than brief lives in the early modern city.

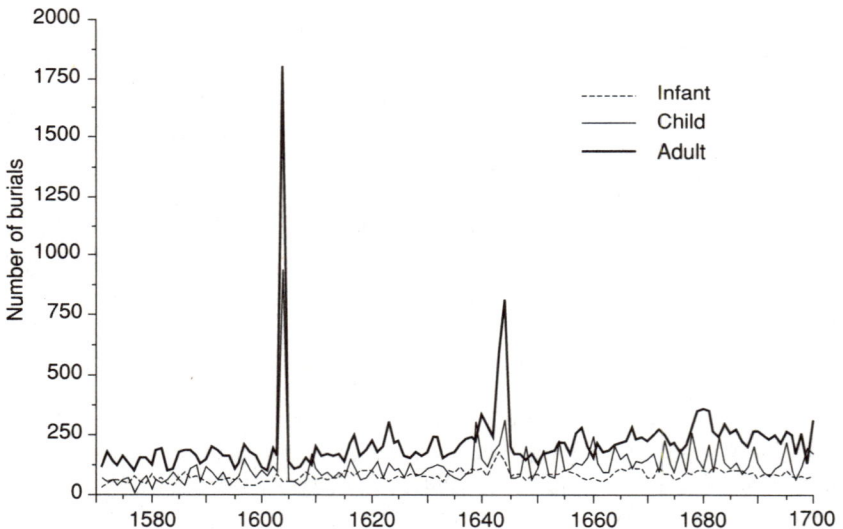

Figure 4.10: Annual infant, child and adult burials, York 1571–1700
Source: original parish registers.

Table 4.13: Adult burials as a percentage of total burials, York 1571–1700

Period	Per cent
1571–80	55.8
1581–90	53.0
1591–1600	54.3
1601–10	56.6
1611–20	51.4
1621–30	52.6
1631–40	50.9
1641–50	56.0
1651–60	47.8
1661–70	49.4
1671–80	51.9
1681–90	52.0
1691–1700	52.5
1571–1600	54.3
1601–40	53.2
1651–1700	50.8

Source: original parish registers.

Broad trends in the number of adult burials emerge by comparing the adult series with those for infants and children (Fig. 4.10). Annual variations occurred, but the series of epidemics that affected children is not replicated in the adult series. Apart from an increase in adult burials c.1680, no obvious pattern emerges.[109] The number of adult burials will have been affected by patterns of adult migration, and consequently it is difficult to identify whether long-term changes were a consequence of changes in mortality or the age-structure. Nevertheless, the overall proportion of adult burials did not change significantly during the period (Table 4.13). The large numbers of adults dying in the 1640s can be attributed to the influx of soldiers to York coupled with the outbreak of typhus, a disease which disproportionately affected adults. Likewise a higher proportion of adult deaths occurred in 1604, and if this year is excluded, the proportion between 1601 and 1640 becomes 51.1.[110] The proportion of adult burials decreased slightly during the seventeenth century, and this is consistent with an increase in childhood mortality. Overall changes within Table 4.13 are small, and since IMRs were also subject to little change, there is no evidence to suggest that adult mortality increased significantly during the period.

Given that migrants were an important section of any early modern urban population and most were born in rural areas, there is the possibility that many may have succumbed to the urban mortality regime.[111] After having spent the early part of their lives in areas of low mortality, it is likely that most will not have been exposed to

109 Similar increases occurred in some parishes in the South; see Dobson (1987), pp. 62–64.
110 Excluding 1604, the proportion in the decade 1601–10 was 48.7.
111 This idea is expressed in McNeill (1980), pp. 28–31.

many of those diseases common amongst urban children.[112] Unfortunately, migrants were not consistently distinguished in the registers, and while individual instances of migrant burials are easy to find, it is not possible to determine mortality rates since the population at risk is not known. Furthermore, while many recently arrived migrants may have been affected by disease, this does not mean that all those who eventually died were buried in the city. Some may have returned home after having fallen ill. The best known example of this is Anne Josselin (Pelling, 1988, pp. 157–59). Anne was bound as a servant in London aged fourteen. Within a few months of her arrival she had contracted smallpox. She stayed in London throughout her illness, but returned home following another illness a year later. She survived, went back to London and suffered two further serious illnesses. The last, five years after having moved to the capital, proved fatal. Before her death she had returned home once again and was buried in the parish of her birth.[113] How typical Anne Josselin was is difficult to tell, but estimates of the mortality of apprentices indentured in London can be given. Rappaport (1989, p. 313) shows that between 1540 and 1589 about 15 per cent of apprentice carpenters died before they could complete their service. This information is difficult to interpret. The ages of these apprentices were not recorded, length of service (usually seven years) could vary and, more importantly, nearly 45 per cent of apprentices left before completing their terms, presumably after acquiring sufficient skills to secure employment.[114] Since the number of apprentices at risk was subject to change as increasing numbers sought employment, the proportion dying will underestimate the numbers who would have died had everyone stayed and finished their apprenticeships.[115] In the case of apprentices born in rural areas, however, the greatest risks would have been encountered during the first years of service, and these should have diminished considerably the longer they stayed in London. Consequently, the level of mortality for London apprentices indicated by Rappaport will probably be close to the true rate since all apprentices were in observation during the first year or so. Similar information was not systematically recorded in York, but if mortality patterns followed West level 6 of the Princeton life tables, then ten per cent of those aged 15 would have died before reaching 25.[116] Since most apprentices were within these ages, the tentative conclusion may be made that mortality rates of apprentices in London were about twice those of York residents, even though comparing this type of information between London and York is

---

112 At the end of the eighteenth century most adult smallpox victims were probably migrants, although the only migrant explicitly recorded as such was a single man from Pickering (St Cuthbert, March 1778). A number of servants and soldiers were also identified, however.

113 Each of Josselin's children who moved to London suffered serious illnesses shortly after their arrival in the capital.

114 Rappaport (1989) shows that of 1,949 carpenters indentured between 1540 and 1589, 39.7 per cent became free, 14.6 per cent died in service, 44.6 per cent left and 1.1 per cent married.

115 Strictly speaking the proportion who died in service must be between 14.6 per cent and 26.9 per cent if only those who completed their service are considered; however, the true rate is probably well towards the lower end of this range.

116 Coale and Demeny (1983), p. 44. If the length of service was seven years, this would imply about seven per cent could expect to die before completing the apprenticeships.

extremely hazardous. During this period London experienced outbreaks of plague in 1563, 1578 and 1582, (Sutherland, 1972, p. 293) and with general levels of mortality in the capital probably being higher than in York, it seems reasonable to infer that the excess mortality of apprentices in York was less than twice that of the resident population. Furthermore, mortality rates between the ages of 15 and 25 were almost the lowest of all age groups, and even if the mortality of rural apprentices was well in excess of native-born apprentices, only relatively small numbers of young servants and apprentices would have been buried each year in a city the size of early modern York.[117]

The evidence about adult mortality is clearly fragile. From the little information that is available there is nothing to indicate that significant changes occurred in early modern York. Overall adult mortality rates were relatively modest, and while rural migrants faced additional risks on arrival in the city, it is unlikely that even this group suffered spectacularly high rates of attrition.

MORTALITY AND THE URBAN DEMOGRAPHIC REGIME

York's burial registers, in common with most, provide few details – usually name, date of burial and relationship to the head of household. Age and cause of death together with supplementary information, such as occupation, are given infrequently, and consequently it is not possible to provide a comprehensive account of mortality in early modern York. Nevertheless, by exploiting these few details, the major characteristics of York's mortality regime become evident. Mortality rates were comparable with those in other early modern towns; they were higher than the national level and lower than in London. The greatest excess was confined to infants and young children. IMRs remained remarkably stable, despite considerable variations in an individual infant's likelihood of survival. There were no substantial variations between parishes. This does not necessary indicate that society in early modern York was uniform, merely that of the myriad of influences affecting infant mortality, none were sufficiently clustered to create significant parochial differences in IMRs. Children suffered high rates of mortality, especially during the seventeenth century when they were affected by smallpox. Once the hazards of childhood had been overcome, the urban disease environment posed less relative risk, although migrants who arrived from rural areas were often affected by the diseases common amongst urban children. However, it is not clear whether all migrants who contracted fatal diseases in the city were also buried there. All urban residents faced the additional threat that the population would be periodically decimated, usually following an outbreak of plague. Individuals were often powerless to influence these events, and once an outbreak had occurred, the only effective course of action to take was to flee the city, although usually only the rich were in a position to be able to do this. York Council was aware of the disruption epidemics could cause and they did everything within their power to avert this eventuality. Sometimes they succeeded, but with little idea about what caused these incidents, often their efforts were in vain.

117 Additionally, about 30 per cent of apprentices came from the city itself see Table 5.9, p. 134.

Despite what appears to be strong evidence, even to contemporaries, that early modern towns were 'urban graveyards', this did not deter migrants flocking to York immediately after an epidemic had ended. Most payed little attention to the high levels of mortality in cities, probably believing that 'it would probably not happen to them', and the potential benefits of living in towns clearly far outweighed any perceived threat to life.

Only childhood mortality rates changed substantially during the period 1561–1700, and it is possible to use the reconstitution evidence to assess how this increase affected York's demographic regime (Table 4.4). Although based on relatively few deaths, these data are sufficiently robust to determine the maximum possible extent of any increase. By examining the number of survivors to age ten from 1,000 births (l_{10}), the greatest change in mortality would have been from the level in St Michael le Belfrey (1565–1602) to that in St Martin Coney Street (1641–1700). Thus, the maximum decrease in (l_{10}) was from 632 to 503, which means that at most an extra 13 deaths per 100 births would have occurred, assuming that the population remained closed. This increase in mortality by itself is insufficient to explain York's changing burial/baptism ratio since an extra 25 deaths per 100 births is required to change it from 0.94 to 1.19 (Table 3.6).[119] Indeed, the actual increase in mortality was probably much lower than this maximum estimate since IMRs hardly changed and a figure below 10 deaths per 100 births would seem to be a more reasonable estimate. A further explanation which may account for some of the change would be, as Sharlin argued, that the number of temporary migrants in the population also changed. In order for York's changing burial/baptism ratio to be explained, an extra 12 deaths per 100 births is required in addition to that caused by the increase in mortality. According to West level 6, out of every 100 births three would expect to die between the ages of 15 and 25; therefore the number of deaths in the age group 15–24 would have to increase to 15 (Coale and Demeny, 1983, p. 44). This would mean a fivefold increase in mortality and such an increase seems highly implausible. Alternatively, a fivefold increase in the numbers aged 15–24 would also account for this change, although if the mortality of migrants were twice that of residents, the number of apprentices and servants in the population would need to have at least doubled between the two periods. There is no evidence to indicate that York's economy underwent the profound changes necessary to explain such substantial increases in the number of servants or apprentices; indeed the opposite may even have occurred (see Table 5.14) and this hypothesis does not therefore appear tenable. Increases in adult mortality could also have occurred, but with no change in the proportion of adult burials being apparent this again seems unlikely. Thus, it is necessary to conclude that increases in mortality cannot account for the full extent of the changes within York's demographic regime. Some increase did occur, but in order to explain York's pattern of natural change, this must also have been accompanied by a reduction in fertility.

118 Even taking into account the effects of possible under-registration, this increase in mortality would not explain a birth/death ratio that changed from 0.91 to 1.08.

Chapter 5

THE RENEWAL OF LIFE

Fertility has been a relatively neglected aspect of early modern urban demography. This has been due to an understandable concentration on the more visible changes wrought by epidemic disease and a result of high levels of migration and turnover which ensures that many aspects of fertility remain difficult to disentangle. It is clear from Chapters 3 and 4, however, that fertility must have played an important role in explaining York's changing demography. While the mechanisms by which fertility changed at the national level have been studied in great detail, less attention has been focused on the local level.[1] One approach to tackling this problem would be to employ Coale's fertility indices to examine the individual components of overall fertility. Thus,

$$I_f = I_m I_g + (1 - I_m) I_h$$

where I_f = total fertility, I_m = the proportion married, I_g = marital fertility and I_h = illegitimate fertility.[2] Throughout early modern England, illegitimacy rates were low (less than four per cent of all births before 1750), and if this condition applies then I_h can be considered approximately equal to zero and the equation effectively reduces to $I_f = I_m I_g$. Most of the changes in overall fertility will therefore be dependent on changes in either the proportion married or the level of marital fertility, but since marital fertility remained virtually constant in early modern English populations, much of any variation will be due to differences in the proportion married (Wilson, 1982). Unfortunately, a number of methodological problems conspire to ensure that it is not easy to provide estimates of either I_m or I_g in the early modern city. Age-specific marital fertility rates (ASMFRs) are difficult to calculate since high turnover rates mean that age at marriage for few women is known, although some estimates of marital fertility can be derived from the parish reconstitutions. Less information is available about the proportion married, since the earliest published listing indicating marital status is the 1861 census.[3] Therefore, in order to determine overall levels of fertility, it is necessary to examine any factor, such as age at marriage, the age/sex structure of the population or changing migration fields, which may have influenced

---

1 Wrigley and Schofield (1981), pp. 242–43 for example.
2 Pressat and Wilson (1985), p. 32. These measures were suggested as a means by which national fertility rates could be compared against a standard – the Hutterites, a religious community who had the highest fertility of any group that had been studied in detail.
3 The proportion married could be calculated from the 1841 and 1851 census enumerators' books; see Armstrong (1974), p. 161. The earlier censuses do not give this information.

the proportion married, and the reasons why fertility changed will only be revealed once all the surviving evidence about fertility, marriage and migration has been examined together.

FERTILITY

It is a relatively simple matter to determine the illegitimate fertility rate provided that such individuals were recorded. Scattered references to illegitimates occur in both baptismal and burial registers; often they were identified explicitly, but sometimes their presence may be inferred if the father's name is absent from the baptism register and only the mother's name is given. No register recorded illegitimates consistently, although some parish clerks appear to have done so diligently and all instances where illegitimates were recorded over a period of years are shown in Table 5.1. It is difficult to assess the consistency with which these registers recorded illegitimates since the numbers involved are small; some will have died before they could be baptized and there may even have been a reluctance by the mother to identify her illegitimate baby. The rates in Table 5.1 should therefore be treated with caution, although there is no evidence to suggest that they are of the wrong order of

Table 5.1: Percentage of illegitimates baptized, York 1580–1700

Parish	Period	Baptisms	Illegitimates	Per cent
Holy Trinity Goodramgate	1618–32	325	11	3.4
St Mary Bishophill Jnr	1622–31	74	5	6.8
	1694–98	110	5	4.5
St Mary Castlegate	1628–38	200	9	4.5
	1691–1700	209	8	3.8
St Michael le Belfrey	1580–88	375	9	2.4
	1633–39	391	6	1.5
	1683–1700	370	6	1.6
All		2,754	59	2.1

Source: original parish registers.

magnitude and substantial numbers of illegitimates went unrecorded.[4] Occasional instances of abandoned infants were recorded, but there was no foundling hospital in York and this problem does not appear to have been severe.[5] It is therefore safe to conclude that illegitimacy rates were low in early modern York, as indeed they were throughout England where nationally levels remained below five per cent of baptisms between 1561 and 1760 (Adair, 1991, p. 63; Laslett and Oosterveen, 1973, p. 260; Wilson and Woods, 1991). The York rates are generally lower than in Laslett

4 Hibberd (1981), p. 363 assumes illegitimates were always recorded and gives rates of 0.9 per cent for St Michael le Belfrey (1660–1719) and 1.5 per cent for St Mary Bishophill Jnr in the same period.
5 For instance, 'Michell Belfreys, a child found in the Minster Yard, nere Bootham, was baptised May 8th (1685)', BIHR PR Y/MB.

and Oosterveen's mainly rural sample, and despite the existence of regional variations, this was probably indicative of a more general trend which is perhaps contrary
to expectation.[6] The reason why urban illegitimacy rates were low is not known, but
rather than indicating differences in levels of pre-marital sexual activity, it may have
been related to skewed urban sex-ratios, a greater dynamism within the urban marriage market or, more likely, many servants often chose or were forced to return
home to the security of their families once they discovered themselves to be pregnant. Given the inconsistency with which illegitimates were recorded in parish registers, the illegitimacy rate is difficult to establish; nevertheless, it seems safe to
conclude that illegitimacy did not make an important contribution to overall fertility
rates in early modern York.

Table 5.2: Birth intervals in months, York 1561–1720

Parish	Period	\[Birth interval\] 0–1	1–2	2–3	3–4	4–5	5–6	\[Average\] 0–6	1–6
St Martin Coney St	1561–1600[a]	11.5	23.3	25.7	22.1	22.3	14.7	19.8	22.7
		(25)	(22)	(18)	(14)	(11)	(7)	(97)	(72)
	1601–40[a]	13.3	19.3	21.2	21.6	24.4	27.5	19.0	21.8
		(34)	(21)	(17)	(14)	(10)	(7)	(103)	(69)
	1641–1700[a]	16.1	21.2	24.1	24.9	19.8	23.2	20.6	22.6
		(32)	(23)	(19)	(11)	(9)	(8)	(102)	(70)
St Michael le Belfrey	1565–1602[a]	13.8	24.4	26.5	26.5	26.3	23.6	21.1	25.5
		(123)	(81)	(54)	(36)	(23)	(13)	(330)	(207)
	1602–1720[b]	13.4	23.1	25.8	24.9	25.5	26.4	20.9	24.7
		(238)	(163)	(118)	(85)	(61)	(47)	(712)	(474)

Note: figures in brackets refer to the number of cases.
Source: a) original family reconstitutions.
            b) Hibberd (1981), p. 355.

A number of measures have been developed to assess marital fertility and many
of these can be calculated from reconstitutions (Wilson, 1982). Perhaps the simplest
and most illuminating are ASMFRs which relate a mother's age to her likelihood of
conceiving. Unfortunately, the necessity of performing a partial rather than a full
reconstitution means that age at marriage is not known and ASMFRs cannot be calculated. Consequently, knowledge about marital fertility is restricted and the only
measure which can be readily estimated is the interval between births (or more correctly between baptisms). Reconstituted birth intervals will overestimate the true
interval if any infants escaped registration entirely; nevertheless, they can still provide a good indication of overall levels of fertility.[7] Intervals by order of birth are

6 Adair (1991), especially pp. 215–37: 'provincial cities in the west and north, where illegitimacy was
   high, had a markedly lower bastardy ratio than their rural hinterlands' (p. 228).
7 Such reservations will also apply to ASMFRs.

Table 5.3: Average birth intervals in months, York 1561–1700

a) Marriage date not given

Parish	Period	Birth interval
St Martin Coney Street	1561–1600	24.6
		(175)
	1601–40	23.8
		(247)
	1641–1700	24.5
		(446)
St Michael le Belfrey	1565–1602	23.8
		(480)

b) All intervals without first births

Parish	Period	Birth interval
St Martin Coney Street	1561–1600	24.0
		(247)
	1601–40	23.4
		(316)
	1641–1700	24.2
		(516)
St Michael le Belfrey	1565–1602	24.3
		(687)
Overall		*24.1*
		(1,766)

Note: figures in brackets refer to number of cases.
Source: original family reconstitutions.

given in Table 5.2 for the two reconstituted parishes. Birth intervals of order greater than six have been excluded due to the small number of cases and the necessarily high rates of fertility that these families must have had in order to produce such a large number of births. The first interval will be affected by any pre-nuptial pregnancies and this may lead to the true rate of marital fertility being overestimated. However, if the first interval is ignored, then the others are remarkably uniform. Within each parish there was little change over time and there are only small differences between parishes. There is little evidence to suggest that attempts were made to space higher order births, and while this issue is highly complicated, it suggests that natural fertility predominated which is consistent with what is known about patterns of marital fertility throughout early modern England.[8] There was, however, some variation in fertility between families, with proximate factors such as the ages

8 Wilson (1984); also see Wrigley (1966).

of parents and levels of coital frequency perhaps explaining some of these differences.[9] One of the most important relates to the length of time that an infant was
breastfed.[10] In St Michael le Belfrey the average birth interval was approximately
two years, but if an infant died before its first birthday, breastfeeding was obviously
curtailed and this had the effect of reducing the following interval to an average of
only 19 months.[11] No record of marriage could be found for nearly three-quarters of
reconstituted families and a large amount of data will consequently remain unused if
these are excluded from the analysis. Average birth intervals for families with no
record of marriage are given in Table 5.3a, and Table 5.3b shows all intervals excluding first births. When these larger amounts of data are examined it becomes clear
that, in spite of some inter-familial variation, there was little difference either
between parishes or over time, with the overall mean birth interval being very close
to two years. As far as it is possible to tell, marital fertility rates in York remained
constant throughout the early modern period.

Table 5.4: Some examples of English birth intervals in months

Parish and period	Birth Intervals					Average	
	0–1	1–2	2–3	3–4	4–5+	0–6	1–6
Urban Quakers[a]	17.4	23.3	24.6	24.7	25.1	22.9	24.5
1650–99	(130)	(113)	(88)	(72)	(187)	(590)	(460)
	17.9	24.7	23.9	25.4	25.3	23.2	24.9
1700–49	(307)	(249)	(202)	(153)	(377)	(1,288)	(981)
Colyton, Devon[b]	11.3	25.2	27.4	30.1		23.3	27.5
1560–1646	(87)	(87)	(84)	(77)		(335)	(248)
	11.1	27.1	31.3	32.5		25.4	30.2
1647–1769	(23)	(23)	(26)	(18)		(184)	(137)
Cardington, Beds[b]	10.8	25.7	27.4	30.9		23.6	28.0
1750–81	(19)	(19)	(18)	(18)		(74)	(55)
Caversham, Mapledurham[b]		24.2	27.5	27.5			26.4
Berks 1630–1706		(103)	(105)	(106)			(314)
York average[c]	13.6	23.1	25.5	24.7		20.7	24.3
1561–1700	(452)	(310)	(226)	(160)		(1,344)	(892)

Note: figures in brackets refer to number of cases.
Sources: a) Vann and Eversley (1992) , p. 161.
        b) Quoted in Finlay (1981c), pp. 135–6.
        c) see Table 5.2.

9 Of the two examples given in Chapter 4, p. 101, birth intervals for Bernard Ellis' children were (in
   months) 6, 11, 17, 15, 11, 16, 24, 18, 14, 12, 17, 18, 16 and 20, while intervals for Mathew Batchelour's children were 10, 13, 20, 23, 12, 23 and 29. In both cases, births of higher order than six were
   excluded from Table 5.2. Also, see Wilson (1986).
10 Wilson (1986), pp. 219–26. Breastfeeding delays the resumption of post-partum ovulation and thereby
   reduces fertility.
11 Hibberd (1981), pp. 129–36, 358. The two short intervals in the Batchelour family followed infant
   deaths.

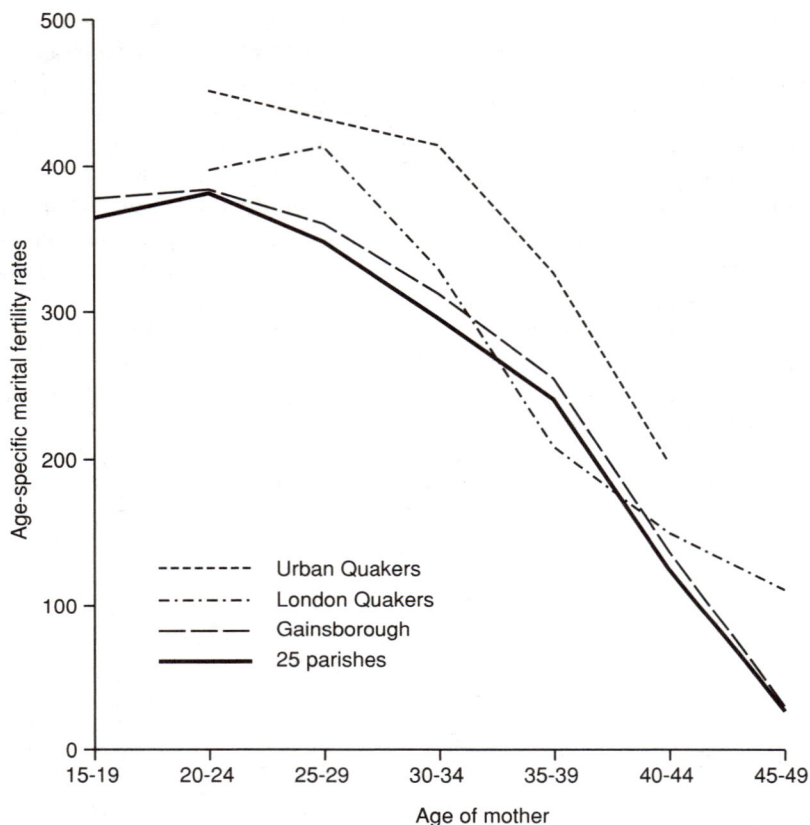

Figure 5.1: Age-specific marital fertility rates for selected English populations, 1550–1849

Sources: Urban Quakers (1650–99), Vann and Eversley, (1992), p. 134
            London Quakers (1700–49), Landers, (1990b), p. 95.
            Gainsborough (1550–1849), Wilson, (1982), Table 2.4.
            25 parishes (1650–99), Wilson and Woods, (1991), p. 405.

Comparative birth intervals calculated from early modern English registers are shown in Table 5.4. The York birth intervals are shorter than those from rural England, but not surprisingly they are very similar to the urban Quakers'.[12] Any differences are small, especially given that the number of intervals reported are few. Wilson, in a study of fertility in 16 English parishes, found little overall variation in his mainly rural sample: 'although the difference between parishes is small, it does seem that the existence of a possible urban–rural difference is suggested'.[13] The shorter urban intervals will in part be a consequence of higher IMRs which caused

12 Landers (1990b), p. 106 reported almost identical intervals for his London Quaker sample, although he does not provide full details.
13 Wilson (1982), p. 21. Wilson's sample included the small market towns of Banbury and Gainsborough.

many shortened intervals following infant deaths. There is also the possibility that there were urban–rural differences in breastfeeding patterns, with a greater proportion of urban mothers not breastfeeding or breastfeeding for shorter periods.[14] Figure 5.1 gives examples of some English ASMFRs, and the possible extent of any variations is shown.[15] There were relatively few geographical variations in marital fertility with most places experiencing rates close to those of the 25 parishes, chosen to be representative of non-metropolitan England, which show the typical pattern of natural fertility with the rates quickly declining with age.[16] Given Gainsborough's high IMR, which was similar to York's, it is perhaps surprising that its ASMFRs are only slightly higher than those of the 25. The London rates appear aberrant, but in part this may result from the much smaller sample sizes. If ASMFRs could be calculated for York, it is likely that they would be close to Vann and Eversley's urban Quaker rates.[17] Thus, while marital fertility rates were high in York, especially by comparison with rural England, they are still consistent with the pattern of natural fertility in the rest of the country. Minor variations or changes which would have been undetected by the birth interval data may have occurred, but it is unlikely that these would have had a major impact on marital fertility rates before 1700.

Evidence about fertility is limited, but sufficient exists to enable three important conclusions to be made: (1) illegitimate fertility was very low; (2) marital fertility rates were high; and more importantly, (3) there is nothing to suggest that significant changes to either illegitimate or marital fertility occurred before 1700. Such results are not surprising and are consistent with what is known about the rest of England.[18] It must therefore follow, referring back to the basic fertility equation, that any changes to York's overall fertility must have been caused by changes in the proportion married (i.e. $I_f \propto I_m$, overall fertility was proportional to the proportion married). Thus, any change in fertility must have been caused either by a change in the over-

---

14 Finlay (1981c), p. 135 discovered a three to four month difference in birth intervals between his 'rich' and 'poor' parishes, which he explained by the widespread use of wet-nurses. It is impossible to be certain about breastfeeding patterns in York or amongst the urban Quakers. Also, see the discussion in Harley, (1995), pp. 199–201.

15 English ASMFRs, including the urban ones, were nevertheless low compared with those in much of early modern Europe; see Wilson (1984), p. 228.

16 Wilson (1984). Fertility rates amongst the Quakers showed some deviation from this pattern after 1750; see Landers (1990b); Vann and Eversley (1992), pp. 129–85.

17 Using estimates of sterility for the 16 English parishes studied by Wilson (1986), p. 211, and the equation $\text{ASMFR}_x = 12/\text{BI}(1000-\text{SR}_x)$, where BI = Birth Interval and SR = Sterility Rate for age group x per 1,000 women, ASMFRs can be calculated for York assuming that a constant birth interval of 24.1 months was maintained throughout the period. This gives the following rates: 15–19, 465; 20–24, 475; 25–29, 453; 30–34, 415; 35–39, 371; 40–44, 188; 45–49, 35. Given that birth intervals will have varied by age and differences in sterility rates no doubt occurred, this procedure will provide only approximate ASMFRs especially at the higher ages; however, they are still only slightly higher than Vann and Eversley's urban Quaker rates.

18 I_g varied little over time and space until the secular decline occurred after 1870, and while I_h was subject to some variation, substantial increases only began to occur during the eighteenth century; see Wilson and Woods (1991), pp. 414–15.

all proportion who married or a change in the age distribution of marriages – if the proportion of young women who married decreased, given their high ASMFRs, then overall fertility rates would do likewise even though the overall proportion married may have remained constant. Determining the incidence and timing of marriage is therefore crucial to understanding why overall fertility fell in York during the second half of the seventeenth century. Such a conclusion is not surprising given that marriage has emerged as the 'principal institutional determinant of aggregate demographic trends and household formation' in English population history (Smith, 1986, p. 43).

MARRIAGE

The decision to marry was influenced by two sets of factors: one related to personal choice, the other to economic circumstance.[19] In addition to the obvious problem of finding a suitable partner, which may not always have been easy given parental pressure, social restrictions or unbalanced sex-ratios, marriage was usually accompanied by the creation of a new household and this meant that some degree of financial security was required before a couple could contemplate marrying.[20] Many couples needed to save in order to marry, and service offered the means by which money could be accumulated, while at the same time it encouraged servants to remain single since contracts were usually terminated on marriage (Laslett, 1988). Most marriages were well planned and carefully considered, but there must have been many exceptions, as when weddings were hastened by pre-nuptial pregnancies. The reasons why individuals decided to marry are clearly complex; however, at the aggregate level, throughout much of north-western Europe few married before their early 20s and large numbers never did so (Hajnal, 1965). During the seventeenth century the mean age at first marriage in England was about 26 for women and 28 for men, and while couples began to marry earlier after 1700, before this date changes to national fertility rates were mainly caused by variations in the proportion marrying (Wrigley and Schofield, 1983, p. 162; Weir, 1983; Schofield, 1984a). Nationally the marriage rate varied against an index of male wage rates, albeit with a generational lag (Wrigley and Schofield, 1981, pp. 425–28; Wrigley, 1985a). The reasons for this lag are not entirely clear, but the link between economy and marriage is well established. The 'Malthusian marriage system' (Macfarlane, 1986, pp. 3–48) therefore ensured that most marriages were undertaken prudently, and nuptiality was regulated by powerful economic forces which overwhelmed personal choice or desire. At all times there were greater numbers wishing to marry than were able to do so; however, those who were able to marry often did so and remarriage intervals could be very short (Macfarlane, 1986, pp. 235–36; Schofield and Wrigley, 1981, pp. 213–19).

19 Macfarlane (1986) provides a perceptive discussion of these issues.
20 Financial security may not have strictly been necessary, but its potential usually was. This point is made by Schofield (1989); also see Wall (1987).

There is little reason to expect that urban couples married for different reasons than the rest of the population; indeed, it has even been argued that an extreme form of the western European marriage pattern was likely to occur in cities.[21] Unfortunately, motives for marrying are difficult to establish. Within cities migration created the possibility that nuptiality could quickly respond to changes in economic circumstance. This happened most notably following epidemics of plague when the considerable redistribution of wealth and status created favourable conditions for marriage. At other times the link between economy and nuptiality is more difficult to establish. High rates of turnover amongst servants created a constant stream of young marriageable women into cities and, if circumstances were favourable, levels of nuptiality would have been high, even though older women and widows may have found it more difficult to marry. Opportunities for economic advancement were plentiful in cities, and while many lived in poverty, the overall proportion of the population who were able to marry was dependent on two factors; one was related to the vitality of the urban economy, the other was influenced by the sex-ratio of unmarried adults, which in turn was affected by net-migrational flows. Such a view of early modern marriage is essentially male-centred. It assumes that most adult females wished to marry and that men had little problem finding suitable partners. Recently it has been pointed out that if women had an appropriate alternative to marriage, for instance when widows were carrying on their former husband's trade, they may have been more reluctant to marry again.[22] Some women undoubtedly did not wish to marry; yet within cities the constant turnover of migrants, many of whom *would* have been women wishing to marry, will have always provided sufficient women to supply the urban marriage market. The overall proportion who were able to marry will of course have been affected by any imbalances in the sex-ratio, but it will have been mainly limited by the number of marriage opportunities that arose. Throughout early modern England, large numbers of women did not marry, and while some of these may have been content with their situation, it is unlikely that there were ever sufficient to substantially influence overall levels of nuptiality, even within cities.[23] Since intentions about marriage are difficult to establish, it is only the events themselves that can be examined, and a number of factors conspire to ensure that some aspects of urban nuptiality are likely to remain obscured.

A couple could choose both where and when a marriage took place.[24] In York they could marry in one of 23 parish churches or the more prestigious Minster, and while

21 Lynch (1991) provides no data from the early modern period about age at marriage or the proportion married to support her case.
22 Such arguments are summarized in Todd (1994); for a different approach see Boulton (1990). Also see Brodsky (1986); Todd (1985). Choices available to women are also explored in Goldberg (1992b).
23 Southall and Gilbert (1996) find a similar relationship between levels of nuptiality and male employment patterns during the nineteenth century. This theme is also examined in Sharpe (1991).
24 Ideally one would require information about those couples who married and then settled in the city. This is not always available. There were two ways by which a couple could marry – either in the local parish, following the reading of banns on three consecutive Sundays, or by licence in almost any nominated church. The licensing system allowed considerable scope as to where a couple could marry.

most will have chosen their local parish, some did not. This caused the individual parish marriage series to be subject to considerable annual variation, especially during the Commonwealth period when couples were forced to marry in certain churches. The aggregate series of marriages is therefore less reliable than those for baptisms and burials. Problems were also caused by York's status as the county capital, which meant that many couples travelled to the city specifically to marry. Likewise, some York couples may have preferred to marry outside the city, and migration for at least one partner was almost a necessary consequence of marriage since it was rare to discover a couple who resided, married and then continued to live in that parish. Indeed, the reconstitutions of St Michael le Belfrey and St Martin Coney Street revealed that only 20 per cent of marriages could be linked to a subsequent baptism or burial.[25] Many of the couples who recorded no other events in the parish may have settled in other parishes in York, but since most marriage registers only provide names and the date of the ceremony, it is impossible to disentangle these marriages from those of couples who subsequently moved out of the city. Finally, there is also the possibility that some couples chose not to marry and instead preferred to cohabit as man and wife (Boulton, 1993; Wrigley, 1973; Wrigley and Schofield, 1981, pp. 263–64). The examination of York's parish registers can therefore only provide a partial guide to both the level and characteristics of marriage in the city.

Despite these difficulties, York's marriage registers can illuminate certain aspects of nuptiality in the city. Occasionally a register indicates a couple's place of origin; for example, 'John Smoughton of Askam Bryan and Em: wheldon of this parishe weire married the 5th day of February (1619/20)'.[26] Figure 5.2 shows the origin of marriage partners from the small number of registers which consistently recorded this information.[27] In at least 20 per cent of marriages, both partners were from outside the city. Nearly all originated from Yorkshire, and many came from very near to York itself. Unfortunately, it is not known if these proportions changed, since most registers recording place of origin date from the late seventeenth century. There were great variations between parishes: in St John Ousebridge (1655–57) the proportion was 55 per cent and in St Michael le Belfrey (1653–60) only one per cent, with the reason for this difference probably being connected to the willingness of certain clergy to marry outsiders by licence on payment of a small fee:

> Marriage licences were used by a wide social strata – not merely nobility and gentry but by almost anyone with claims to standing above the labouring class; moreover, until Lord Hardwicke's Act came into operation in 1754 it seems to have been customary for those with social pretensions to marry away from their home parishes, often in the neighbouring market or county town (Webb, 1981, p. 34).

---

25 By comparison, 83 per cent of baptisms and 52 per cent of burials could be linked to at least one other event.

26 BIHR PR Y/MG. It is not clear whether this information refers to place of origin or residence.

27 The recording of place of origin depended on the parish clerk and most registers included this information only for short periods. The total sample comprised 1,119 marriages; see Galley (1991) p. 172 for details of the individual registers.

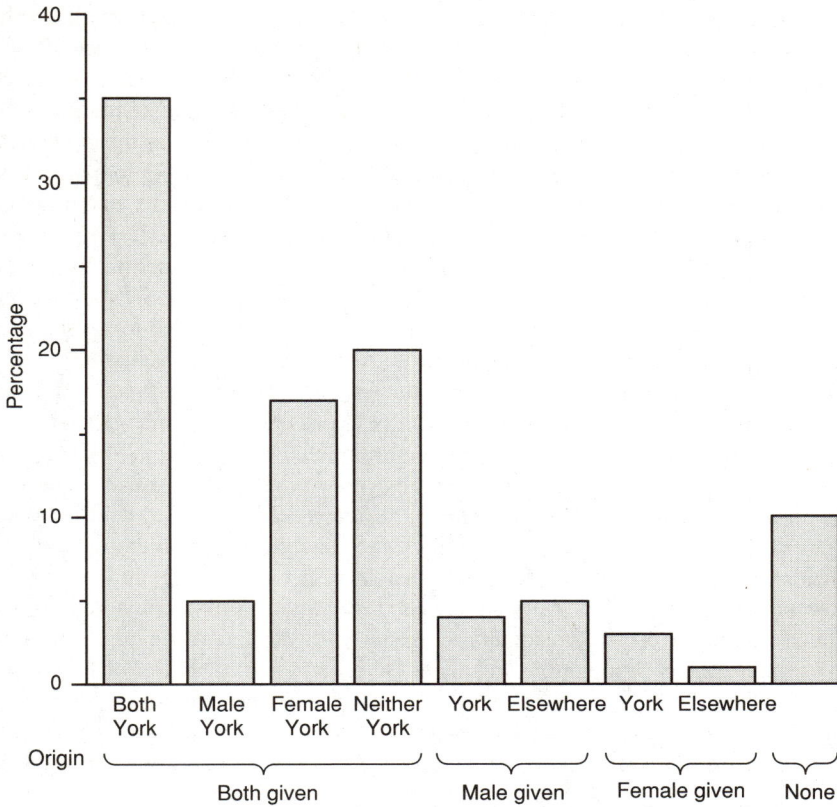

Figure 5.2: Place of origin for brides and grooms in York marriage registers, 1614–1700
Source: original parish registers.

Not surprisingly, therefore, 32 per cent of marriages in the Minster (1681–1700) were of non-York couples. The marriage licensing system enabled many to marry where they wished, and for those wishing anonymity, towns were ideal. Figure 5.2 also shows that in only 35 per cent of marriages were both partners from York. No origin was given in 10 per cent of marriages, and details about only one partner were provided in 13 per cent of marriages, and in these cases it is not known if this information was intended to apply to both. Most marriages (64 per cent) involved someone from York and 45 per cent of marriages where the origin of both partners was given were of a York couple. At least 22 per cent of marriages were of a York resident together with someone from outside the city, and while some of these couples may have settled elsewhere, it is clear that marriage was an important way by which the migrant could be absorbed into the city.[28] Given the high and possibly changing

28 Friedrichs (1985) makes the same point about seventeenth-century Nordlingen.

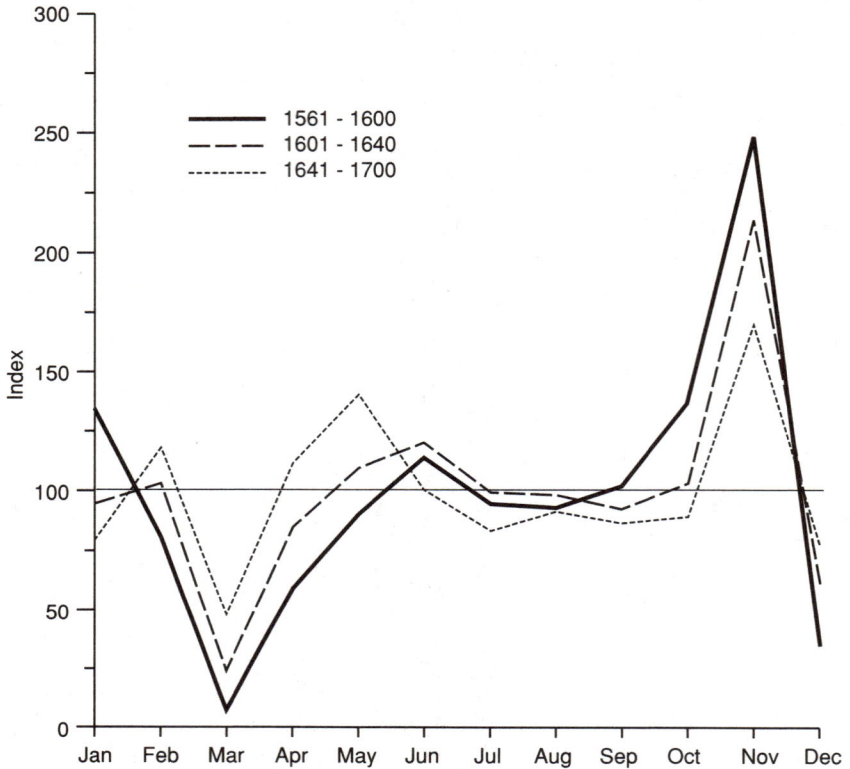

Figure 5.3: Seasonality of marriages, York 1561–1700
Source: original parish registers.

proportions of exogenous marriages, analysis of the city's registers remains difficult; nevertheless, the importance of migrants to York's marriage market is clear and there was considerable scope for change in the numbers who were able to marry.

Influences on nuptiality can be examined via marriage seasonality (Fig. 5.3). The pattern is striking, with large numbers of marriages occurring in November and correspondingly few in March. Change occurred during the seventeenth century as the peak and trough became less intense, although there was less variation throughout the rest of the year. Broadly, seasonality in York was similar to the national pattern, which was heavily influenced by the prohibition of marriage in Lent and Advent.[29] While pregnant brides no doubt were able to persuade priests to marry them at any time, March weddings were very rare during the sixteenth century. Kussmaul (1990, pp. 52–63, 193–94), when examining regional trends in marriage seasonality, dis-

---

29 Wrigley and Schofield (1981), pp. 298–300. They also show that an increase in May marriages occurred during the second half of the seventeenth century.

Table 5.5: Female status from marriage registers, York 1571–1638

| Parish | Period | Number of marriages by female status | | | | Per cent servant marriages |
		Servant	Widow	Daughter	None	
St Martin Coney Street	1596–1606	21	4	9	24	36
	1623–25	9	1	4	5	47
St Martin cum Gregory	1571–5	7	3	1	0	64
	1617–25	25	4	4	25	43
	1628–38	22	5	1	29	39
St Michael le Belfrey	1580–87	29	19	7	48	28
Total		113	36	26	131	37

Source: original parish registers.

covered considerable spatial variations which she explained by differences in work patterns. Rural agrarian parishes near to York were 'autumn marrying', with the majority of marriages taking place after the autumn harvest, while in contrast many West Riding parishes had less seasonal marriage patterns. Between 1561 and 1600 York was also 'autumn marrying', although a more non-seasonal pattern emerged during the seventeenth century. Exactly why York should have experienced an essentially rural pattern of marriage seasonality during the sixteenth century is not clear, since Kussmaul suggests that towns should exhibit less seasonality.[30] At least 20 per cent of marriages taking place in York were effectively rural ones transposed to the city, and much of the seventeenth-century change was due to a greater number of marriages occurring in Lent and Advent. A further reason for the autumn peak in marriages was that many involved servants, and annual contracts often terminated at Martinmas (11 November) (Goldberg 1986, p. 149). For servants planning and saving towards marriage, an autumn wedding would be ideal and the seasonality of servant marriages certainly reflects this, even though all servants did not marry at this time of year.[31] The importance of servant marriages can be further examined since status was occasionally given in the registers Table 5.5.[32] At least 37 per cent of all marriages involved female servants, and this figure must represent an absolute minimum since in 43 per cent of cases status was not recorded. Not all servants would have been migrants, but for many, service provided the opportunity for female migrants to marry and remain permanently in the city. Remarriages were also important and comprised at least 12 per cent of all marriages (or 21 per cent of the mar-

30 Kussmaul (1990), p. 30. Work in towns was less seasonal than in rural areas. There were clearly powerful national forces regulating demographic events in York since the seasonality of baptisms was also similar to the national pattern; see Galley (1991), 189.
31 Monthly indices for 113 female servant marriages were: Jan(35), Feb(141), Mar(12), Apr(84), May(105), Jun(36), Jul(23), Aug(140), Sep(48), Oct(187), Nov(350), Dec(47).
32 Male status was rarely recorded.

riages where status was given).[33] It is not possible to examine the proportion of remarriages or servant brides over time since it was only in the eighteenth century that many registers began to systematically provide information about occupation, place of origin, status or age. For many the most appropriate time to marry was late autumn, and while conclusions about who married in early modern York must remain tentative, the importance of both migrants in general and servants in particular to the city's marriage market is clear and consistent.

Table 5.6: Age at first marriage from licences (both York residents), 1640–1700

Period	Age in years	
	Male	Female
1640–41	25.1	26.2
	(12)	*(20)*
1661–70	31.6	25.4
	(192)	*(141)*
1671–80	30.4	23.4
	(160)	*(139)*
1681–90	28.4	24.6
	(102)	*(78)*
1691–1700	26.8	23.7
	(185)	*(187)*
1640–1700	29.3	24.3
	(651)	*(565)*

Note: numbers in brackets refer to number of cases.
Source: Paver's marriage licences.

An alternative source to parish registers are marriage licences, and while few originals from York survive, during the nineteenth century William Paver made notes from the licence registers and these have been published (Clay, various years). The use of marriage licences is not without problems. Up to three parishes where a wedding could take place were nominated, and unless the parish registers are checked, it is not known where or even if the wedding took place.[34] The greatest drawback with using licences is that it is not known whether those who married by licence form a representative sample of all those who married. Whilst the poor rarely married by licence, Brodsky argues that there is 'no reason to regard the ages reported in [licences] as being particularly unrepresentative of all single women marrying at the time' (Brodsky, 1981, p. 82). In York there are no licences between 1645 and 1660

33 Few registers contain consistent, accurate data about remarriages. Nationally the proportion of those marrying who were widows and widowers was as high as 30 per cent in the sixteenth century and this steadily fell to 11 per cent by the mid-nineteenth century; Wrigley and Schofield (1981), pp. 258–59.
34 Only those cases where York parishes were nominated were examined.

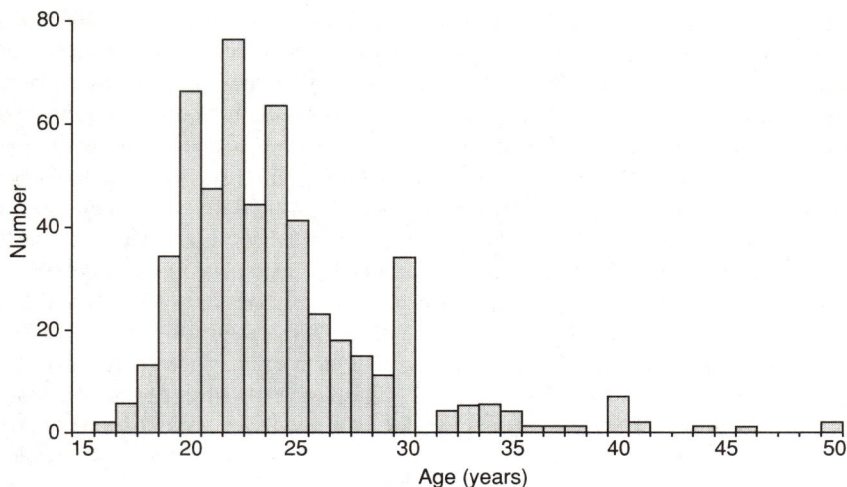

Figure 5.4: Distribution of female ages at first marriage (both York residents)
Source: Paver's marriage licences.

and the earlier ones are less detailed, but from 1661 female status (spinster or widow), place of origin and age were given for most couples. Figure 5.4 shows the distribution of female marriage ages and Table 5.6 shows age at first marriage for couples who both gave their place of origin as York.[35] Ages given in early modern documents are notoriously unreliable, and testing marriage ages poses particular problems since there will have been substantial grouping around the modal age. Figure 5.4 shows that there are problems with these data – age heaping at 30 and 40, fewer than expected married at ages 21 and 23 compared with 20 and 22; however, these are not severe since the overall distribution of ages is as expected, approximately normal and slightly skewed towards the higher ages. Most York women married at comparatively young ages and only a few after 30. The mean age of first marriage was about 24 for women and 29 for men during the second half of the seventeenth century.[36] The accuracy of these estimates may be open to some question, but similar low marriage ages occurred throughout the rest of Yorkshire. Between 1661 and 1670, women married on average at 24.4 (2,127 marriages), and Drake in an analysis of 7,242 Yorkshire marriages between 1662 and 1714, which will have included some of these marriages, showed that age at first marriage for women was about 24.5.[37] Furthermore, non-York women who married York men also married

---

35 The ages given are in completed years, and in order to calculate the mean age it is necessary to add 0.5 to the mean of the given ages since the true age of someone described as 22 can be from 22 years 0 days to 22 years 364 days.

36 A better measure would be the singulate mean age at first marriage which is calculated from the proportion remaining single in each age group.

37 Drake (1961–62), p. 444. Drake does not calculate the mean age at first marriage, but instead provides a distribution in five-year intervals of the numbers marrying, from which an average may be estimated.

early, average age 24.0 (1661–1700, 186 marriages). Brodsky (1981, p. 87) found that female migrants to London married at an almost identical low age, but that London-born women married even earlier (20.5 years, 496 marriages). By comparison, Wrigley and Schofield showed that in 13 parishes between 1651 and 1700 the mean age at first marriage was 28.1 for men and 26.2 for women.[38] These differences may be accounted for given a preference for the wealthy to marry by licence. Such a group would be less reliant on service as a means of accumulating sufficient funds to marry and hence they may have been likely to marry earlier. Low marriage ages in York are also confirmed by Hibberd, who calculated a mean age at marriage of 23.2 years for 43 women she traced in St Michael le Belfrey between 1600 and 1720.[39] Cowgill (1970, p. 75) in a wider examination of age at marriage also found that York women married early, with the average age at first marriage increasing from 23.2 (1538–1601) to 25.6 (1602–1701) (Table 5.7). Despite what appears to be conclusive proof about age at marriage, Cowgill's work has been subject to considerable criticism.[40] While the calculation of age at marriage should be relatively straightforward, provided that the links between baptisms and marriages have been made correctly, it is worrying that Cowgill was able to calculate the ages of 180 brides between 1602 and 1701 in St Michael le Belfrey while Hibberd, after performing a reconstitution, only managed to trace 43 for much the same period. This discrepancy could have arisen if Cowgill allowed links to be made across the parishes in her sample; however, she is not explicit on this point and her results need to be treated with scepticism. Licences also enabled the proportion of remarriages to be examined (Table 5.8). Reservations again need to be be applied to this evidence since those remarrying may have been more or less likely to marry by licence. Nevertheless, by the end of the seventeenth century up to a quarter of all marriages were remarriages and any changes over time were relatively small. Remarriage was an important feature of York's marriage regime, as indeed it was throughout the whole country. Such rates were small, however, by comparison with London where, possibly as a consequence of high levels of crisis mortality, between 1598 and 1619 remarriages involving widows formed up to 35 per cent of women marrying by licence (Brodsky, 1986, p. 129).

The evidence about nuptiality in York is difficult to interpret and inconclusive. Moreover, it has not been possible to show that there were any changes in the proportion who married. The evidence about age at marriage suggests that the York marriage market was dynamic and many were able to marry at young ages.[41] Such conclusions need to be tempered with caution since ages in marriage licences may

38 Wrigley and Schofield (1983), p. 162. Also, see Schofield (1984a) for slightly revised estimates of age at marriage. These do not substantially alter the trend in age at marriage.
39 Hibberd (1981), p. 347. The reconstitution of St Michael le Belfrey during the sixteenth century could not add significantly to this sample since it was only by the end of the 1580s that it would be possible to know brides ages.
40 Her work on mortality suffered from the fundamental flaw that her calculations did not take into account the possibility of migration; see Cowgill (1967) and the reply by Henry (1968).
41 Such a conclusion does not exclude the possibility that there may have been social differences in both the ability and willingness of individuals to marry.

Table 5.7: Female age at first marriage, York 1538–1751

Parish	Age in years		
	1538–1601	*1602–1701*	*1702–51*
All Saints Pavement	21.7	24.8	27.1
	(13)	*(45)*	*(19)*
Holy Trinity Goodramgate	–	24.4	28.9
		(31)	*(49)*
St Crux	24.0	24.3	–
	(25)	*(56)*	
St Lawrence	–	30.0	25.7
		(4)	*(10)*
St Martin Coney Street	23.4	28.0	27.7
	(11)	*(58)*	*(15)*
St Mary Bishophill Jnr	–	27.0	28.0
		(25)	*(51)*
St Michael le Belfrey	23.0	25.4	30.3
	(16)	*(180)*	*(69)*
St Olave	24.8	25.5	–
	(22)	*(31)*	
Overall	*23.6*	*25.6*	*28.7*
	(87)	*(430)*	*(213)*

Note: number of cases are given in brackets.
Source: Cowgill (1970), 75.

be inaccurate and those calculated by reconstitution may be affected by truncation if migration influenced the timing of marriage.[42] Similar low ages at marriage occurred in London during the early sixteenth century, with Finlay finding a mean female age at marriage of 23.1 years, although after 1650 Landers found Quaker marriage ages much closer to those of Wrigley and Schofield.[43] While high levels of migration ensured that marriage remains a difficult variable to quantify, urban nuptiality could and did respond to changing economic circumstances both at the individual and aggregate level. The importance of servant marriages is evident and it was relatively easy for most women to find a husband in early modern towns.

42 Ruggles (1992). Wrigley (1994) shows that such effects do not apply in the English case. However, the very high turnover rates in urban parishes may mean that differences will still have arisen.
43 Finlay (1981c), p. 137. Landers (1990b), p. 93 gives female marriage ages of 27.1 (1650–99) and 25.6 (1700–49). Male marriage ages were 31.0 and 29.4 for the same periods.

Table 5.8: Proportion of remarriages by licence, York 1590–1700

Period	Remarriages
1590–1600	23.8
	(19)
1601–10	22.9
	(27)
1611–20	13.7
	(14)
1631–40	20.5
	(66)
1641–44	24.2
	(24)
1660–70	28.6
	(68)
1671–80	22.2
	(37)
1681–86	23.5
	(24)
1691–1700	18.3
	(42)
1601–40	19.7
	(107)
1660–1700	23.1
	(171)

Note: number of cases are given in brackets.
Source: Paver's marriage licences.

MIGRATION

For many, migration was a common experience in early modern England, but no
English source consistently recorded the movement of migrants. Instead, information about migration has to be gleaned from a variety of documents: for example,
Freemen's lists, apprenticeship and parish registers may indicate place of origin, witnesses giving evidence in court were sometimes asked to give a short account of their
lives, and prosecutions for vagrancy necessarily provide evidence about a special
type of migration.[44] Evidence about migration is therefore limited and often biased.
It is mainly confined to single males and consequently relatively little is known about
female migration or the extent to which families were likely to move (Clark and
Souden, 1987, pp. 18–20). Most rural–urban migrants are considered to be young
and single, with many remaining on a temporary basis; but to what extent this picture is a consequence of deficiencies in the source material is difficult to determine
since so little is known about many aspects of migration. Circular migration must

---

44 See the case studies in Clark and Souden (1987); Beier (1985) Clark and Souden provide the best intro-
    duction to the topic of migration in this period.

have occurred to some extent and seasonal migration began to be increasingly important for some cities during the second half of the seventeenth century.[45] Even estimates of overall migration flows cannot be given since virtually nothing is known about out-migration.[46] In York a legal document from 1680 testifies to the possibilities that were available for those wishing to leave the city.[47] It concerns William Smith, a petty thief who was indentured to emigrate to Virginia via Hull. The details of the case are not relevant, but the document shows that movement between York, Hull, London and even America was commonplace since an eye-witness recalls seeing William Smith in London and letters received from Virginia confirm his subsequent appearance in the New World. Another example from the diary of William Edmunson (born 1627) who was apprenticed in York reveals that he 'was strongly importuned to settle in Dublin, trading being then very brisk, and houses on easy terms, it being not long after the plague'.[48] These two examples are probably far from typical, with most instances of out-migration being more mundane, but since York, like most towns, was at the heart of a complex trading system, opportunities to migrate, both into and out of the city, would have arisen frequently.

Table 5.9: Place of origin from apprenticeship registers, York 1609–1700

| Company | Date | Place of origin | | | |
		York	Yorkshire	Other	None
Merchant Taylors[a]	1609–40	27	61	9	3
		(236)	(538)	(76)	(25)
	1641–1700	26	55	8	11
		(204)	(434)	(63)	(86)
Merchant Adventurers[b]	1678–1700	29	58	13	
		(46)	(92)	(21)	
Eastland Company[b]	1678–1701	36	63	1	
		(31)	(55)	(1)	
General Register[c]	1586–1640	33	54	8	4
		(349)	(572)	(83)	(47)
	1641–87	25	55	7	12
		(90)	(195)	(24)	(44)
All registers	1586–1640	30	58	8	4
		(585)	(1,110)	(159)	(72)
	1641–1700	27	56	8	9
		(371)	(776)	(109)	(130)

Note: figures in brackets refer to the number of cases.
Source: a) BIHR MTA 4.1.2.
             b) Merchant Adventurers Minute Book.
             c) YCA D12.

45 Souden (1984b), p. 142 show that about one-fifth of widowed women over 50 were recent in-migrants. Aveling (1970), p. 97 notes that many of the Catholic gentry only stayed in York during the season.
46 de Vries (1984), pp. 200–21. Reher (1990), pp. 245–98 discusses out-migration for the pre-industrial town of Cuenca. He shows that while young adults were more likely to migrate, annual rates of both in- and out-migration were greater than ten per cent for all ages (Figs 7.1 and 7.2).
47 BIHR CPH 3497.
48 Quoted in Ben-Amos (1991), p. 164.

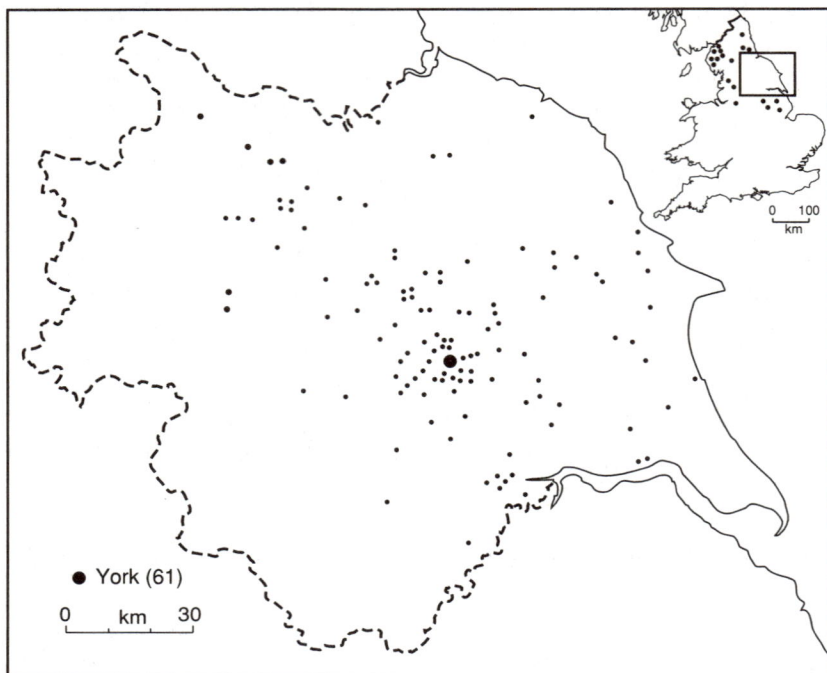

Figure 5.5: Place of origin of 200 York apprentices, 1621–30
Source: YCA D12.

Migration fields can be established from a variety of sources. Palliser's analysis of the origin of 361 men who were made 'Free' between 1535 and 1565 showed that most had only moved short distances to reach the city (Palliser, 1985). About 28 per cent of Freemen were born in the city itself, just over 50 per cent came from the rest of Yorkshire and the other 20 per cent came from further afield, with a substantial number originating from Cumbria, an area with well established trading links with York. An alternative perspective is provided by Goldberg's discussion of female migration to medieval York, and despite his sample being small and covering a long period of time few differences are revealed between male and female migration fields (Goldberg, 1986, pp. 147–49). While York's migration field extended through-out the country, it mainly recruited locally, often from parishes very close to the city.[49] It is not possible to replicate Palliser's or Goldberg's work for the early mod-ern period since place of origin was not given in later Freemen's lists or preambles to cause paper evidence. Migration fields can be established for seventeenth-century

---

49 This was a pattern common to many towns; see Kitch (1986), pp. 228–38; Buckatzch (1949–50); Patten (1976); Holman (1980). London's size meant that it recruited throughout the country, although
most migrants moved relatively short distances; see Smith (1973); Ramsay (1986); Wareing (1980).
The consequences of London's demand for migrants is considered in Wrigley (1967).

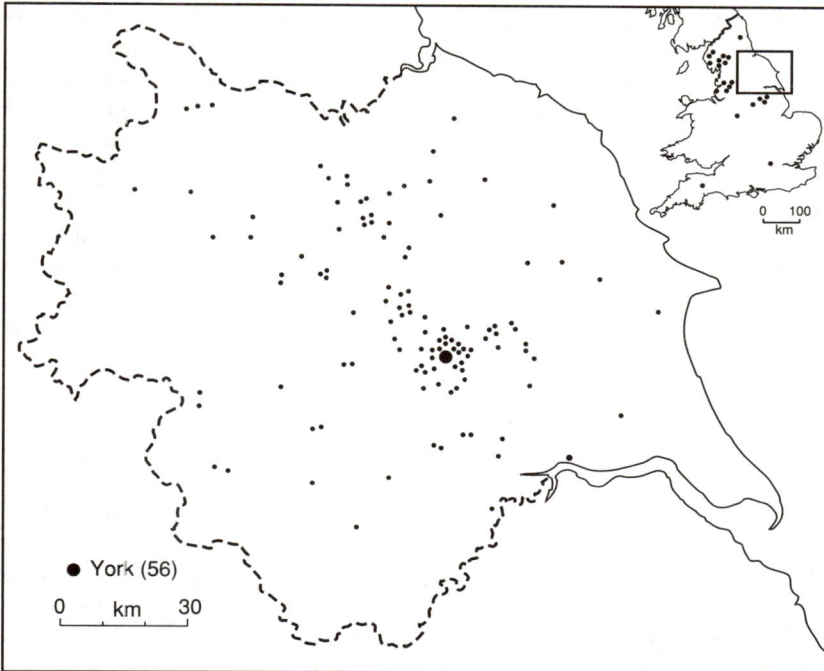

Figure 5.6: Place of origin of 200 York apprentices, 1661–70
Source: YCA D12.

York using apprenticeship registers (Fig. 5.5 and 5.6).[50] Few differences are revealed between the 1620s and the 1660s, and overall there are many similarities between these apprentices and Palliser's Freemen.[51] Many apprentices were recruited from the city itself or close by, and relatively few came from the populous West Riding parishes or those close to Hull where alternative opportunities were available. Rural parishes, especially those in the less populated parts of the North Riding, sent many apprentices to York.[52] Within these areas York had few rivals, and consequently it was the focus for much rural–urban migration. Some masters even preferred to recruit from the same villages and often the same families. York attracted migrants from all over the country, yet most of those migrating from outside Yorkshire came from the north-west, an area which had long since exported its wool through York. As far as it is possible to tell given such a small and biased sample, York's migration fields changed little during the seventeenth century. Table 5.9 presents a more sys-

50 Three apprenticeship registers have survived: BIHR MTA 4.1.2, Merchant Adventurers Minute Book, YCA D12. Two of the registers, the Merchant Taylors and Merchant Adventurers, were companies involved in trade. The other was kept by the council and lists apprentices from a wide variety of occupations.
51 Palliser (1985), p. 115. Migration fields in the rest of the seventeenth century are similar.
52 A few apprentices also came from smaller market towns such as Ripon or North Allerton.

tematic analysis of the apprenticeship data and little change is again apparent. About 30 per cent came from York, 60 per cent from Yorkshire and 10 per cent from outside the county. The proportion originating from the three areas is similar to the Freemen data, with the exception that twice the proportion of Freemen came from outside Yorkshire. This may reflect York's declining national importance, but it may have been caused by Palliser's smaller sample containing a number of wealthier adults who were prepared to travel long distances to establish businesses in the city.[53] York attracted apprentices from as far afield as London, Scotland, Northampton, Worcester, Oxford, Lincoln and Durham, yet nearly half of those apprentices migrating from outside Yorkshire originated from Westmorland or Cumberland and many others came from Lancashire. The vast majority of migrants came from areas with few or only small urban settlements, and throughout the seventeenth century York recruited migrants from areas where it was economically dominant or had traditional trading links. From the medieval period onwards York's migration fields hardly changed and the city appears to have experienced few problems recruiting rural apprentices.

Movement was not confined to those entering or leaving the city. Within individual urban parishes there was considerable population turnover and this can be estimated from parish rate books.[54] Church rates were used to maintain the clergy and the fabric of the building. They were set annually and it was usual for the churchwardens to list each head of household together with any assessment. Rate books do however pose problems of interpretation. They include an unknown proportion of the total population, the very poorest may be missing from some lists and, in a few cases, individuals were not named.[55] Despite these shortcomings linking names to subsequent assessments will yield reliable estimates of residential persistence.[56] It

53 It was possible to become free by apprenticeship, patrimony (having a father who was free) or by redemption (payment). A greater proportion of longer-distance migrants may reflect that those who were willing to take the greater risks were the ones more likely to succeed.
54 Rate books are discussed in Wright (1985) (1989); Alldridge (1986) exploits these and similar sources to produce a population profile of Chester.
55 Houses were occasionally listed as empty, and 'unpaid' was written at the side of some entries. Absence from home, nonconformity or poverty could all contribute to reasons why individuals failed to pay these rates. In Holy Trinity Goodramgate in 1673, 44 out of 141 (31 per cent) of householders are listed as 'unpaid'. Of these, 15 appear as having paid in the 1674 list, 10 are listed as 'unpaid' and the remaining 19 do not appear again; BIHR Y/HTG 12:546–48. This rate of non-payment seems to have been exceptional since in other years a much lower rate was recorded and sometimes individuals were marked 'unpaid' even though they had made a part payment towards the rate. Thus, it is uncertain if rate books listed all householders, or just those liable for payments. Alldridge (1986), pp. 119–20 concluded that in Chester the rate books give a virtually complete list of householders, although he does admit that some of the very poorest may have been omitted.
56 The method follows that of Boulton (1987a), pp. 208–14. Nominal record linkage is hazardous when only first and last names are available. This did not cause serious problems because the size of both parishes ensured that different householders possessing the same name would occur very infrequently. In performing two reconstitutions there was only one case where it was impossible to assign children to the correct parents because the head of two families shared the same names.

Table 5.10: Percentage annual turnover rates in three York parishes

Parish	Period	Turnover
Holy Trinity Goodramgate	1621–22	14
		(51)
	1631–32	39
		(64)
	1641–42	23
		(61)
	1651–52	39
		(51)
	1661–62	26
		(50)
	1671–72	13
		(113)
	1681–82	26
		(147)
	1691–92	21
		(166)
St Michael le Belfrey	1639–40	15
		(137)
	1681–82	26
		(138)
St Martin Coney St	1587–88	18
		(61)
All Parishes		21
		(1,039)

Note: figures in brackets refer to number of cases.
Source: BIHR PR Y/HTG 12; Y/MB 34; Y/MCS F1/3.

should be noted that this technique measures persistence of householders, not households, since if a householder died it is often difficult to establish whether other members of that household continued to live in the same parish. Persistence of households will therefore be greater than persistence of householders and turnover rates calculated from these types of sources will always be higher than the actual rates. Two York parishes, St Michael le Belfrey and Holy Trinity Goodramgate, have well-kept rate books, and Tables 5.10 and 5.11 show annual and decadal turnover rates respectively.[58] It is immediately apparent that large numbers of householders were absent from subsequent lists as the overall annual turnover rate was near to 20 per cent. These levels of turnover were similar to those found in seventeenth-century London, which is encouraging since even short distance movement in York, with its small

57 BIHR Y/MB 33, 34; Y/HTG 12. Rating assessments also exist for St Martin Coney Street, 1557–58 (BIHR Y/MCS F1/3) and All Saints Pavement, 1666 (BIHR Y/ASP F14/11). The 1621 list was compared with the 1622 list and then with the 1630 list to calculate decadal rates (strictly nine years). The process was repeated for the other decades.

Table 5.11: Percentage decadal persistence and turnover rates in two York parishes

Parish	Period	Decadal persistence	Average annual turnover	Turnover excluding first year
Holy Trinity Goodramgate	1559–68	39 (57)	9.9	–
	1590–1600	46 (35)	7.5	–
	1611–20	12 (40)	21.0	–
	1621–30	47 (51)	8.0	7.3
	1651–60	25 (51)	14.2	10.3
	1661–70	30 (50)	12.5	10.7
	1671–80	30 (113)	12.5	12.4
	1681–90	23 (147)	15.0	13.5
	1691–1700	12 (166)	21.0	21.0
St Michael le Belfrey	1681–90	36 (138)	10.9	8.8
All parishes		28 (848)	13.8	12.5

Note: figures in brackets refer to number of cases. The lists for 1560, 1591 and 1612 are missing.
Source: see Table 5.10.

parishes, would often have resulted in crossing parish boundaries.[58] If such rates remained constant then only 13 per cent of householders would still have been resident after nine years. This did not happen and Table 5.11 shows that after nine years nearly 30 per cent of household heads remained in the parish. Such results are not surprising given that the process of reconstitution yielded substantial information about many families. If the high turnover of the first year is excluded, then average annual turnover rates were near to 12 per cent. Thus, there must have been two types of households in York, one which was highly mobile, the other exhibiting greater levels of parochial persistence. Given that familial rates of turnover will have been

---

58 Boulton (1987a), p. 211 found an average annual turnover rate of 21 per cent in seventeenth-century Southwark, with 25 per cent still being in residence after 10 years. Finlay (1981c), pp. 46–47 quotes slightly lower rates of turnover for three London parishes.

lower than those indicated in Table 5.11, sufficient will have persisted within areas of the city to allow a number of close-knit communities to develop.[59]

It is difficult to determine, given the limitations of rate books, exactly what the characteristics of these 'movers' and 'stayers' were.[60] A clue is given by Hibberd, who analysed population turnover between the Hearth Tax returns of 1671 and 1672 (Hibberd, 1981, p. 407). She found that 25.6 per cent of those listed by parish in 1671 could not be found in 1672. Of those who were missing, 3.9 per cent were accounted for by the death of the householder and 4.8 per cent were due to inter-parish movement and problems arising from landlords owning more than one property making it difficult to link names. This meant that the overall turnover rate was 16.9 per cent which, added to the 3.9 per cent of householder deaths, produces a figure close to that derived from the rate books. Hibberd also argued that movement varied across the city, with lower rates being associated with the 'richer' central parishes (Hibberd, 1981, p. 442). Differential mobility can be tested, albeit crudely, by comparing the turnover rate of the ten richest householders in each rating list with the poorest ten. For the lists included in Table 5.10, the richest householders experienced a turnover rate of 14 per cent compared with 34 per cent for the poorest.[61] With old age being a primary cause of poverty, there was probably some differential mortality between the two samples, but whilst the poor were always in search of good, cheap accommodation, poverty by itself was not the only cause of these differences (Pound, 1988, p. 130). Opportunities for moving were probably more restricted for the very rich since they would already be living in some of the best housing. Many were also likely to be serving, or have served, as parish officials and this would have reinforced neighbourhood loyalty and contributed towards greater stability. Yet, even for the most stable sections in society, parish turnover rates were still in the region of 10 per cent.

Like most early modern urban societies, York's population was highly mobile and turnover amongst those of highest mobility, such as servants and lodgers, cannot even be measured. Movement into and out of the city was frequent, parochial turnover rates were high, yet at the core of each parish, and by implication throughout the city as a whole, there was much greater stability. The overall flow of migrants was controlled by economic forces. In periods of dearth some sought to move to towns in the hope of finding work or charity, and in exceptional circumstances councils ensured that the city was not overwhelmed by expelling poor migrants. Thus, while concentrations of poverty certainly existed, these were kept under control by local initiatives, and despite considerable levels of turnover, most towns were able

---

59 This occurred to some extent in London; see Boulton (1987a), especially p. 227. The stability of the capital's population is one of the themes of Rappaport (1989).

60 These terms are taken from Souden (1984).

61 More sophisticated methods were employed to test this association, but the overall link between wealth and mobility is at best weak. One of the many problems, even with accurate lists of rating assessments, was to produce a workable definition of 'rich' and 'poor'. Turnover amongst the poor was very high in 1631 and 1651; in other years it was closer to that of the rich, and without these two exceptional years the rates would have been rich 12 per cent: poor 24 per cent.

to prosper throughout the seventeenth century.[62] Even after a period of severe crisis mortality, the city's economy continued to function. Within a few years of the 1604 plague, the city had returned to normal, demographically at least. Many migrants must have moved to York for the same reasons that William Edmundson moved to Dublin. These migrants appear to have been quickly and easily assimilated into the population. At the same time the Council attempted to ensure that those merchants who had fled the city in 1604 returned as soon as possible in order to resume trade; however, no attempts were made to specifically recruit migrants.[63] Freemen admissions show that whilst there was a huge increase in the numbers admitted after 1604, the proportion of those who qualified by patrimony did not significantly differ from earlier periods.[64] In many cases it would appear that the death of a Freeman created the opportunity for his heir to set up in business. Where this was not possible an apprentice or journeyman, who may have already been residing in the city, would have taken the opportunity of becoming 'Free', which in turn created the need for additional apprentices. The availability of casual employment provided some opportunities for the poor to migrate, although there is no evidence to suggest that a mass influx occurred and it would seem safe to conclude that most migrants moved to York only if there were jobs for them to do. In many instances these in-migrants literally stepped into 'dead men's shoes', replacing those who had died in the plague. The prospect of economic advancement was obviously a tempting proposition for many, and despite the obvious threat to health, vacancies of all kinds were soon filled. This also meant that many were suddenly able to marry. Initially, a younger population structure was probably created, but such changes were short-lived, with high mortality and turnover rates ensuring that the population structure reverted to normal very quickly. Migration was a powerful agent in the early modern city. While lodgings were plentiful and opportunities for casual work existed, it was only towards the end of the sixteenth century that a serious threat emerged that York would be swamped by an influx of poor migrants. At other times migration flows were effectively controlled and determined by internal economic demand.

---

62 Slack (1988), pp. 162–82 shows that by the end of the seventeenth century most towns were spending greater amounts on poor relief, yet in comparison with a century earlier there is nothing to suggest that poor migrants were flooding into the city. Action was taken by the Council throughout the seventeenth century to ensure that the number of poor remained under control: 'The main attack, however, was directed against "undersettlers" or "inmates" who might easily become a charge on the rates; repeated attempts were made to reduce the numbers of undesirable lodgers ... The problem remained unresolved, however, and provoked renewed action at the end of the century' (Tillott 1961, p. 171.

63 YCA B32 345, 369.

64 From 1605 to 1610 the proportion who qualified by patrimony was 38 per cent (272 out of 720). This was identical to the period 1591–1600 (222 out of 590).

THE EFFECT OF MIGRATION ON YORK'S POPULATION STRUCTURE

Lack of sources ensures that many aspects of migration will remain unknown, but some of its effects on York's population structure may be determined. Without migration, any imbalance in the sex-ratio of the population will have been small and caused by sex-specific mortality differentials. In Lichfield, however, imbalances were due to differential migration and these were concentrated amongst young adults and the very old. By the end of the seventeenth century many towns contained an excess of females, and this is often attributed to wealthier urban residents employing large numbers of female domestic servants. The sex-ratio of servants, especially if apprentices are included, could vary considerably as trades involving heavy manual work tended to employ male servants.[65] Evidence on the sex-ratio is sparse, although analysis of the 1377 Poll Tax revealed an adult sex-ratio of 90.5 males per 100 females in York.[66] Goldberg's analysis showed considerable variation between individual parishes, with the number and type of servants probably being the key to explaining differential urban sex-ratios.[67] Once again it is difficult to examine the age/sex-structure without listings, and the only way that changes in the sex-structure

Table 5.12: Sex–ratios at burial (males per 100 females), York 1561–1700

Period	Children	Number	Adults	Number	All	Number
1561–70	149	(112)	89	(142)	113	(745)
1571–80	130	(287)	101	(362)	113	(1,146)
1581–90	128	(225)	99	(511)	114	(1,620)
1591–1600	100	(498)	102	(629)	108	(1,936)
1601–10	111	(1,167)	102	(1,274)	108	(3,512)
1611–20	116	(1,203)	126	(1,561)	121	(2,866)
1621–30	109	(1,295)	108	(1,469)	109	(3,122)
1631–40	100	(1,664)	106	(1,776)	101	(3,643)
1641–50	110	(1,634)	146	(2,284)	129	(4,092)
1651–60	101	(1,688)	107	(1,709)	104	(3,397)
1661–70	111	(1,968)	99	(1,971)	105	(3,939)
1671–80	110	(2,097)	98	(2,378)	104	(4,475)
1681–90	111	(2,193)	92	(2,426)	101	(4,619)
1691–1700	114	(1,902)	90	(2,439)	99	(4,341)
1561–1600	117	(1,122)	100	(1,644)	111	(5,447)
1601–40	108	(5,329)	110	(6,080)	109	(13,143)
1641–50	110	(1,634)	146	(2,284)	129	(4,092)
1651–1700	110	(9,848)	96	(10,923)	102	(20,771)

Source: original parish registers.

65 Phythian-Adams (1979), pp. 208–12. Also see Kussmaul (1981).
66 Goldberg (1990), p. 200. The 1381 return which is damaged gives a sex-ratio of 106.1, and the conclusion that medieval York had an excess of females should therefore be treated cautiously.
67 Goldberg (1990). Servant sex-ratios show much greater variation than non-servant ratios.

can be determined is via the sex-ratio at burial.[68] The sex-ratio at baptism in York between 1561 and 1700 was 104, and this is sufficiently close to that experienced by modern populations to have confidence in the accuracy of York's registers in recording sex.[69] The use of sex-ratios at burial has to be tempered by possible sex-specific mortality differentials. In the early nineteenth century, sex-ratios at burial were 100 (1801–10), 99 (1811–20), 104 (1821–30) and 103 (1831–40) which compare with actual sex-ratios of 77 in 1801, 80 in 1811, 84 in 1821, 84 in 1831 and 87 in 1841.[70] Higher male mortality caused these differences, and while adults experienced some differential, infants and children experienced considerable excess male mortality.[71] Thus, sex-ratios at burial will only provide a very approximate indication of the sex-ratio of the population; nevertheless, any changes in the sex-structure, should be reflected by changes in the sex-ratio at burial. In order to use sex-ratios at burial to investigate the changing sex-structure it is therefore necessary to separate adult from child burials (Table 5.12).[72] The decade 1641–50 is treated separately since the influx of military personnel during the Civil War created a uniquely distorted population structure and caused a substantial excess of male burials (see pp. 83–87). Overall there was an excess of male burials throughout the whole period, but once burials are separated into adults and children a different pattern emerges. The child ratios reveal the expected excess of male burials at all times; the adult ratios are more interesting and indicate possible changes to York's population structure. Once the figure for the 1640s has been excluded, the adult sex-ratio at burial shows a modest fall from a balanced population in the sixteenth century to one favouring women by the late seventeenth century. During the early seventeenth century and in both decades following mortality crises, men predominated, but after 1650 York increasingly became dominated by women, with decadal sex-ratios from 1651–60 to 1691–1700 being 107, 99, 98, 92 and 90.[73]

There was some variation in the adult sex-ratio between parishes (Table 5.13). The presence of gaols in St Mary Castlegate and St John Ousebridge explains much of the excess male mortality in these parishes as the vast majority of prisoner burials were male.[74] There were excess female burials in some suburban parishes which may

68 Without sex-specific migration, the sex-ratio should be fairly balanced. For examples of urban sex-ratios see Souden (1984b) and for variations by county see Souden (1987).
69 York's registers recorded 20,395 male and 19,683 female baptisms. Wrigley and Schofield (1981), pp. 126–28, 224–25 also found that sex-ratios at baptism were close to 104. The main problem in calculating sex-ratios was with assigning a sex to the names Francis and Frances since examples of both spellings occurred to both males and females.
70 *1801 Census. Parish Registers* (London, 1802); *1811 Census. Parish Registers* (London, 1812); *1821 Census. Parish Register Abstract* (London, 1822); *1831 Census. Parish Register Abstract* (London, 1833); *1841 Census* (London, 1843).
71 Schofield and Wrigley (1979), p. 65. Compared with a sex-ratio at birth of 104, the sex ratio of children (under 15s) was only 95 in 1841.
72 Children were not always differentiated from adults.
73 Based on 1,709, 1,971, 2,378, 2,426 and 2,439 burials respectively.
74 In St Mary Castlegate, if those burials which were explicitly stated as being from the Castle are excluded, the ratios become 105 and 114 respectively. Tillot (1961), pp. 521–28 discusses York's prisons.

Table 5.13: Adult sex–ratios at burial (males per 100 females) by parish, York 1561–1700

Parish	Sex–ratio at burial		
	1561–1600	1601–40	1651–1700
All Saints North Street	100	89	71
All Saints Pavement	–	94	92
Holy Trinity Goodramgate	127	108	92
Holy Trinity Kings Court	–	74	106
Holy Trinity Micklegate	–	87	104
St Crux	–	98	109
St Cuthbert	–	–	48
St Denys with St George	–	68	109
St Helen Stonegate	120	101	78
St John Ousebridge	106	167	115
St Lawrence	–	97	73
St Margaret Walmgate	65	101	85
St Martin Coney Street	179	117	109
St Mary Bishophill Jnr	–	105	88
St Mary Bishophill Snr	–	–	78
St Mary Castlegate	–	188	144
St Maurice	–	–	78
St Michael le Belfrey	97	109	107
St Michael Spurriergate	–	118	99
St Olave	105	103	73
St Sampson	–	–	114
St Saviour	–	–	71

Source: original parish registers.

be explained by the presence of an above average number of widows, a group which would have had an acute effect on the sex-ratio at burial.[75] By the second half of the seventeenth century, in St Olave and St Mary Bishophill Snr, both parishes with excess female burials, almshouses had been set up for the maintenance of poor widows.[76] More important than variations between parishes, Table 5.13 confirms that the sex-ratio in most parishes declined from the beginning to the end of the seventeenth century. Furthermore, if only the parishes that were in observation for all three periods are considered separately, then adult sex-ratios at burial were 99, 110 and 95 respectively, which again confirms the changes to York's sex-structure.[77] Even though overall changes in the sex-ratio were small, the imbalance may have been much greater amongst young adults, the section of the population most easily

---

75 Not all widows would have been old. Evidence from poor relief payments shows concentrations of payments to lone women in some parishes, and presumably many of these would have been widows; see YCA E70–4.

76 Tillot (1961), pp. 423–24. BIHR Y/SO, BIHR Y/SMBpSnr.

77 Numbers of burials (male/female): 1561–1600, 821/833; 1601–1640, 1,699/1,547; 1,651–1,700 1,953/2,057.

affected by changes in migration. In an early modern urban population, about 40 per cent would have been children and one-third married (see Tables 1.3, 6.1). This would mean that in a town of 12,000 there would be 4,800 children and 7,200 adults, of whom 4,000 would be married. An adult sex-ratio of 95 would therefore imply that there were about 1,500 unmarried males and 1,700 unmarried females. Between 1831 and 1840 the overall sex-ratio at burial was 102, but the sex-ratio of the adult population was only 83: now, since the sex-ratio at burial between 1651 and 1700 was 102, an adult ratio of 83 would infer that there were 1,266 unmarried males and 1,934 unmarried females.[78] Such calculations can at best only be illustrative, but much of any imbalance will have been concentrated amongst 20 to 30 year olds and the increasing feminization of York's population will have meant that marriage opportunities for some female migrants became more restricted, especially given that the economy and population was stagnant. York had a balanced sex-ratio during the sixteenth century which gave way to an excess of males from 1610, and by the end of the seventeenth century the sex-ratio had skewed significantly towards females. Given that there were no significant sex-specific variations in adult mortality and large numbers of widows or old spinsters did not move into the city, the main cause of a decreasing sex-ratio would be a greater proportion of young females in the population, many of whom would have been servants. Such a thesis is likely given that York was developing into a social centre during the seventeenth century.

The impact of sex-specific changes in migration on York's demographic history is such that it is important to discover possible variations in the employment of servants. Burials of servants and apprentices were occasionally indicated in the parish registers, but for urban-born residents relatively few deaths would have occurred between 15 and 30, the commonest ages of servants. Rural migrants, however, may not have been exposed to the variety of diseases which were endemic in the city, and the mortality of this age group may well have been greater than that predicted by model life tables (see pp. 111–13). The proportion of servant and apprentice burials is given in Table 5.14. Since servants and apprentices were not consistently recorded, the large excess of males is probably indicative of low female status rather than the actual ratio of servants in York. Most registers recorded only small numbers of servant burials and the accuracy of the rates must be subject to a wide margin of error. As the evidence about parochial sex-ratios indicated, occupational zoning would also have caused concentrations of different types of servants throughout the city. Table 5.14 shows that servant and apprentice burials amounted to between four and 29 per cent of all adult burials. Given this wide variation, it is appropriate to use the median figure of 8.5 per cent to represent the average.[79] Throughout the whole city, only ten per cent of adult deaths were described as servants and there were no increases after 1650; indeed the opposite occurred. The number of servants in York

---

78 All imbalances must have occurred within the unmarried population.

79 Mode equals 8, Mean equals 8. Excluding the very high figure from St Helen Stonegate, at most 20 per cent of adult burials were caused by servants, and this represents only about 10 per cent of all burials.

Table 5.14: Burials of servants and apprentices in selected York registers, 1561–1700

Parish	Period	Servants and apprentices				Adult burials	% of servant burials
		M	F	U/K	Total		
All Saints North Street	1602–09	3	4		7	69	10
	1615–25	4			4	63	6
All Saints Pavement	1632–36	3	2		5	51	10
Holy Trinity Goodramgate	1590–96	5	1	1	7	54	13
	1610–22	12	2		14	106	13
	1677–84	4	3		7	119	6
	1689–92	2	4		6	66	9
Holy Trinity Kings Court	1618–24	4	4		8	70	11
	1632–44	5	8		13	123	11
	1659–70	4	5		9	125	7
Holy Trinity Micklegate	1608–14	3	2		5	85	6
St Helen Stonegate	1566–78	12	3		15	52	29
St John Ousebridge	1598–1616	14	10		24	319	8
	1623–30	2	4	1	7	98	7
St Martin Coney Street	1591–95	4	1		5	31	16
	1601–23	18	16	2	36	192	19
	1635–40	5	1		6	49	12
St Martin cum Gregory	1625–32	5	1		6	38	16
	1681–89	3	2		5	66	8
St Mary Castlegate	1621–34	3	5	1	9	224	4
St Michael le Belfrey	1566–1602	29	25		54	659	8
	1637–44	12	2	1	15	327	5
	1662–73	12	8		20	279	7
St Olave	1622–28	7			7	84	8
Overall	1561–1602	50	30	1	81	796	10.2
	1601–44	100	61	5	166	1898	8.7
	1651–1700	25	22		47	655	7.2
	1561–1700	175	113	6	294	3349	8.8

Source: original parish registers.

is not known, but by the end of the seventeenth century many cities had about ten per cent servants in their populations.[80] Thus, while the death rates amongst servants may have been high, it would appear that they were not sufficiently high to alter the demographic balance. The graph of baptisms, burials and marriages (Figure 3.4) reveals that during 1651–1700, the period of greatest natural decrease, burials exceeded baptisms by 18 per cent, and if it were possible to remove all servant burials from the series, a large shortfall would still have existed. Furthermore, changes in the numbers of servants do not explain York's changing patterns of baptisms and burials.

80 Souden (1984b), p. 150 gives the following percentage of servants in late-seventeenth-century towns: Bristol (10), Leicester (8), Lichfield (8) and Southampton (10).

While not all 'temporary migrants' would have been apprentices and servants, many were, and in order for all the excess mortality to be explained by the number of servants in the population, the percentage of servant burials would have to be 15.5 per cent of *all* burials. This is far greater than Table 5.14 indicates, and this result has important implications for Sharlin's model since he considered most of the excess deaths in cities due to temporary migrants to have been servants and apprentices.[81] Furthermore, with no increase in the proportion of servant burials during the seventeenth century, it does not appear that an increase in the proportion of temporary migrants in the population can explain York's pattern of natural change. Changes to York's population structure certainly occurred, but these mainly affected nuptiality by reducing the proportion of the population who were able to marry.

FERTILITY, MARRIAGE AND MIGRATION IN EARLY MODERN YORK

Chapters 3 and 4 showed that increases in mortality could not entirely explain the pattern of natural change in York, and consequently there must have been a complementary reduction in fertility during the seventeenth century. Since marital and illegitimate fertility hardly changed, any reduction in overall fertility must have been caused by changes in the incidence and timing of marriage. Precise measures of nuptiality cannot be given, but there are indications that fewer were able to marry in the seventeenth century. First, even though evidence about age at marriage is difficult to interpret, women married later in the seventeenth century than they had done in the sixteenth century. Secondly, the sex-structure increasingly became dominated by females after 1650. Such imbalances restricted marriage opportunities and thereby lowered the proportion married. Thirdly, and of greatest importance, economic growth after 1650 was at best slight. This meant that fewer opportunities to marry arose and this further depressed levels of nuptiality. Throughout the entire early modern period York's demographic history was directly influenced by its economy. Economic demand within the city essentially determined how many people were able to live in the city; but it also influenced the age-sex profile of net migration and the proportion of the population who were able to marry.

Figure 5.7, which has been adapted from Figure 2.3, summarizes how the principal features of York's demography affected each other and, more importantly, how they changed between 1561 and 1700. The exogenous influences on the system are crucial to understanding this change. Throughout early modern York, rates of mortality were high. With the possible exception of the 1631 plague which was controlled by the imposition of a *cordon sanitaire*, knowledge of how diseases spread was limited and large numbers living in close proximity together with poor levels of sanitation ensured that levels of mortality remained high. Fertility also changed. Economic recovery from the 1560s created the conditions in which many could con-

---

81 Sharlin (1978). Temporary migrants may also have worked as journeymen, but numbers are difficult to estimate. Phythian-Adams (1979), p. 104 shows that in Coventry the number of journeymen was variable and could have been greater than the number of masters; however, Ben-Amos (1991) found that most apprentices did not work for long periods as journeymen.

1561-1600

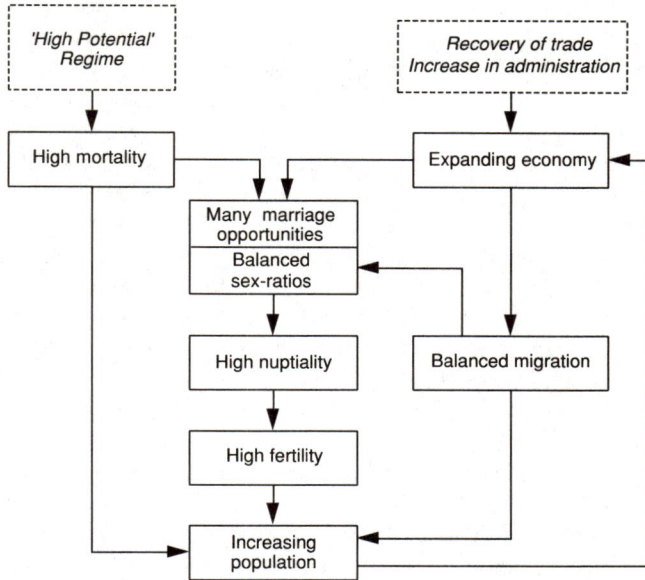

1650-1700

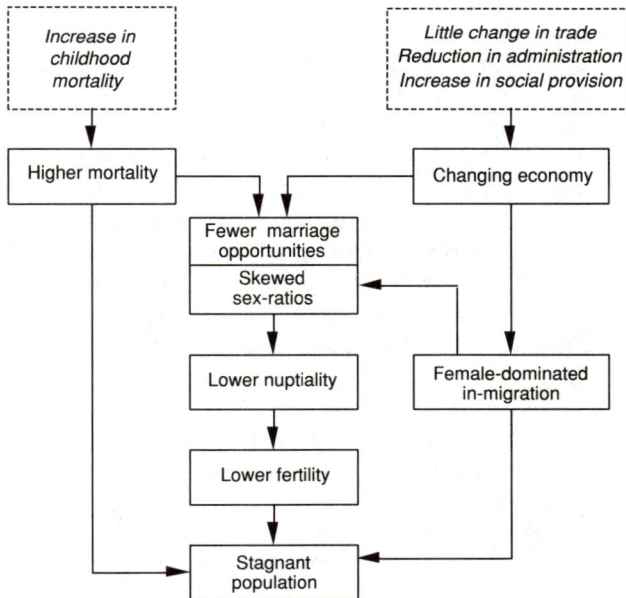

Figure 5.7: The changing relationship between York's economy and demography
Source: original parish registers.

template marriage, and this they did with enthusiasm. Moreover, York's economy created a demand for migrants that resulted in a population that was not substantially skewed towards one sex. This meant that the proportion married was high, and so was fertility. The rising population created a feedback mechanism which further stimulated the economy and created additional marriage opportunities. For a period of 40 years or so there were more births than deaths in York. This fact by itself has little relevance to York's demography and in some ways it is merely an accident of the accounting system, although it does reveal that given a 'booming' economy it was possible for fertility, at least in the short term, to outpace the urban mortality penalty. The propensity for much of the population to migrate, due in part to restricted marriage opportunities throughout the country, ensured that there were always sufficient who would be eager to move either into or out of cities in order to exploit economic opportunities, and thus, levels of net migration were much more important in determining the overall size of York's population than levels of natural change.

By the end of the seventeenth century, York's demography had undergone a number of subtle changes. York's 'high potential' mortality regime had been intensified by increases in childhood mortality. Of equal, if not greater, impact, its economy had also changed as administration became less important and the city began to evolve into a social centre. York still remained wealthy, but its economy had ceased to grow. Its population remained stationary, and any feedback mechanism in which population increase encouraged economic growth, which further encouraged population increase, had ended. Many were still able to marry, but the 'boom' had come to an end and marriage opportunities were now only created in the natural course of events by death, retirement or out-migration. These changes also resulted in the stream of migrants becoming skewed towards females, although this may also reflect, in a period of general population stagnation, greater opportunities for males in their home parishes.[82] The skewed population further reduced the proportion who were able to marry, and hence lowered overall levels of fertility. The increase in mortality and the decrease in fertility now created natural decrease. Again this was largely irrelevant to York's demographic history and the city was maintained, as it had been in the sixteenth century, by a steady flow of migrants into York. The period between 1600 and 1640 can be viewed as one of transition. The 'boom' had begun to fade as both economic and population growth was only modest, although there appears to have been a resumption in the late 1630s. Fewer marriages occurred and for a short period there were more males in the population. These slight changes now meant that births and deaths were roughly in balance. Once again the level of natural change did not affect whether or not the city grew.

Piecing together the jigsaw of York's demographic history has necessarily involved some speculation since substantial limitations are imposed by the source

82 Wrigley and Schofield (1981), p. 528 show that the national population was 5.2 million in 1651, 4.9 million in 1681 and 5.1 million in 1701.

material. In spite of some aspects of York's demography remaining hidden, what is clear is that it is dangerous to view single aspects of demographic regimes in isolation. The links between mortality, fertility, nuptiality and migration are many and complex, and it will only be by examining the urban demographic regime as a whole that progress can be made towards fully understanding the population dynamics of early modern cities.

CONCLUSION

Chapter 6

A DYNAMIC MODEL OF
EARLY MODERN URBAN DEMOGRAPHY

The primary objective of the preceding three chapters was to find out precisely what could be discovered about the demography of York between 1561 and 1700. The two major techniques of the historical demographer – aggregative analysis and family reconstitution – were used on the city's registers and these revealed a variety of demographic experience. The aggregate series of baptisms, burials and marriages showed that changes to York's demography occurred during the seventeenth century as mortality increased relative to fertility. Reconstitution, together with the simpler technique of linking baptisms to infant burials, then enabled accurate estimates of infant and childhood mortality and marital and illegitimate fertility to be given, although adult mortality and nuptiality were more difficult to assess. This limited range of measures was insufficient to fully explain York's changing demographic regime, yet enough could be discovered to conclude that by the second half of the seventeenth century, mortality had increased, a smaller proportion of the population was able to marry and overall fertility had decreased.

An inability to fully reconstruct the demographic characteristics of English urban populations ensures that certain aspects of urban demography are still hidden. In particular, factors influencing the ability to marry are difficult to disentangle and the role of the migrant remains elusive. Until further research is carried out on the demography and economy of other cities, all conclusions will necessarily be tentative; nevertheless, sufficient has been discovered about York to show that demographic analysis in other large provincial cities will provide rich rewards for future research.

URBAN DEMOGRAPHY – SOURCES AND METHODS

All analysis of past societies is limited by the often chance survival of appropriate sources, and the most important for the demographer of pre-Victorian England is the parish register. The quality of urban registers has been questioned on a number of occasions.[1] While undoubtedly *some* registers in *some* parishes were of very poor quality, there is little reason to suspect that the best-kept urban registers are any less reliable than the best-kept rural registers, at least until the eighteenth century. By the beginning of the nineteenth century, registration in many parishes especially in the cities, had become inadequate and this eventually led to the creation of a national civil registration system. John Rickman, when commenting upon the results from the first census in 1801, revealed:

---

1 See the discussion in Galley *et al*. (1995).

Concerning The Registry of Burials.

The Registry of Burials may be supposed to be deficient on the following considerations.

1. Many Congregations of Dissenters, inhabiting Towns, have their own peculiar Burying Grounds; as have the Jews, and the Roman Catholics, who reside in London.

2. That some persons, from motives of Poverty or Convenience, inter their Dead without any religious Ceremony; this is known to happen in the Metropolis, in Bristol, and Newcastle-upon-Tyne, and may happen in a few large Towns.

3. Children who die before Baptism are interred without any religious Ceremony, and consequently are not registered.

Concerning the registry of Baptisms

The Registry of Baptisms is deficient from the same causes as that of Burials, and from the first of those causes by a greater Degree.

1. Many Dissenters of every Denomination who usually bury in the Cemeteries of the established Church, do not baptize in it. This cause alone is sufficient to prevent the Number of Registered Baptisms from approximating to the Number of Births.

2. Some irreligious Persons do not cause their Children to be baptized at all. This is supposed to happen chiefly in the large towns.

3. Some Children, whose Parents are of the established Church, die immediately after Birth, unbaptized; and a much greater number who are privately baptized, are not afterwards brought to the Church for Public Baptism, and therefore are not always registered. The practice of the clergy is not uniform in this Point, as the Canon concerning Registers applies to *Christenings:* which word is supposed to mean *Public* Baptism only. In parts of the County of Northumberland it is supposed that One Third of the whole Number of Baptisms is omitted from this cause; and doubtless in many other Counties, Omissions from the same cause also take place. (Rickman in Glass, 1973, n.p.)

After 1750 therefore, rapid population increase, nonconformity and the opening of private burial grounds caused registration to deteriorate in a number of towns. It is therefore frustrating that least is known about urban demography during the period when industrialization may have caused demographic patterns in some towns to have diverged from those in the remainder of the country. Moreover, increasing levels of urbanization meant that what happened in those towns increasingly affected the national trend, and it is crucial therefore to discover more about urban demography especially between 1750 and the commencement of Civil Registration in 1837 (Woods, 1985). By the end of the eighteenth century, detailed Bills of Mortality had been compiled for a number of towns, and while these may be no more accurate than parish registers, they indicate increasing interest in population issues and their exploitation has allowed mortality trends to be determined in some towns.[2] The most impressive series are, of course, those for London. These have been used to provide a wide ranging analysis of mortality change in the capital and their accuracy is testified to by the derivation of annual IMRs consistent with those from the early years of Civil Registration (Landers, 1992, p. 56; Laxton and Williams, 1989, p. 126). The Bills revealed that mortality decreased dramatically during the eighteenth century so

---

2 Armstrong (1981). Often Bills of Mortality refer simply to totals of baptisms and burials, for example White (1792). More detailed ones giving age and cause of death include those for Carlisle – Heynsham (1973): Chester – Haygarth (1981): Liverpool – Enfield (1773); Langton and Laxton (1978). See Glass (1973b) for a discussion of the growing interest in issues relating to population during the eighteenth century.

that, by the mid-nineteenth century, infant mortality was similar to national levels, although childhood mortality was higher and expectation of life at birth was about four years lower.[3] Much less is known about other towns and indeed, it remains to be shown whether demographic analysis in provincial cities and large industrial towns between 1750 and 1850 is a practical proposition.[4]

Chapter 3 showed that once a series of checks on the quality of registers has been carried out, aggregative analysis can be used to create series of births, deaths and marriages for early modern cities. Family reconstitution is more difficult to employ in an urban environment. In small market towns such as Banbury or Gainsborough which were entirely contained within a single parish, this technique has been successfully used and any additional problems, compared with rural parish reconstitutions, only relate to scale. Reconstitution requires that the register is of the highest quality, and since most towns were subdivided into many small parishes, it is unlikely that a complete set of registers from a large provincial city will have survived that is both complete and of sufficient quality. All the major early modern cities were split into large numbers of parishes: London had over 100, Norwich 33, Bristol 18 and Ipswich 13.[5] Even a smaller town like Worcester had 12, and of the largest provincial towns the only exception is Newcastle-upon-Tyne with four parishes (Humphery-Smith, 1984). The heart of the great cities of Victorian England often comprised single ancient parishes, and while new ones were created to combat the problems of rapid population increase, registration often remained inadequate.[6] Reconstituting single urban parishes is therefore often the only alternative. The amount of time expended in extracting useful data, which is high in all forms of reconstitution, is much greater if only one parish is used, since high parochial turnover rates cause the complete demographic history of few families to be contained in a single register.[7] Moreover, if there were differential turnover rates between rich and poor, then the representativeness of the reconstitutable minority may need questioning since those families captured by reconstitution would be proportionally richer than the population as a whole. However, such issues are complex, and while age at marriage may have varied by wealth, it is not certain if other demographic measures did likewise: for instance, it is unlikely that wealth would have been responsible for significant variations in marital fertility or infant mortality since breastfeeding was such a powerful influence on both these variables and there is little evidence to suggest that either artificial methods of infant feeding were regularly employed or wet-nursing was practised on a large scale outside London.[8] Such issues

---

3 Woods (1985), p. 650 gives e_0s of 37 for London and 41 for England and Wales in 1861.

4 Huck (1994) provides an attempt to do this. However, reservations need to be expressed about the methods Huck used to calculate infant mortality; see Galley (1995b).

5 Even if these registers were found to be complete and of high quality, the size of the enterprise may prove too daunting.

6 See Lewis (1993) for a discussion of the limitations of demographic analysis in such places.

7 This point is aptly made by means of a lexis diagram in Woods (1989), p. 91. Even the largest urban parishes will suffer from this problem, more so if the city is undergoing rapid population change.

8 Galley et al. (1995); Woods and Williams (1995). Variations may have occurred during the nineteenth century.

remain difficult to resolve, and given the limitations inherent in English parish registers it is likely that the range of demographic measures that have been calculated
for York will be replicated if other urban registers are used.[9] Parish registers sometimes, however, include a wealth of supplementary detail and more may be discovered about topics such as age and cause of death, illegitimacy, occupation and the
origin of migrants by investigating a wider range of urban registers. This information is often included only for short periods, but if used sensitively it could illuminate many aspects of urban society, especially when combined with other
demographic material.

Serious limitations on the range of measures that could be calculated for York
were imposed by the lack of a complete population listing before 1841. Sources such
as Hearth Tax returns, the Compton Census and parish rate books proved useful,
although at best each only provided an enumeration of households and household
heads. Similar sources survive for most cities, but occasionally more detailed censuses made for a variety of purposes, such as a household count in Chester (1645–46)
and an enumeration of the poor in Norwich (1570), have survived.[10] That for Lichfield compiled by Gregory King is unique in that it covers the entire population and
also includes ages.[11] A number of cities including London, Bristol and Hull do however have listings made in response to the Marriage Duty Act at the end of the seventeenth century (Glass, 1966; Ralph and Williams, 1968; Hull City Record Office,
1990). It should therefore be possible to combine these with parish register data, perhaps also incorporating material from the Hearth Tax or similar sources, to provide
an exhaustive analysis of an urban population at the end of the seventeenth century.[12]
Such an approach would be similar to that of 'total reconstitution' where the results
of a family reconstitution are linked to the widest possible variety of other sources
(Macfarlane, 1977). In this way it may be possible to address the relationship
between economic prospects, household formation, marriage and migration within
an urban context. The ease by which migrants could move into and out of the city

---

9   With the exception of London, it would be surprising to discover any English towns where levels of
     infant and childhood mortality were substantially greater than in York or Gainsborough or where ille-
     gitimate and marital fertility differed significantly from national patterns. A possible exception may be
     Norwich, which had a relatively poor population and experienced substantial growth throughout the
     seventeenth century. The greatest differences occurred in London, where the extremely high levels of
     mortality in the eighteenth century are well established. Similar levels may have occurred in the period
     before 1650, although the frequency of plague epidemics considerably complicates the picture.

10 Details of many local listings are given in Gibson and Medlycott (1992).

11 Censuses including ages were rare in early modern England. Gibson and Medlycott (1992) give few
     before 1801: Cardington – 1782–91 (Bedfordshire); Buckfastleigh, Ringmore – 1698, Wembworthy –
     1779 (Devon); Corfe Castle – c.1790 (Dorset); Ardleigh – 1796 (Essex); Ealing – 1599 (Middlesex);
     Great Brington, Little Brington and Nobottle – 1781 (Northamptonshire); Trent – 1745 (Somerset);
     Lichfield – 1695, Stoke on Trent – 1701 (Staffordshire); Chilvers Coton – 1684 and 1781, Astley –
     1782 (Warwickshire); Wetherby – 1776 (Yorkshire). Of these, only Lichfield can be considered urban
     since Stoke on Trent in 1701 comprised little more than a group of villages. In the eighteenth century,
     enumerations of many places were undertaken, although few details other than population totals have
     survived. Some examples are given in Chapman (1991).

12 It is unfortunate, therefore, that this period was untypically one of demographic stagnation.

will always mean that many left little trace of themselves in urban sources, and since no English source consistently recorded the movement of migrants, many questions crucial to a full understanding of the dynamics of urban demography are likely to remain unanswered.

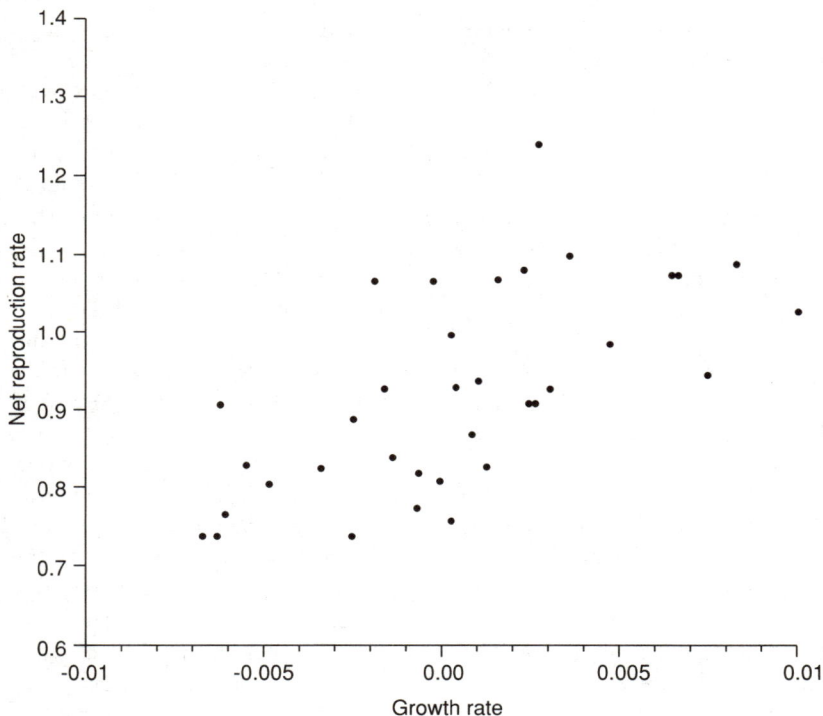

Figure 6.1: The relationship between the growth rate and the net reproduction rate, Amsterdam 1680–1860
Source: van Leeuwen and Oeppen (1993), p. 87.

European cities may provide some of the answers that are not forthcoming from English towns. de Vries (1984, pp. 185–98) in a wide ranging analysis of urbanization across Europe examined a variety of demographic material, especially with respect to marriage. He showed that in many cities, over half of all brides were migrants and there were also differences in age at marriage between migrant and native-born brides. In particular he reviewed evidence from Amsterdam, a city with a persistent excess of burials, and stressed the importance of nuptiality to the city's demographic regime. He concluded that 'total urban fertility may have varied over time because of changes in the sex-composition and total volume of rural–urban migration' (de Vries, 1984, p. 197). By implication this lends support to the work of van der Woude, who:

argues that Amsterdam before 1650 had a surplus of men eager to marry, a large number of children and a relatively young age structure. The crude birth-rate must have been higher before the
mid-seventeenth century than was thereafter the case, and it might well have been sufficiently
high to generate some measure of natural increase.[13]

Whether short periods of natural increase were the result of in-migration creating
unusually large numbers of young families of childbearing age cannot be discovered
since data on family formation in European cities are also limited. It is clear that fertility varied considerably, and much of this was a consequence of changes in migration. Exciting new possibilities have recently been revealed by the application of the
technique of Generalized Inverse Projection to the population of Amsterdam (van
Leeuwen and Oeppen, 1993). Using information about births, deaths and age structure and making assumptions about net migration, it is possible to derive estimates
of mortality, fertility and age-structure at intervals throughout the period.[14] This type
of analysis will obviously be sensitive to the quality of the input data; nevertheless,
a considerable degree of consistency is apparent. Both mortality and fertility were
subject to change, and on many occasions before the mid-nineteenth century the city
was able to replace itself since the net reproduction rate (the average number of
daughters who survived to begin reproduction) was greater than one. Levels of fertility varied substantially and there was some correlation between population growth
and high fertility (Fig. 6.1).[15] Such results support de Vries and van der Woude by
suggesting that changes in migration could boost overall levels of fertility; however,
they also reveal that the urban demographic regime was far from static and resulted
from the complex interaction between mortality, fertility and migration. After 1860
mortality decreased substantially and from then until 1920, when the study ends,
Amsterdam always replaced itself.[16] Identical sources exist for other Dutch towns,
and once a similar analysis has been undertaken, it will be possible to determine
whether Amsterdam's demographic regime was unique in this respect. As yet no
early modern European town has been shown to have experienced fertility rates consistently in excess of mortality over the long term. de Vries provides a number of
examples to demonstrate the extreme levels of mortality in some cities and he is
finally forced to conclude that while urban fertility may have varied, 'It is, however,
by no means clear that this argument can contribute to a dethronement of mortality
as the chief determinant of urban natural decrease' (de Vries, 1984, p. 197). Moreover, levels of mortality varied between cities, countries and over time, and it is
likely that as more towns are examined, an even greater variety of demographic
experience will be discovered.[17] Support for this point of view is provided by Alfred
Perrenoud's work on Geneva which showed significant differences in demographic

13 de Vries (1984), p. 196. Also, see van der Woude (1982).
14 The technique is described in Oeppen (1993).
15 The line of least squares regression is $y = 0.92 + 22.43x$, $(R^2 = 0.44)$.
16 Van Leeuwen and Oeppen (1993), p. 87. During the 1850s e_0 was about 31.5 while in the next decade
    it had increased to 37.2.
17 For examples see Corsini and Viazzo (1993); Vögele (1994).

behaviour by class, origin and over time (Perrenoud, 1979; 1982). Throughout the whole period 1625–1810, the city was unable to replace itself, but curiously, as mortality fell and the city became more healthy, the net reproduction rate declined from 0.87 between 1625 and 1644 to 0.65 between 1800 and 1810 (Fig. 6.2). Given that both mortality and fertility were subject to considerable change, it is difficult to determine which was more important in causing this low net reproduction rate. Indeed, as mortality fell throughout the eighteenth century, celibacy increased and marital fertility also fell. There were significant differences between classes, with mortality being especially high for the lower classes in the seventeenth century. There were also class-specific differences in age at marriage and levels of fertility. Some sections of the population managed to replace themselves for short periods at least and Geneva's overall demographic regime can therefore, in part, be viewed as a consequence of its class composition, and given the often diverse experiences of these different classes, it is difficult to make generalizations. However, it is important to emphasize that small changes to either the age at marriage or the proportion married, especially in the period before 1705, could easily have created natural population growth, although once the number of children born to each family began to fall in the eighteenth century, this became increasingly unlikely.[18] Moreover, since all the data are derived from family reconstitution, the effects of any short-term changes in migration are difficult to determine and the demographic behaviour of those families who cannot be reconstituted will of course remain elusive. It does appear, however, that the main characteristics of Geneva's demography were both high mortality and low fertility.

This brief excursion into European urban demography has revealed the differing experiences of individual towns and the need to examine a wide range of examples. As yet it has not been possible to fully assess the contribution that migrants made to urban demography, and until this has been done, the debate conducted in *Past and Present* by Sharlin and Finlay will not be concluded. The potential to resolve many of these issues exists for some Scandinavian cities. In Sweden, in addition to parish registers, population registers (*husförhörslängd*) were also kept which listed every person in the parish and included information about the movement of individuals (Kälvemark, 1977; Jeub, 1993). This means that in theory at least it should be possible to trace entire cohorts of an urban population through time, thereby determining the precise demographic characteristics of each section of the population, including migrants. Such an undertaking would require a considerable investment of time and be dependent on a complete series of registers having survived for a particular town. Throughout Sweden, mortality declined steadily during the nineteenth century and this means that eighteenth-century registers would probably need to be used; however, the creation of the *Tabellverket* (Statistical Commission) in 1749, which collected and published annual population data, means that such limitations

---

18 Perrenoud (1982), p. 589. Most early modern cities did not experience a similar decline in marital fertility.

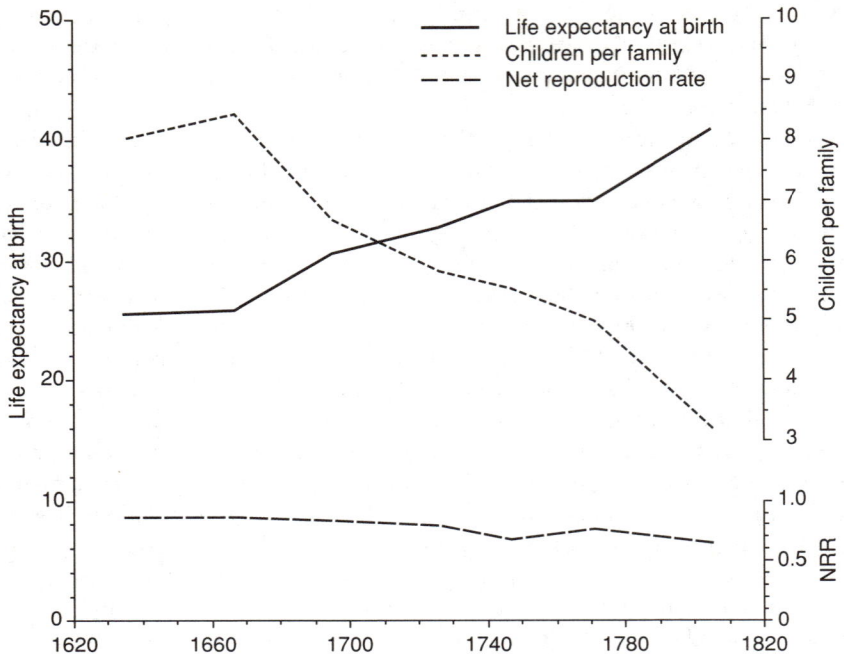

Figure 6.2: The demography of Geneva, 1620–1820
Source: Perrenoud, (1982).

should easily be overcome.[19] By 1750 there were only two major cities in Sweden – Stockholm and Gothenburg – and Stockholm's extremely high levels of mortality appear to have made it exceptional.[20] Many of Sweden's smaller towns were also subject to high mortality rates, and demographic analysis in such places would considerably reduce problems of record linkage.[21] Given that European cities experienced such apparently diverse demographic patterns, it is unlikely that the analysis of a single town would finally resolve matters; but given the richness of Swedish sources, such a study may be able to establish the boundaries of possible demographic variations amongst individual sections of the population – it would certainly provide fresh insights and renew interest in the topic.

19 Parish registration was regulated in 1686, by which time most dioceses were keeping some registers. Improvements to the system were made during the nineteenth century; see Jeub (1993), pp. 5–7. The excellent quality of Swedish demographic sources during the nineteenth century means that the earlier period has been somewhat neglected by Swedish historical demographers.
20 de Vries (1984), p. 270 gives the population of Gothenburg as 8,000 and Stockholm as 60,000 in 1750 see Söderberg *et al.* (1991), pp. 150–200 for a discussion of Stockholm's high mortality.
21 The town of Linköping with a population of 2,680 in 1800 and IMRs just below 300 would appear to possess the necessary credentials for such a study; see Bengtsson (1995); Sundin (1995).

In spite of a number of shortcomings, the analysis of York's population history has demonstrated the feasibility of performing a demographic study in an early modern English city. While much remains speculative and some questions are likely to remain unanswered sufficient is now known about urban demographic regimes for a general model of urban demography to be proposed and discussed. This model emphasizes that while mortality was perhaps the single most important feature of urban demography, fertility was also subject to variation and under certain circumstances it could exceed mortality, causing natural population growth. However, it is important to stress, as do Sharlin, van der Woude and de Vries, that the dynamics of urban demography can only be fully understood if the individual components of mortality, nuptiality, fertility and migration are considered together – each interacting with the others to create a city's individual regime.

A MODEL OF EARLY MODERN URBAN DEMOGRAPHY

In order to move beyond the boundaries of a single city, it is necessary to propose a model of early modern urban demography, one that unifies much that has been written on the topic. The model accepts that in detail there were many distinctive forms of the urban demographic regime, as indeed there were of rural ones, and is best viewed by means of a diagram (Fig. 6.3). The scales on each axis have been omitted,

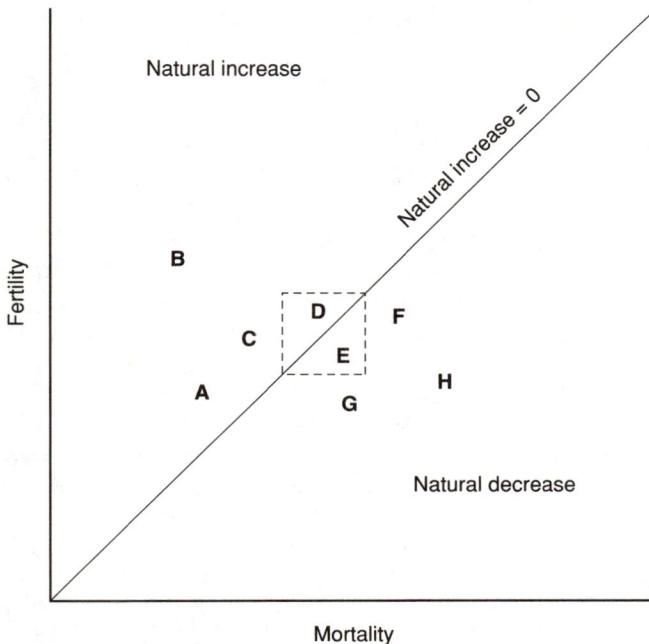

Figure 6.3: A model of early modern urban demography

because specific measures of mortality and fertility do not adequately reflect the complex picture found in early modern cities, but also because the extent to which mortality and fertility may have varied is not known. If fertility was greater than mortality (any point above the diagonal) then natural increase would have occurred. By means of several examples it is possible to show the range of demographic experience. The points labelled A-C represent rural parishes. Mortality and fertility varied, but since most rural parishes experienced low mortality, fertility usually exceeded mortality and natural increase occurred, despite a large proportion of the population remaining unmarried.[22] Examples F-H represent cities experiencing high mortality and natural decrease. In the case of F and G only modest increases in fertility would have been required to cancel out any natural decrease. However, H represents a city where mortality was so high that unrealistic levels of fertility would have been required to achieve natural increase. London may well have been located at H since there, IMRs were well in excess of 300 during the early eighteenth century (Landers 1990a, p. 39). Examples D and E are more interesting. They represent York between 1561 and 1700, with the box showing the extent to which mortality and fertility were likely to vary in the medium term. D is York in the late sixteenth century. Mortality was high, but fertility was even higher. After the Civil War (example E) mortality increased slightly, and following a reduction in fertility, natural decrease occurred. York's demography was therefore finely balanced, with only relatively small changes required to turn modest natural increase into substantial natural decrease. By contrast, because of the exceptional levels of mortality in London, an unacceptably high proportion of the population would need to have been married in order for natural increase to have occurred. However, the capital was so exceptional both in its size and rate of growth that the experience of other English cities may have been closer to York's than to London's. With mortality being subject to greater variation than fertility, it was still the most important influence on natural change, and once a threshold had been crossed natural decrease became virtually inevitable.

It is possible to speculate about the extent to which the populations of towns could increase naturally using model life tables. Reservations have already been expressed about the extent to which these will accurately reflect the experiences of past populations, and the 'high potential' mortality regime in towns will probably exacerbate any differences since much of the excess mortality was experienced by infants and young children. Nevertheless, similar results will be forthcoming whichever set of tables is used. Assuming there is no net migration and mortality remains constant, the proportion of the population at various ages will remain stable and whether the population increases or decreases will depend on the birth rate.[23] For each level of

---

22 High mortality and natural decrease also occurred in some rural areas. Indeed, low-lying marshy parishes in the Fens experienced perhaps the highest rates of all outside London and their demographic regimes would be closer to H than A, B, or C; see Dobson (1989), pp. 410–11 and (1992), p. 82.

23 Both assumptions are of course unrealistic for the early modern period. The following calculations do, however, indicate the levels of fertility required for a population to achieve natural increase given various levels of mortality.

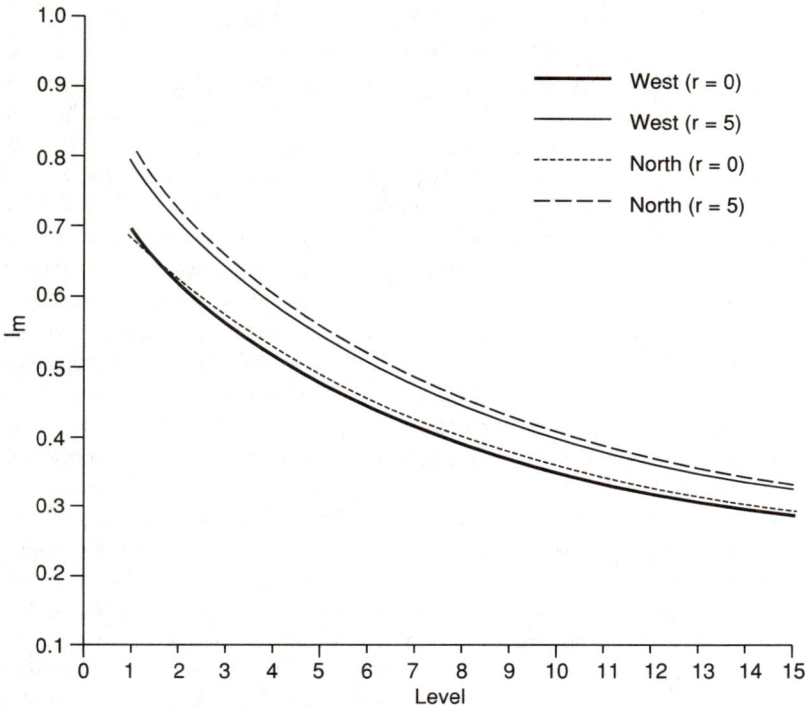

Figure 6.4: Estimates of I_m necessary to maintain a stable population
Note: 'r' is rate of growth per thousand population.
Source: Coale and Demeny, (1983).

models West and North of the Coale-Demeny life tables, Figure 6.4 shows the proportion of females that would need to be married in order for the given rates of growth to occur, assuming that ASMFRs were identical to the average in early modern England and illegitimate fertility was negligible.[24] Figure 6.4 is at best illustrative since in real towns the age-structure of mortality and ASMFRs may have varied from these assumed patterns; it does, however, show that (1) there is little difference between the two life tables, and (2) populations were theoretically capable of enduring the harshest mortality regimes (West level 1 is equivalent to an IMR of c.393 per 1,000 live births and e_0 of 19), even being able to experience a small amount of natural increase. In cities such as medieval Florence, where a non-western European marriage pattern occurred and marriage was almost universal, very high levels of mortality could be endured with only modest amounts of natural population decrease

24 The ASMFRs used were 15–19, 359; 20–24, 376; 25–29, 354; 30–34, 298; 35–39, 242; 40–44, 127; 45–49, 25; Wilson and Woods (1991), p. 406, figures for 25 parishes 1600–49 quoted. Since illegitimacy rates were up to five per cent, a slightly lower proportion married was needed to sustain these rates of growth.

occurring.[25] At lower levels of mortality far fewer would needed to have married. For instance, if mortality followed the pattern of West level 5 (IMR = 276, e_0 = 29), then births would balance deaths if the proportion married was 0.48, and if it was 0.54 then the annual growth rate would be five per 1,000. From this theoretical perspective, whether towns experienced natural increase or decrease essentially depended on three factors: the level of mortality, the proportion of the population that were able to marry, and the age at which they were able to do so. In England as a whole, I_m varied from 0.39 to 0.60 for quinquennia between 1541 and 1700, although it was mostly close to 0.5.[26] If such values were typical, this would suggest that mortality between levels two and three was the threshold at which towns could increase naturally (IMR = 359, e_0 = 21; IMR = 329, e_0 = 24, respectively); yet to what extent more or less were able to marry in cities is impossible to tell. Given the relationship between economic prospects and marriage it is not unreasonable to expect that the economic vitality of some towns created relatively high proportions married, although there may have been considerable variation between cities and over time. Providing a probable range for I_m is therefore difficult, and clearly the culture of late age at marriage means that it could not have been too high, but values near to 0.6 which occurred nationally between 1790 and 1830 appear plausible, especially if individual urban economies were vibrant and expanding.[27] Figure 6.4 also provides an answer to a question that is often posed in discussions of early modern urban demography – 'in the absence of migration, would early modern towns have increased or decreased in size?'. For a particular city the answer can be read straight from the graph and, of course, is dependent on the level of mortality and the ability to marry. There is, however, an entirely different answer to this question; one that acknowledges that the survival of towns depended on trade and that movement of both goods and individuals was commonplace. Towns prospered because of the willingness of migrants to move into or out of the city in order to exploit economic demand, and attempting to examine the demography of towns in the absence of migration is therefore a theoretical, ahistorical exercise since, irrespective of their underlying demographic regimes, towns would quickly wither and die without migrants. A more interesting, but more difficult problem, is to determine how migrants affected urban demographic regimes.

25 Herlihy and Klapisch–Zuber (1985); Smith (1981b). Herlihy (1977), p. 160 suggests that fertility rates were by no means constant, but accurate demographic information from this period is sparse. Florence would, however, only have been able to maintain its population in the face of constant outbreaks of plague by means of in-migration.

26 Wilson and Woods (1991), pp, 414–15. Average values of I_m were 1541–50, 0.58; 1551–75, 0.52; 1576–1600, 0.50; 1601–25, 0.48; 1626–50, 0.47; 1651–75, 0.41; 1676–1700, 0.48.

27 Wilson and Woods (1991), p. 415. I_m is a composite measure and it is not identical to the proportion of the overall population that was married. It is calculated by comparing the number of legitimate births in a population with the maximum possible, assuming that all women of reproductive age were married. With a high mean age at first marriage and young women experiencing the highest rates of fertility, very high levels of I_m are impossible, especially if up to ten per cent of women remained unmarried by the age of 45.

Table 6.1: Overall proportion of the population married from some English population listings

Place	Date	Per cent married	Number
Norwich (poor)	1570	41.9	(2,359)
Ipswich(poor)	1597	30.4	(415)
Southampton (6 parishes)	1696/97	30.4	(2,043)
Stoke-on-Trent	1701	30.8	(1,208)
Lichfield	1695	30.9	(2,861)
Shrewsbury	1695	32.0	(3,864)
London (80 parishes within the walls)	1695	32.3	(57,648)
Gloucester	1696	32.4	(4,756)
Leicester (2 parishes)	1697	32.9	(2,178)
Bristol	1696	33.4	(20,139)
Bury St Edmonds	1695	33.9	(3,153)
61 English listings	1574–1821	33.4	–
30 English listings	1650–1749	34.8	–
29 English listings	1750–1821	32.4	–

Sources: Norwich – Pound (1971), pp. 95–6.
    Ipswich – Webb (1966), pp. 121–40.
    Lichfield – Glass (1965) p. 181.
    London – Glass (1966).
    Bristol – Ralph and Williams (1968).
    Gloucester – King, (1973), pp. 70–71.
    Southampton – (St John, Portswood, Holy Rhood, St Lawrence, All Saints within, All Saints without); Leicester (St Martin, St Mary); Shrewsbury; Bury St Edmonds (St James); Stoke–on–Trent – photocopies of original documents consulted at the Cambridge Group for the History of Population and Social Structure.
    English listings – (61) Laslett (1972), p. 145; (30) and (29) Wall (1977), p. 92.

The calculations on which Figure 6.4 were based necessarily assume that a stable population distribution was achieved, but this was unlikely to happen as migration would have radically altered the age-sex structure, making values for the proportion married often meaningless. Table 6.1 examines the overall proportion of the population that was married for a range of early modern towns. It should be noted that this measure is not identical to I_m, since I_m relates the fertility of married women aged 15–49 to the potential fertility of all women, while the lack of ages in most English listings means that it is only possible to calculate the number who were married divided by total population. Strictly speaking, high levels of I_m could be consistent with low numbers of births if there were relatively few women of fertile age in the population, and increases in the number of married women aged over 50 could cause the overall proportion married to increase without affecting I_m. Table 6.1 shows little variation in the proportion married, yet two provisos need to be given. The group of mainly rural listings from the sixteenth to the nineteenth centuries mask considerable variation between individual settlements, and overall trends are difficult to discern.[28] The complete urban listings were all made in response to the Marriage Duty Act at the end of the seventeenth century, when nationally I_m was relatively modest. During this period most cities contained an excess of females and it is not unreasonable to expect higher proportions married in other periods. It is unfortunate that the lack of suitable urban listings precludes an examination of this subject, and the Norwich listing is therefore especially interesting. While this list of poor families includes an unrepresentative section of the population, it may indicate that conditions for marriage were favourable in sixteenth-century Norwich, especially as Slack showed that, as these censuses incorporate a greater proportion of the population, the characteristics of poor households increasingly resemble those of the whole population (Slack, 1988, pp. 73–76). The Norwich census represents about 22 per cent of the English population in the city. That for Ipswich enumerated only 13 per cent of the population, which, if Slack is correct, appears to support high levels of urban nuptiality in the late sixteenth century; however, it is difficult to be certain.[29] Table 6.1 provides no indication of the age-structure of the married population, and this is crucial to determining the relationship between the proportion married and overall fertility.

Table 6.2a seeks to explore this relationship by examining York in 1861, the earliest date at which estimates of the numbers married by age can be given.[30] By the mid-nineteenth century, marital fertility rates had changed little and it is a relatively straightforward exercise to estimate the number of births that should result given these ASMFRs.[31] Table 6.2a predicts that there would have been 1,875 legitimate births in York Registration District in 1861. The number registered was 2,002, although 151 of these were illegitimate, leaving 1,851 legitimate births.[32] This difference is small and probably a consequence of the proportion of married women within the age-groups varying slightly, although there may also have been slight differences between the actual and assumed ASMFRs. This method of estimating births therefore appears satisfactory and shows that a combination of late age at marriage and low fertility for older women meant that about half of all births were to women aged 25–35. Table 6.2b explores the relationship further by examining the age-sex structure of

---

28 Laslett (1972), p. 145. The standard deviation for the 61 listings giving this information was 6.3.
29 Slack (1988). Slack also gives examples from other towns, with the figures in brackets representing per cent married and poor as a proportion of total population respectively: Worcester – 1557 (28.6, 18); Warwick – 1587 (27.1, 12); Huddersfield – 1622 (32.6, 20–25); Salisbury – 1635 (23.2, 5). Widowhood was one of the primary reasons for poverty.
30 The figures given are for York Registration District, not the city; see pp. 000–00 for a discussion of the differences. In 1861, marital status was only published for the age-groups 15–, 20–, 25–, 35–, 45–, etc. and in order to decompose the age-groups 25– and 35– into 25–, 30– and 35–, 40– respectively it was necessary to assume that the proportions within each group were the same as in 1881, when this age breakdown was provided.
31 Wilson and Woods (1991), pp. 414–15. ASMFRs were assumed to be those reported for 1600–49, see Table 2, 406.
32 *Annual Report of the Registrar General for 1861* (London, 1863), p. 75.

Table 6.2: Estimating levels of fertility

a) York 1861

Age	Married women	ASMFR	Legitimate births
15–19	92	0.359	33.028
20–24	892	0.376	335.392
25–29	1,620	0.354	573.480
30–34	1,380	0.298	411.240
35–39	1,361	0.242	329.362
40–44	1,308	0.127	166.116
45–49	1,065	0.025	26.625
Total			1,875.243

b) Lichfield 1695

Age	Single/ widows	Married women	ASMFR	Legitimate births
0–14	511	0		0
15–19	170	1	0.359	0.359
20–24	125	22	0.376	8.272
25–29	75	69	0.354	24.426
30–34	30	81	0.298	24.138
35–39	51	87	0.242	21.054
40–44	19	43	0.127	5.461
45–49	14	46	0.025	1.150
50+	122	94		0
Total	1,117	443		84.860

Source: see text.

Lichfield in 1696. If these calculations are correct, then only about 85 births per year should have occurred, but examination of the registers revealed an average of 106 baptisms between 1690 and 1700 (Galley, 1995a, pp. 466–67). It is unlikely that this discrepancy was caused by illegitimacy since, while illegitimates were not identified in the registers, at most only four or five per year would have been expected. A difference in ASMFRs of about 25 per cent is also unrealistic given the stability of rates throughout early modern England, and the most likely explanation is that there was considerable mis-reporting of age or age-heaping in King's census. Glass (1965, p. 181) noted 'the marked concentration of ages in the second half of each ten year age group' and Table 1.3 showed that there were large numbers of older married females. If some of these were to be transposed into younger age-groups then the differences could be explained. The importance of these theoretical calculations is not only in providing a check to the accuracy of King's census they also demonstrate how numbers married at various ages determine overall levels of fertility. In both York and Lichfield the age-group 25–40 contributed the majority of births (70 per cent and 82 per cent respectively), although in York 20–24 year olds were responsible for 18 per cent of births. Obviously, as the numbers married within the various age-groups altered, the number of births changed accordingly and relatively small increases within the younger groups could cause significant increases in fertility. In spite of problems with its listing, the crude baptism rate in Lichfield was high at about 37 per 1,000 population, and comparison with other towns reveals that its overall proportion married was relatively low.[33] Table 6.1 shows that in both London and Bristol, which were expanding rapidly at this date, larger proportions of the population were married, which means that in these cities the birth rate could have been even higher, although much, of course, will have depended on the ages of these married women.

Table 6.3 broadens the discussion by incorporating mortality into the calculations using York's age-structure in 1861 as a starting point. It is relatively straightforward to estimate the number of deaths from each age-group providing that an appropriate life table is used, and Table 6.3 was constructed by making the following assumptions: the infant and childhood mortality rates, chosen to represent York in the sixteenth century, were IMR = 260, 1–4 = 200 and 5–9 = 110, and adult mortality corresponded to either West level 4 or 6.[34] For infants and young children, difficulties arise because the 1861 census did not separate infants from young children and both groups suffered very high mortality rates. However, by assuming that 2,000 births occurred each year, estimates of those dying before the age of five can be made by applying the infant and early childhood mortality rates successively to these births.[35] Table 6.3 predicts that there would have been either 1,867 or 1,719 deaths, depending on the structure of adult mortality. The actual number of deaths recorded in York was only 1,440, but this was because mortality, unlike marital fertility, had fallen considerably by 1861.[36] These calculations reveal that natural increase would have occurred despite these relatively high levels of mortality; indeed, for natural decrease to have taken place infant and early childhood mortality would need to have increased by 25 per cent or adult mortality to West level 2. Whatever the true level of mortality in early modern York, Table 6.3 demonstrates the effects that age-structure had on the overall number of deaths.[37] The most important contributions were made by children under ten, who were responsible for 40 per cent of all deaths, and of these 28 per cent were infants. Relatively small changes in infant and childhood mortality will therefore have caused considerable changes to total deaths, while large changes in adult mortality were needed to account for a similar change since mor-

---

33 (106/2,861) x 1,000 = 37.05.

34 See Table 4.4. No precise rates are representative of the period as a whole, although West level 4 will take into account any excess adult mortality.

35 This procedure assumes that there was no net migration within this age group, but since infant deaths dominated this is not unreasonable.

36 *Annual Report for 1861*, pp. 114–15. Also, see pp. 181–83.

37 A similar exercise using the same child mortality rates and West level 4 on the age-structure of Lichfield predicts about 84 deaths, which is nearly 10 per cent higher than the recorded average of 77 burials. This difference was likely to have been due to Lichfield having had lower levels of mortality.

Table 6.3: Estimates of mortality and fertility using York's age/sex structure in 1861

Age	Males	Females	Annual deaths			Married women	Annual births
			Total	Level 4	Level 6		
0–	3,796	3,741	7,537	594.0	594.0		
5–	3,323	3,234	6,557	145.0	145.0		
10–	2,851	2,980	5,831	46.7	38.8		
15–	2,771	3,080	5,851	62.2	52.1	92	33.3
20–	2,472	2,942	5,414	76.4	64.1	892	335.4
25–	2,258	2,606	4,864	76.8	64.3	1,620	573.5
30–	1,994	2,126	4,120	74.2	62.2	1,380	411.2
35–	1,778	1,903	3,681	75.0	63.0	1,361	329.4
40–	1,760	1,798	3,558	82.4	69.6	1,308	166.1
45–	1,455	1,554	3,009	77.7	66.4	1,065	26.6
50–	1,320	1,417	2,737	89.1	76.9		
55–	984	1,068	2,052	81.7	71.5		
60–	762	896	1,658	90.2	79.5		
65–	490	669	1,159	81.0	72.5		
70–	412	538	950	88.1	80.1		
75–	217	317	534	64.4	59.5		
80–	101	154	255	37.2	35.4		
85–	40	72	112	19.3	18.7		
90–	10	16	26	4.9	4.9		
95–	2	2	4	0.8	0.8		
100–	0	1	1	0.2	0.2		
Totals	28,796	31,113	59,909	1,867.3	1,719.5	7,718	1,875.2

Source: 1861 census; Table 6.2; Coale and Demeny (1983).

tality rates for adults, except at high ages, were low by comparison with the infant and childhood rates. Modelling populations in this way has its limitations, especially if particular groups such as temporary migrants experienced mortality rates well in excess of those expected from life tables. Nevertheless, Table 6.3 demonstrates that in spite of high levels of mortality, early modern towns were capable of achieving natural increase, and consequently urban natural decrease must therefore be viewed as much as a consequence of low nuptiality and distortions in the age-structure as of high mortality.

Figure 6.5 incorporates migration into the model by showing the female population by marital status and age together with the main migration flows. Few women, if any, married before 16 and almost all the births were contributed by the group M_{15-49}, although S_{15-49} and W_{15-49} were responsible for the small number of illegitimate births. All other sections of the population only contributed deaths. Most came from the group S_{0-14}, the majority being infants or very young children, with numbers directly proportional to births and depending on the level of mortality. In a typical early modern city up to a half the children would have died before their fifteenth birthday, and a city recorded natural increase or decrease depending on whether the

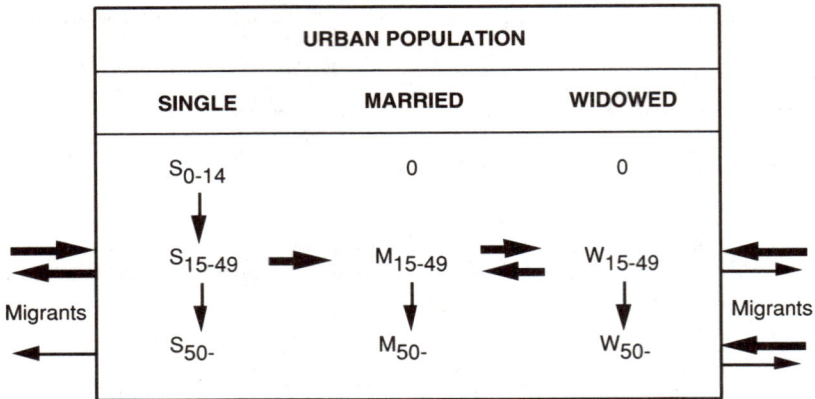

Figure 6.5: The female population of an early modern town

deaths from the other age-groups, including males who of course only contributed towards deaths, were greater than those who survived childhood. Two further factors were important – the ease with which individuals were able to marry and the effects of migration, both in- and out-, in distorting the age-sex structure. Both these variables were inextricably interlinked, and since male economic prospects were a crucial factor in a couple's decision to marry, imbalances in the age-structure of males were an especially important influence on overall levels of nuptiality. The arrows in Figure 6.5 show the probable direction of migration flows; however, little is known about the propensity of some sections of the population to migrate and further research may provide a radically altered perspective. The age-specific nature of migration is crucial to the resulting population structure, and when opportunities for marriage were restricted many migrants were only able to move to cities on a temporary basis, and as Sharlin noted, their overall effect on the balance between births and deaths was negative. By contrast, with an expanding economy and population, many migrants would have been able to settle permanently. Moreover, with most of these migrants concentrated into ages when their reproductive value was high, their net effect on the balance between births and deaths was likely to be positive.[38] Axiomatic to the construction of Figure 6.5 is the assumption that there were always sufficient migrants able to move into cities. If this was not the case, then the age-sex structure may have become even more distorted and marriage been restricted further. However, throughout the sixteenth and seventeenth centuries, levels of celibacy

38 Keyfitz and Philipov (1981), p. 289 provide an interesting discussion of reproductive value in Mexico and give values ranging from 1.2 for ages 0–4 to 1.9 for 15–19 and 0.2 for 40–44. Migrants aged over 45 will clearly only contribute towards deaths. Similar values could be calculated for early modern cities, assuming that the appropriate information could be discovered. Many migrants will be concentrated at ages when their reproductive value was high, and while the actual levels will depend on mortality rates, the differentials are likely to remain similar.

remained high and for any rural 'excess' the opportunities available in towns were very attractive. Consequently, even though Table 1.6 appeared to show that urban growth acted as a brake on the rise of England's population before 1750, by accepting that towns were capable of recording natural increase and that patterns of urban nuptiality were subject to variation, it is probable that in many instances towns had a positive influence on population growth, especially given that there were always large numbers of unmarried potential migrants within the rural population.[39] More importantly towns also stimulated demand, and rather than viewing towns simply as 'consumers of men', it may be more appropriate to consider them as centres of innovation where the potential rewards for migrants far outweighed the additional threat to life (Wrigley, 1978; 1990).

'URBAN GRAVEYARDS' – AN APPROPRIATE DESCRIPTION FOR EARLY MODERN TOWNS?

The pursuit of a simple explanation has often hindered a full understanding of the distinctive nature of early modern urban demography. Too much effort has been spent in seeking to explain urban natural decrease because, as with modern populations, little can be discovered by simply examining the balance between births and deaths.[40] Thus, in many ways it is still necessary to reiterate Sharlin's plea for greater knowledge about the components of urban demography:

> It would clearly be valuable to know a great deal more about migration in early modern cities and its effect on fertility, mortality and social structure. For example, how long did temporary migrants remain in the cities and what proportion of migrants became permanent residents? Even to have age-specific mortality rates for one city with a population of over 10,000 would mean a great step forward (Sharlin, 1978, pp. 137–38).

However, while the process of migration into the early modern city remains difficult to quantify, following the analysis of York's demography, sufficient can be gleaned about urban demographic regimes to make a number of generalizations.

Four factors combined to explain the distinctiveness of early modern urban demography – under-registration, mortality, migration and marriage. *Under-registration* is strictly speaking of only technical importance. Urban registers, if chosen carefully, can provide an accurate reflection of the baptisms, burials and marriages that occurred in a parish. In most registers more baptisms than burials were lost, and this exacerbated the tendency towards natural decrease being recorded. In some urban parishes the combination of high neonatal mortality rates and concentrations of nonconformity created substantial levels of under-registration, and consequently

---

39 Even if urban natural decrease occurred, with most migrants being single the effect on the rural hinterland would have been minimal.

40 In the American retirement community of St Petersburg, deaths greatly exceed births, yet health care provision is excellent; see de Vries (1984), p. 181. Likewise the crude death rate in England and Wales in 1983 was 11.7 compared with 7.1 in Mexico where mortality was higher; Newell (1988), p. 64.

the reliability of urban registers needs to be established before demographic analysis is undertaken. *Mortality* was high in all early modern towns, especially by comparison with some rural places. Much of the urban excess was confined to infants and young children with poor levels of sanitation and high population density creating an environment where the transmission of disease was easy. Geographical variations in mortality were great, and while rural parishes could experience IMRs below 100, in towns IMRs were typically above 250. There was no simple rural/urban gradient since rural parishes could also be subjected to high mortality rates and urban mortality rates were not necessarily constant. *Migration* is the least known element in the demographic regime, yet its importance was crucial. Much was temporary, and while this group was subjected to higher mortality rates than native-born individuals, any excess was insufficient to alter the demographic balance. Of much greater importance was how both in- and out-migration regulated the demographic system by immediately responding to changes in the urban economy. As a necessary by-product of this process, distinctive urban age/sex-structures evolved and these in turn influenced the ability to marry, with many who were unable to find a marriage partner eventually moving elsewhere. *Marriage*, its incidence and timing, regulated much of England's population history before 1700 and this was also true in the early modern city. The ability of individuals to marry was mainly determined by economic factors, although the age-sex structure of the population and net migration flows were all important influences.

Mortality has dominated most discussions of early modern urban demography and this has been partly due to the relative ease with which evidence about it can be discovered, especially when compared with the difficulties that arise when assessing migration or nuptiality. Figure 6.6 illustrates the relative wealth of data about mortality that is available for the early modern town. It gives survivors by age calculated from a selection of early life tables and shows that there was some variation in experience. That for London was calculated by Graunt in 1662. It reveals horrendous levels of mortality (less than five out of every 100 would have survived to reach 60), but is best thought of as an interesting statistical exercise rather than providing an accurate picture of mortality in the capital (Glass, 1950). Infant mortality is certainly underestimated, but for adults subjected to repeated outbreaks of plague when up to 25 per cent of the population may have died in a single year, this level of mortality could be of the right order. The tables from Geneva, Breslau and York appear more plausible, with mortality rates in York being assumed to be the same as in Table 6.3 (adult mortality at West levels 4 and 6 being given for comparison). There is a remarkable degree of similarity between the Geneva and Breslau tables and this may be no more than coincidence. Of greater interest is the comparison between these cities and York. Infant and childhood mortality was higher in Geneva and Breslau, although adult mortality was lower. These differences were not substantial and mortality in York can be considered broadly comparable to seventeenth-century Geneva even though the population history of that city followed an entirely different course. Thus, with no substantial differences in mortality between these places, the conclusions derived from Table 6.3 about the relationship between mortality, fertility and

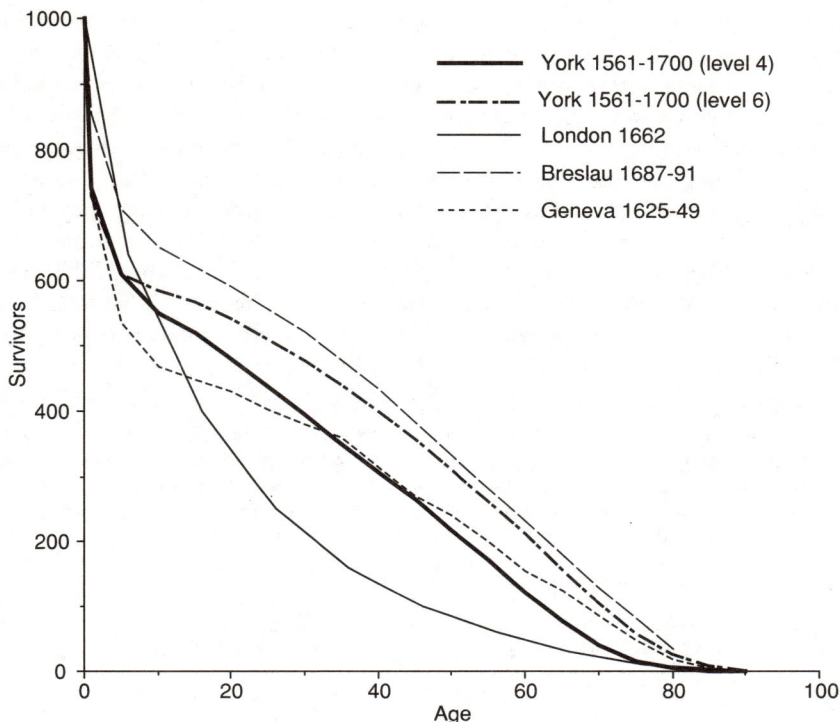

Figure 6.6: Survivors by age calculated from a selection of early life tables.
Source: York – Table 6.3.
London – Glass (1950).
Breslau – Halley (1692).
Geneva – Perrenoud (1982).

age-structure are likely to be applicable to other European cities, and in conclusion it is hard to disagree with Sharlin, who argued:

> that age-specific mortality was usually higher in cities than in the country, but not nearly so much higher as to justify the image of the early modern city as an extremely unhealthy environment that acted as a drain on population growth … the counts of births and deaths should be understood as the result of a dynamic social process rather than some static law of nature (Sharlin, 1978, p. 138).

It is commonplace to describe early modern towns as 'urban graveyards'; yet by focusing on only one aspect of urban demography, other important features relating to nuptiality and migration become neglected. The urban mortality penalty was certainly universal, especially for infants and young children, and in the age of plague, the devastating impact of this disease was capable of wiping out any accumulated natural increase within the space of a few short months.[41] In non-crisis years, mortality was far less important and in many instances births could and did outstrip deaths. The spectacular nature of crisis mortality and the presence of urban natural decrease in many towns during the early eighteenth century, when there was burgeoning interest in demographic matters, has meant that many have sought only to explain the most obvious feature of urban demography – high mortality. Likewise, from Graunt's analysis of mid-seventeenth-century London's demography to later concern over increasing levels of urban vice, cities have tended to be viewed in extremes, with engravings such as Hogarth's 'Gin Lane' providing a harrowing depiction of urban life. However, alternative views of the city can be found, with 'Beer Street', the companion piece to 'Gin Lane', depicting the city as provider of plenty (Paulson, 1975). According to Arthur Weitzman:

> In the period between 1660 and 1800, feelings of fear and despair toward the city were anticipated by the writers whom we think of as the quintessence of cosmopolitan politeness: Pope, Swift, Fielding, and even Dr. Johnson in some of his moods. On the other hand, what one also finds among the Augustans is a real sense of an urban ideal, a heightened longing for a life possible only in the city – what Johnson meant by his apothegm: 'When a man is tired of London, he is tired of life.' (Weitzman, 1975)

Thus, Rousseau's view of urban life:

> Of all animals man is least capable of living in flocks. Penned up like sheep, men soon lose all. The breath of man is fatal to his fellows ... Cities are the burial pit of the human species[42]

needs to be balanced by that of Voltaire:

> Rival of Athens, London, blest indeed
> That with thy tyrants had the wit to chase
> The prejudices civil factions breed.
> Men speak their thoughts and worth can win its place.
> In London, who has talent, he is great.[43]

In many ways early modern urban demography has also been viewed in extremes, and until recently, few have sought to provide positive urban images. But, by focusing on elements within the urban demographic regime such as nuptiality, migration and fertility rather than mortality alone, a more optimistic picture emerges. Whether the term 'urban graveyard' is an accurate description of early modern towns is clearly a matter of degree. Further research may clarify matters, but this research needs to avoid only concentrating on mortality – it must take notice of the complex relationships within cities and seek to provide a more rounded picture of the demography of early modern towns.

41 In London during the 100 years before 1665 plague was responsible for more than 18 per cent of deaths. The numbers were estimated from Figure 1.3 by assuming that plague deaths in crisis years can be calculated by subtracting the mean of the surrounding years from the total deaths in crisis years. This method is very approximate. There were major epidemics in 1593, 1603, 1625, 1636 and 1665, although some plague deaths were also recorded in other years.
42 Quoted in Weitzman (1975), p.469 from Emile ou de l'éducation (Paris, 1854), I, p. 36.
43 Quoted in Weitzman (1975), p. 475 from Verses on the Death of Adrienne Lecouvreur.

Chapter 7

CITIES AND ENGLISH
POPULATION HISTORY

Before travelling to Chester, Daniel Defoe made a quick trip over the Mersey to Liverpool, the 'Bristol of this part of England' (Defoe, 1971, p. 391). On a subsequent visit he provided a lengthy description of the town and revealed why Chester was unable to compete with its expanding neighbour:

> Liverpoole is one of the wonders of England ... the town was, at my first visiting it, about the year 1680, a large, handsome, well built and increasing or thriving town, at my second visit, anno 1690, it was much bigger than at my first seeing it, and, by the report of the inhabitants, more than twice as big as it was twenty years before that; but, I think, I may safely say at this my third seeing it, for I was surprised at the view, it was more than double what it was at the second; and I am told, that it still visibly increases both in wealth, people, business and buildings. What it may grow to in time, I know not (Defoe, 1981, pp. 540–41).

Liverpool was very different from Chester: it did not have many of the traditional features of towns such as walls or a Cathedral, but there were few restrictions on trade; shipping and commercial activities flourished and this rapid economic growth created considerable wealth in the city:

> there is no town in England, London excepted, that can equal Liverpoole for the fineness of the streets, and beauty of the buildings; many of the houses are all of free stone, and completely finished; and all the rest (of the new part I mean) of brick, as handsomely built as London it self (Defoe, 1971, p. 543).

Chester, like York, managed to survive and in some sense it prospered. However, the economic vitality of the likes of Liverpool and the northern industrial towns ensured that during the eighteenth century many of the established regional capitals lost their former dominance and were overtaken by what became the great towns of Victorian England.

This shift was also accompanied by increasing levels of urbanization throughout the country. England was still overwhelmingly rural in 1700; only 17 per cent of its inhabitants lived in towns with a population greater than 5,000, and of these, 11 per cent lived in London (Wrigley, 1985b, p. 688). By 1750 the urban population had increased to 21 per cent, by 1801 27 per cent lived in towns and by 1850 over 50 per cent of the population could be considered urban (Wrigley, 1985b, p. 688; Law, 1967, p. 126). The urban mortality penalty persisted into the twentieth century and it is clear that, even given the reservations about universal urban natural decrease discussed above, no country could have supported this level of urbanization and have experienced large-scale population increase, from five million in 1700 to 5.7 million in 1750, 8.6 million in 1800 and 16.5 million in 1850, if cities consistently recorded natural decrease (Wrigley and Schofield, 1981, p. 534). Furthermore, the increasing importance of the urban sector and the relatively small number of urban parishes included in Wrigley and Schofield's parish sample may mean that their series is not representative of increasing levels of urbanization given persistent urban/rural differentials in demographic rates. This problem is likely to have been acute during the first half of the nineteenth century, especially as so little is known about demographic trends in the large industrial towns. Much needs to be done in order to discover more about the demography of towns during this period; however, a cursory examination of longer-term trends in York's demography will shed light on some of these issues.

DEMOGRAPHIC TRENDS IN YORK, 1561–1871

The change from ecclesiastical to civil registration in 1837 has meant that most historical demographers have concentrated their efforts on either the pre- or post-civil registration period. Moreover, since the quality of sources is paramount to any demographic analysis, much work has focused on either the second half of the nineteenth century, by which time civil registration was working well and the vast majority of births and deaths were captured, or the early parish register period when birth-baptism delay was short and nonconformity caused fewer problems. Consequently, the second half of the eighteenth and first half of the nineteenth century has suffered relative neglect, especially in towns, and few have attempted to bridge the gap between the two registration systems.[1] Indeed, in many ways, for towns at least this period remains a 'Demographic Dark Age'. It is, however, a relatively straightforward exercise to extend the York aggregate series of baptisms and burials to 1837. The eighteenth-century registers have survived well and the technique employed in Chapter 3 can be used to fill the few gaps in registration.[2] The quality of the registers appears

Table 7.1: Birth-baptism intervals, St Michael le Belfrey, York 1653-1812

Period	Interval in days by which stated per cent of births were baptized				Number of observations	Per cent incomplete
	25	50	75	90		
1653-57	4	6	8	9	171	2
1779-86	3	13	29	55	404	0
1787-94	28	39	85	120	427	1
1795-1802	27	50	76	124	388	0
1803-12	3	7	25	57	585	0

Source: original parish register.

1 The notable exception is Wrigley and Schofield (1981).
2 See p. 65. The following registers were deficient – Baptisms: All Saints Pavement 1739–95, St Michael Spurriergate 1764–73; Burials: All Saints Pavement 1739–1807, St Maurice 1761–1812, St Michael Spurriergate 1764–73.

good, but inspection alone cannot detect if substantial under-registration occurred. One of the most likely causes of under-registration was increasing birth-baptism delay, although this problem is far from straightforward. Table 7.1 shows the changing interval between birth and baptism in St Michael le Belfrey. Between 1787 and 1802 the interval had increased substantially from the Commonwealth period, with only 25 per cent of infants having been baptised within four weeks. During 1779–86 and 1803–12 it was much shorter, even though up to 25 per cent of infants were still baptised after four weeks. There is no indication in the registers to suggest that any disruption to registration occurred, and the most likely explanation for these substantial differences is that a change in the way private baptisms were recorded took place. These baptisms were usually conducted in the individual's home and it was usual to bring these infants for formal church baptism some time later. For instance, in the parish register of St Olave there is the following entry from 1778: 'Mary Harriot born 18th June baptised 28th June was admitted into the Church Aug 30th'.[3] Clearly the length of delay will be influenced by which baptism date was recorded, and this in turn may create additional problems in determining levels of under-registration due to infants dying before baptism.

Nonconformity also created problems. From the middle of the eighteenth century separate registers began to be kept by the nonconformist churches and these can easily be incorporated into the series.[4] Some nonconformists will be missing from the series in the early eighteenth century, but most nonconformist registers recorded relatively few births or baptisms, and levels of under-registration were likely to have been at similar levels to those of the late seventeenth century.[5] Only St Saviours Gate and Lendal chapels recorded burials and some burial loss may have occurred, although this is difficult to determine since the Anglican registers do not specifically indicate nonconformist burials. Furthermore, it is not known whether individuals from outside the city used these churches for baptism. The Catholic register in particular contains a suspiciously high number of baptisms, averaging nearly 65 per year during the 1820s. While further work needs to be done to determine the true extent of under-registration in eighteenth-century York, the aggregate series of baptisms and burials between 1700 and 1840 should broadly reflect the trend of births and deaths in the city.

3 BIHR PR Y/OL.
4 Four nonconformist chapels have surviving registers, Lendal Chapel (1799), PRO R4 4055, 4451; St Saviours Gate Chapel (1721), PRO R4 3780; New Jubbergate Chapel (1779) PRO R4 3518; New St (1821), PRO R4 3973. In addition there were Catholic registers at Micklegate Bar and Little Blake St; see Hanson (1936), and a Quaker register (1776); Brotherton Library I 1,2,3,4.
5 The following number of events were recorded in the first decade of registration: Lendal Chapel – (1801–10) 56 baptisms, (1821–30) 17 burials; St Saviours Gate – (1731–40) 16 baptisms, (1801–10) 10 burials; New Jubbergate – (1791–1800) 25 births; New St – (1821–30) 50 baptisms; Micklegate Bar – (1781–90) 63 baptisms; Little Blake Street – (1771–80) 196 baptisms; Quaker register – (1781–90) 38 births, 75 burials.

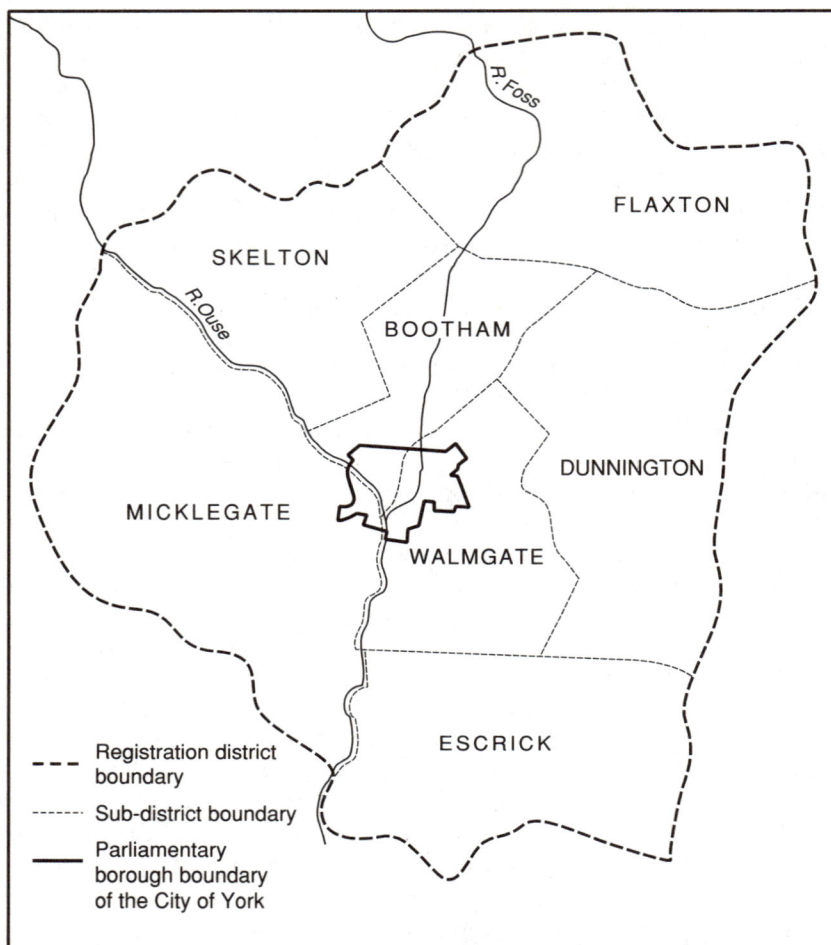

Figure 7.1: York Registration District
Source: Armstrong (1974), p. 71.

   Problems are also encountered when constructing a series of births and deaths for
the city of York in the Civil Registration period. There is general concern that in its
early years the system was not perfect and that more births than deaths were lost
(Glass, 1951). Whatever these inadequacies may have been, Civil Registration was
soon better than the ecclesiastical system that preceded it, and by 1860 few serious
problems remained. Unfortunately, individual entries from English and Welsh birth
and death registers are not at present open for inspection, and consequently it is not
possible to determine the precise numbers who were born and died in the city of
York. Instead it is necessary to rely on data published in the *Annual Reports of the*

Registrar General. This information was classified by county, registration district (RD) or sub-district, and the RD which contains the city of York also included a considerable rural hinterland: in 1841 the population of the city was 28,842, while that of the RD was 47,778 (Fig. 7.1).[6] York RD was divided into seven sub-districts, four of which were entirely rural. Thus, by using the births, deaths and population totals in the rural sub-districts it is possible to estimate birth and death rates in the rural portion of the RD.[7] Then, by assuming that the rates in the rural sub-districts, were identical to those in the rural parts of the sub-districts that comprised the city of York, the urban births and deaths can be separated from those in the rural hinterland. Once this procedure has been completed, the annual series of births and deaths from 1838 to 1871 can then be joined to the end of the aggregate series of baptisms and burials.[8]

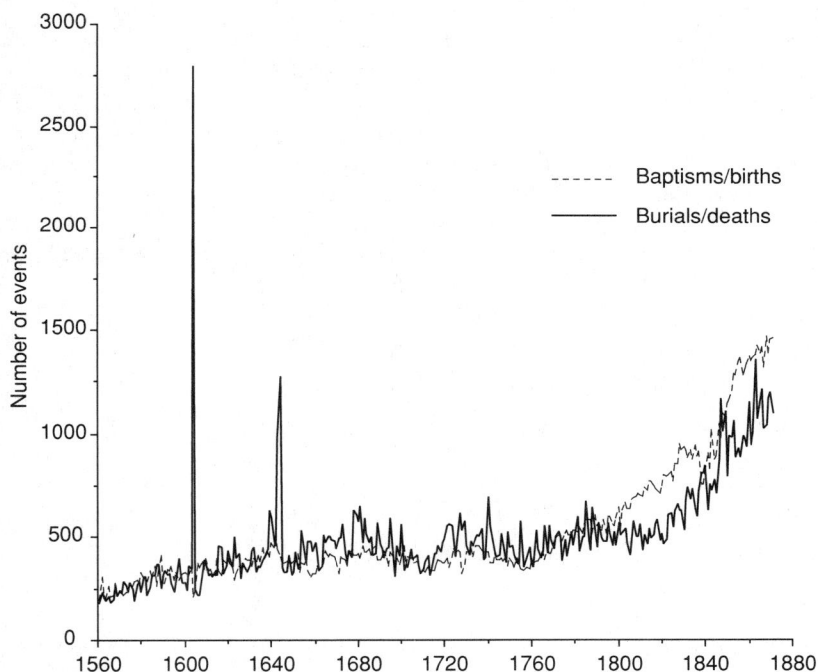

Figure 7.2: Annual series of vital events, York 1561–1870
Source: see text.

6 *1851 Census, Division IX*, pp. 2, 10.
7 Not surprisingly, the urban death rate was considerably greater than the rural one. The urban birth rate was also greater, although only by a small amount.
8 It is possible to replicate this procedure to produce a series of marriages, but the variability of the previous marriage series, caused in part by individual choice over where the event could take place, meant that this was not undertaken.

Figure 7.2 shows the trend of vital events in York between 1561 and 1871. No attempt was made to convert baptisms and burials into births and deaths, and given the complexities of the procedure, it is reassuring that no serious anomalies are revealed. The number of births, registered in 1839, the first year in which annual totals are available, was only 760 compared with 916 baptisms in 1837; however, by 1841 births had recovered and the large number of Catholic baptisms occurring during the 1830s may mean that the aggregate series over-estimates the true number of York baptisms. For five-yearly intervals between 1826 and 1850, the average annual numbers of baptisms or births were 904, 911, 826, 980 and 1,075 respectively. Given that the population was increasing throughout this period, there are obvious problems between 1836 and 1840, but overall these do not appear to be substantial.[9] It is immediately apparent that no event after 1700 compares with the great mortality crises of the seventeenth century, especially the 1604 plague. Mortality was high in 1740 and the 1720s, but from then onwards fluctuations became less severe. York did suffer epidemics in the nineteenth century, most notably outbreaks of cholera in 1832 and 1849 and one of typhus in 1847. These events can be identified in Fig. 7.2 and while politically they were important in that they focused attention on the need to adopt public health measures, demographically they were less significant, especially when compared with the devastation wrought by plague.[10]

Figure 7.3 presents the same data as Figure 7.2 for the period 1700–1840. Together these figures reveal the changing relationship between mortality and fertil-

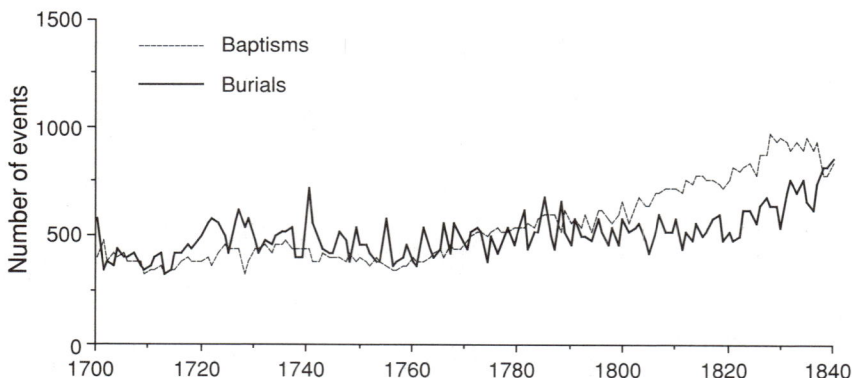

Figure 7.3: Annual series of baptisms and burials, York 1700–1840
Source: original parish registers.

9 The birth rate in 1841 was 31.5 per 1,000, which compares with 32.1 in 1801, 36.8 in 1821 and 33.4 in 1861. Such figures do not suggest substantial under-registration of births. There appear to be less problems with the series of burials and deaths – 697 burials were recorded between 1831 and 1835 compared with 722 deaths between 1841 and 1845. A more sophisticated analysis is necessary to determine the full extent of under-registration.
10 Only 185 deaths were caused by cholera in 1832, 25 per cent of the total for the year; see Durey (1974), p. 8.

ity. They show that the period of natural decrease lasted from 1640 to c.1770, when natural increase became the norm. By the nineteenth century, births outstripped deaths by a considerable amount, and this was also true of other towns and cities. The reasons for these changes warrant their own monograph, but some basic features of the city's demography can easily be determined. It is apparent that the date at which natural increase reasserted itself also coincided with increases in the city's population. Throughout the eighteenth century York's economy changed little. It remained a major social centre, but toward the end of the century, probably as a result of an increasing population within its hinterland, York's markets began to expand, trade increased and a number of small-scale manufactures were established in the city. Overall growth was modest, however, and industrialization did not affect York until after the advent of the railways in 1839 (Hutchinson and Palliser, 1980, pp. 69–76). It is likely that this economic and population expansion created the conditions in which marriage became easier, with the result that overall fertility increased correspondingly during the late eighteenth century. Of perhaps greater importance in explaining the shift in the balance between births and deaths is that mortality fell considerably at some point between 1700 and the middle of the nineteenth century (Wrigley and Schofield, 1983).

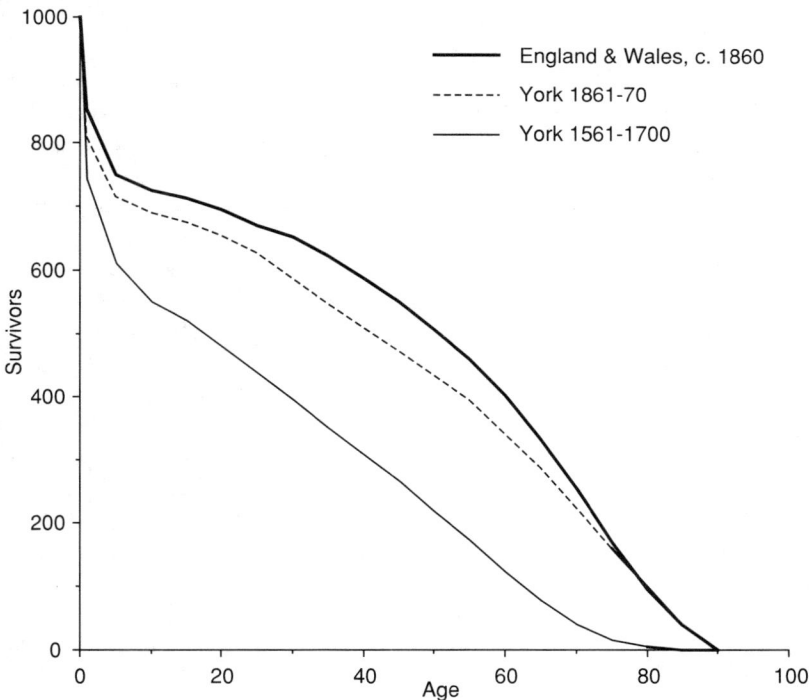

Figure 7.4: York's changing mortality, 1561–1870
Source: see text.

Figure 7.5: Infant mortality rates, York 1561–1950
Source: see text.

Figure 7.4 depicts the overall change in York's mortality by showing survivors by age for the seventeenth century (with adult mortality at West, level 4) and the 1860s, compared with the average for mid-nineteenth-century England and Wales.[11] By the 1860s mortality in York was still higher than the national average, but it was considerably lower than in the seventeenth century at virtually all ages. These differences represent a gain in life expectancy at birth of almost ten years from a level of about 30 years, and in terms of infant mortality the rate declined from over 260 in 1700 to 195 in the 1840s.[12] Single 'snapshots' at the beginning and end of a period cannot of course provide a chronology of the decline, nor can they delineate whether mortality at different ages declined at the same rates. It is possible, however, to investigate the changing pattern of infant mortality during the period relatively easily (Fig. 7.5). The rates before 1700 were taken from Table 4.4; those between 1700 and 1840 were calculated using the technique of linking infant burials to baptisms on the parish registers of Holy Trinity Goodramgate, St Martin Coney St and St Michael le Belfrey; those between 1840 and 1896 from the *Annual and Quarterly Returns of the Registrar General* and those after 1896 from the *Annual Medical Officer of Health Reports*.[13] A number of technical problems were encountered when con-

11 For the seventeenth century see Figure 6.6. The life table for the 1860s was calculated for the RD from data contained in *The Supplement to the Annual Report for 1872* (London, 1874). The England and Wales figures were calculated by taking the mean of the third, fourth and fifth English life tables; see Woods and Hinde (1987), p. 33.
12 E_0 was about 43 in mid-Victorian England and Wales and the IMR was about 150.
13 After 1840 the values are presented as seven-year moving averages.

structing the series. From 1897 the rates refer to the city; between 1840 and 1896 the data were only published for the RD and the rural births and infant deaths had to be excluded from the data.[14] Further problems arose during the period 1700–1840, since it became increasingly obvious that as the eighteenth century progressed, fewer infant burials were being recorded, and consequently mortality appeared to decline substantially. However, when civil registration began, the rate increased from an estimated 131 between 1801 and 1840 to nearly 200 in the 1840s. Such results were disappointing, and while the series was not corrected for the under-registration of infant burials, this must have occurred on such a scale to make the IMRs between 1700 and 1840 increasingly unreliable. Therefore, it is difficult to determine when the eighteenth-century infant mortality decline began, and while investigation of other York registers may yield a more reliable series, it seems unlikely.[15] Despite what may be insurmountable problems concerning the reliability of infant burials during the eighteenth and early nineteenth centuries, Figure 7.5 does indicate the direction of long-term changes in infant mortality in York. Until 1700 there was relative stability, even though annual rates were subject to considerable variation. At some stage before 1840, infant mortality must have declined by about 70 deaths per 1,000 births, and Figure 7.2 indicates that unless fertility also decreased before 1760 or there were compensating increases in mortality in other age groups, then much of the decline was likely to have occurred after this date. By the second half of the nineteenth century annual variations still occurred, but overall decline was slow until 1900 when it accelerated and was sustained.

Much remains to be done, especially with respect to determining levels of under-registration, in order to provide accurate demographic rates for eighteenth-century York. However, it is clear from this brief investigation into the city's demography after 1700 that, even allowing for under-registration, natural decrease did not effectively occur after 1780, as indeed was the case with most other English cities.[16] The reason for this is not known; but it would appear that it coincided with a period of both mortality decrease and fertility increase which again may reflect wider national patterns. Certainly by 1800 mortality had fallen sufficiently to ensure that natural decrease became very unlikely, and while mortality change was less dramatic during the nineteenth century, it was by then sufficiently low to ensure that towns could no longer be described as 'urban graveyards' even if they still retained the ability to shock and appal contemporary commentators.

14 See above for the technique. This had the effect of increasing the IMR from 157 in the RD to 166 in the city between 1886 and 1890.
15 While the calculation of infant mortality is difficult, this should not affect estimates of natural change since most of the missing infant burials were also likely to be absent from the baptism register; see the discussion in Galley et al. (1995). Previously it was thought that the Quaker register would be able to provide accurate IMRs between 1776 and 1837, thus enabling the gap to be filled. A full investigation of the register revealed an IMR of 151 (based on 191 births), so even this register appears to suffer from some under-registration since burials rather than deaths seem to have been recorded. However, too few York births were included to enable definite conclusions to be made.
16 See Table 1.3.

CITIES AND ENGLISH POPULATION HISTORY

The effects of population redistribution on national demographic patterns can be illustrated relatively simply by reference to variations in nineteenth-century IMRs (Fig. 7.6). The IMR in England and Wales remained remarkably stable at about 150 deaths per 1,000 live births. This general stability is partly illusory since it masked considerable urban-rural differentials in infant mortality throughout the period. The lines marked Colyton and Hartland show the Devon RDs containing these parishes and can broadly be said to be representative of those rural areas that experienced amongst the lowest IMRs in this period. There was little change in mortality in many

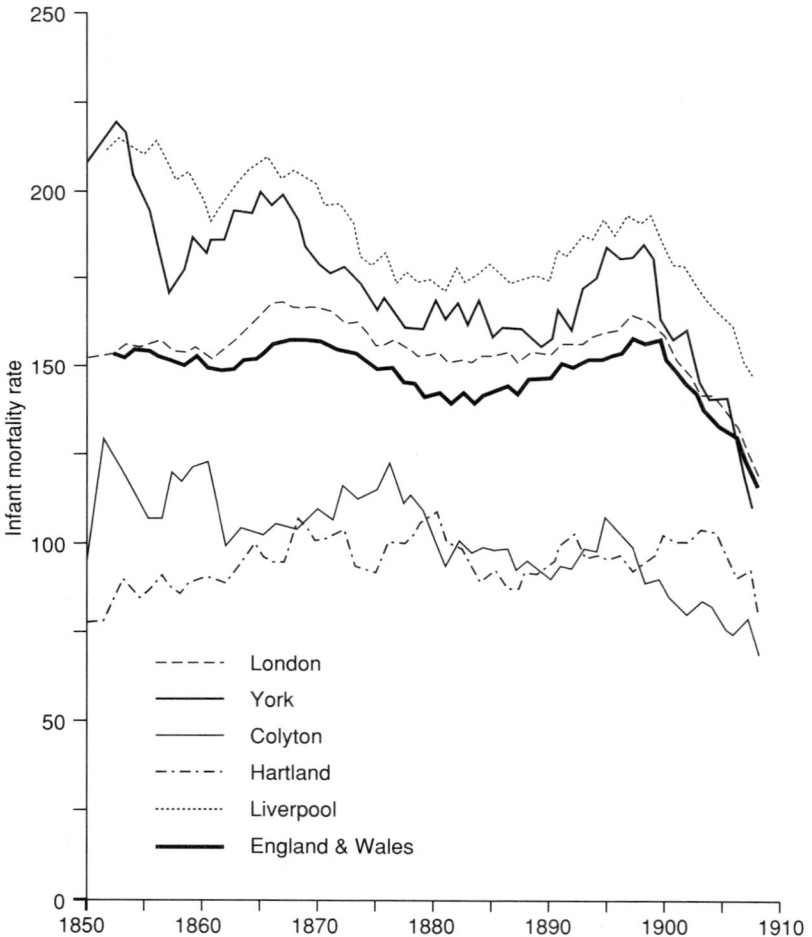

Figure 7.6: Infant mortality rates in selected places, 1850–1910
Source: Annual reports of the Registrar General.

of these places. By comparison, in large towns such as Liverpool and York, which experienced some of the highest rates, there were greater annual fluctuations, although in London, the largest city of all, IMRs were very near to the average for the whole country. Most places lay between these extremes and in parts of the country the overall trend in infant mortality was downwards (Williams and Galley, 1995, pp. 410–11). However, as an increasing proportion of the population lived in the larger towns, this redistribution of population offset any gains elsewhere. Moreover, a series of very hot summers towards the end of the century caused substantial increases in urban IMRs, thereby delaying the secular decline in national infant mortality until the beginning of the twentieth century (Woods *et al.*, 1989). Thus, the national trend was composed of a number of diverse patterns and its overall stability can only be fully understood after the full extent of the geographical variations has been examined.

Figure 7.7 extends Figure 7.6 backwards as far as possible and reveals longer-term trends.[17] A number of methodological issues have been skirted over rather quickly in order to make these comparisons. Perhaps the most important is whether it is appropriate to compare IMRs derived from single parish reconstitutions with those in the corresponding RD, which may contain upwards of 30 parishes, especially given that geographical variations in infant mortality could be substantial.[18] In spite of these difficulties, Figure 7.7 reveals the broad direction of any trends and it shows the full extent of urban/rural differentials in infant mortality. Broadly speaking, IMRs in places such as Colyton and Hartland underwent little change in the 350 years from 1550, even though there were likely to have been some annual or periodic variation. By contrast, towns such as York experienced considerable change and the decline in London's IMR after 1750 was nothing short of spectacular. It is also possible to speculate on what happened in towns such as Liverpool. By the middle of the nineteenth century these places had the harshest environments in which to raise infants, yet IMRs there were much lower than in early modern York or eighteenth-century London. Thus, however bad conditions were in the industrial towns, they were likely to have been an improvement on those a century earlier. During the eighteenth century, decreases in mortality occurred throughout the country, but they were much more pronounced in the towns. While it is impossible to say what levels of infant mortality were like in Liverpool immediately before 1850, it seems likely that they followed a pattern similar to York rather than London, given that it was a relatively small town during the seventeenth century. London's contribution to England's overall IMR was very important. For instance, if the IMR in provincial England remained constant at say 180 per 1,000 live births, then once London is included the overall

---

17 Sources – from 1850; see Figure 7.6: before 1850; for London see Landers (1990a), pp. 39–42; York, see Figure 7.5; Colyton, see Wrigley (1972), p. 261; Hartland, see Smith (1978), p. 210.
18 Parish register reconstitutions do not include illegitimates, and since illegitimate IMRs were up to twice those of legitimates, the parish register estimates also need to be inflated to take this into account.

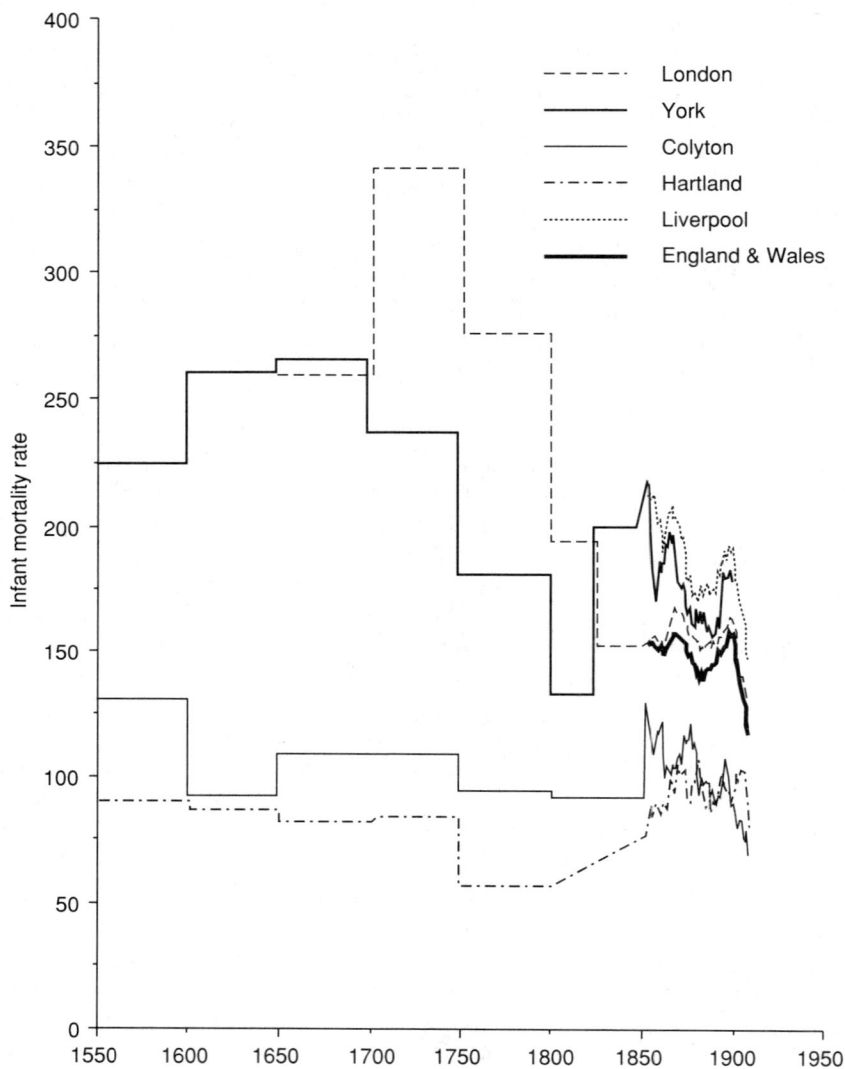

Figure 7.7: Long-term trends in infant mortality
Source: see text.

rate rises to 186 in 1670, 198 in 1700, 197 in 1750 and 181 in 1801.[19] Thus, substantial changes in the national IMR could be accounted for purely by the impact of urbanization. The provincial towns were likely to have had less of an impact on overall rates since IMRs there were more modest and most growth occurred after 1750, by which time mortality rates were beginning to fall.

The inclusion of some urban parishes together with market towns such as Gainsborough, whose mortality profile was very similar to York's, suggests that compositional effects caused by urbanization were less likely to have affected Wrigley and Schofield's national parish sample, especially given the emergence of urban natural increase in eighteenth-century towns. Of course, more studies need to be carried out in order to verify whether York was representative of other towns in this period, and the greatest challenge for historical demographers still remains to derive accurate demographic rates for the emerging industrial towns. The impact of the towns on national demographic patterns will only be fully revealed once the extent of geographical variations in mortality and indeed of other demographic variables has been discovered. London's demography remains crucial and much depends on the accuracy of Bills of Mortality, since they are usually used as the basis for determining the city's population history. However, these have been subject to considerable scepticism, and as Boulton showed, there is general concern that nonconformity and birth-baptism delay affected a number of London parishes (Landers, 1993; Boulton, 1992). With inter-parish variations probably being substantial and the decline in fertility revealed by Figure 1.3 not having been fully explained, clearly more work needs to be done in order to delineate demographic trends in the capital, especially in the period before 1700. Table 1.6 showed that towns in general and London in particular could only grow in the late seventeenth century at the expense of the rest of the country. While this caused rural depopulation for a short period, at other times towns were less of a drain on national population resources, especially given that urban nuptiality and fertility were also subject to variation. In many towns there is little evidence for long-term natural decrease and with patterns of nuptiality being subject to local variation this was just as important a characteristic of towns as the urban penalty. Indeed, it would appear that towns together with their local hinterlands experienced some form of population homeostasis: urban mortality and fertility were often in more harmony than is commonly acknowledged and the whole region existed in mutual demographic symbiosis (Lee, 1985). Such systems existed because large numbers remained unmarried and much of the population were willing to migrate. However, it was only after urban mortality rates had begun to fall that both rapid urbanization and substantial national population increase became possible.

More is known about the population history of England than of any other country; yet much still remains to be discovered about urban demography, especially in the

---

19 These figures have been calculated using the population totals given in Wrigley, Table 2, p. 680 and the IMRs for London Quakers in Landers (1990a), p. 42. Clearly while the actual values may be subject to debate the contribution of London to the national trend was substantial.

eighteenth century, and as the country developed into the first industrial nation, it is likely that if anywhere deviated from national trends it would have been the towns. But, as was the case with early modern towns while differences or variations in demographic rates no doubt occurred, these seem unlikely to be of sufficient magnitude to alter the overall direction of national population trends.

Appendix 1

ADMISSIONS TO THE FREEDOM IN YORK, 1500–1699

A. Textile industry

Occupation	1500–24	1525–49	1550–74	1575–99	1600–24	1625–49	1650–74	1675–99
Clothier, clothdresser, clothworker	–	3	2	1	1	13	31	8
Coverlet weaver	–	1	–	–	–	1	2	4
Darnixweaver	–	–	–	–	–	2	–	–
Dasher	2	–	–	–	–	–	–	–
Dyer	26	8	11	4	11	12	13	17
Flaxdresser	–	–	–	–	–	1	–	2
Fuller	16	5	6	–	–	–	–	–
Fustianweaver	–	–	–	–	2	–	–	–
Hempdresser	–	–	–	–	–	–	11	7
Jerseyman, jerseyworker	–	–	–	1	1	1	–	–
Linendresser	–	–	–	–	1	1	–	–
Linenweaver	8	12	1	11	35	39	55	32
Linenweaver & woolenweaver	1	1	–	–	–	–	–	–
Seargeweaver	–	–	–	–	–	–	1	1
Shearman	5	2	7	2	3	2	–	–
Silkweaver	–	–	1	4	31	39	30	23
Spinster	1	1	2	2	2	–	–	1
Stapler	–	–	–	–	–	–	–	3
Tapiter	38	68	34	22	16	14	7	–
Weaver	20	10	25	14	–	5	1	8
Woollenweaver	3	5	2	–	1	–	–	–
Worstedweaver	–	–	–	–	2	1	–	–
Others*	4	1	1	–	–	–	–	1
Totals	**124**	**117**	**92**	**61**	**106**	**131**	**151**	**107**
Percentages	**9.7**	**8.3**	**6.3**	**3.8**	**6.0**	**7.5**	**7.3**	**5.7**

*1500–24 hairweaver & porter; linenweaver & porter; weaver & pinner; woolman. 1525–49 hairweaver; 1550–74 silkman; 1675–99 seargemaker.

B Clothing trades

Occupation	1500–24	1525–49	1550–74	1575–99	1600–24	1625–49	1650–74	1675–99
Capper	16	14	11	–	–	–	–	–
Feltmaker	–	–	–	17	45	15	5	3
Feltmaker and haberdasher	–	–	–	4	–	–	1	3
Hatter, hatmaker	5	2	13	12	–	1	–	1
Hosier	10	8	2	–	–	–	1	7
Imboderer	1	1	3	7	17	12	5	1
Millioner	–	–	2	10	14	21	21	11
Pointer, pointmaker	2	–	–	–	–	–	–	–
Semester, simstresse	–	2	1	–	–	–	–	4
Tyrewomen	–	–	–	–	–	–	–	2
Tailor	85	112	154	170	220	190	193	59
Tailor and labourer	2	–	–	–	–	–	–	–
Vestmentmaker	6	3	1	–	–	–	–	–
Others*	2	–	–	–	–	–	–	–
Totals	**129**	**142**	**187**	**220**	**296**	**239**	**226**	**91**
Percentages	**10.1**	**10.1**	**12.8**	**13.6**	**16.8**	**13.6**	**11.0**	**4.9**

* 1500–24 hayster, labourer & tapiter; tailor & hosier.

C. Leather industry

Occupation	1500–24	1525–49	1550–74	1575–99	1600–24	1625–49	1650–74	1675–99
Artizen skinner	–	–	–	–	–	1	2	2
Bottler, bottlemaker	1	3	4	2	–	–	–	–
Cobbler, translator	3	3	8	8	8	13	29	40
Conyour	3	1	–	–	–	–	–	–
Cordwainer, shoemaker	62	65	69	80	90	117	142	101
Currier, leatherdresser	9	13	13	19	10	11	13	13
Fellmonger	–	–	–	–	–	2	13	27
Glover	27	28	45	54	56	41	25	10
Jirkinmaker	–	–	2	–	–	–	–	–
Leather gilder	–	–	–	–	–	–	15	2
Parchmener, parchment maker	6	13	13	16	14	12	5	–
Saddler	11	14	25	29	34	22	27	22
Saddler & cardmaker	1	–	–	–	1	–	–	–
Skinner	12	6	11	7	7	5	13	3
Tanner, barker	39	62	62	65	69	71	95	69
Trunkmaker	–	–	–	–	–	6	8	5
Others*	3	–	–	–	–	–	–	1
Totals	**177**	**208**	**252**	**280**	**289**	**301**	**387**	**295**
Percentages	**13.9**	**14.8**	**17.3**	**17.4**	**16.4**	**17.2**	**18.9**	**15.7**

* 1500–24 bagmaker; glover & labourer; lesshmaker. 1675–99 bridlemaker.

D. Building trades

Occupation	1500–24	1525–49	1550–74	1575–99	1600–24	1625–49	1650–74	1675–99
Bricklayer	–	–	–	8	35	35	62	68
Brickmaker	–	–	–	2	–	3	6	1
Carpenter	27	29	36	34	34	23	57	68
Firemason	–	–	–	2	–	–	–	–
Freemason	–	–	–	–	1	–	1	4
Glazier	12	5	9	11	9	4	15	16
Mason	5	3	–	–	–	–	1	2
Sawyer	8	2	1	12	2	–	1	–
Tiler	18	30	36	29	7	–	–	–
Tilemaker	1	6	7	1	–	–	–	–
Wright	5	6	1	–	–	–	–	–
Others*	1	–	–	–	–	2	–	–
Totals	**77**	**81**	**90**	**99**	**88**	**67**	**143**	**159**
Percentages	**6.0**	**5.7**	**6.2**	**6.1**	**5.0**	**3.8**	**7.0**	**8.5**

* 1500–24 alblasterer. 1625–49 hourglassmaker; millwright.

E. Woodworking trades

Occupation	1500–24	1525–49	1550–74	1575–99	1600–24	1625–49	1650–74	1675–99
Basketmaker	–	1	–	1	1	1	8	3
Bowyer	10	7	3	1	8	3	–	–
Cartwright	6	2	–	–	–	–	–	–
Carver	7	18	–	–	2	2	–	2
Cooper	8	14	10	17	14	32	23	36
Fletcher	10	5	4	4	–	–	–	–
Heelmaker, woodheelmaker	–	–	–	–	–	–	2	1
Joiner	3	5	20	38	48	33	23	48
Organmaker	–	2	–	–	1	–	–	–
Shipcarpenter, shipwright	5	5	6	3	4	4	2	–
Turner	2	2	–	–	2	1	2	–
Upholster	1	–	1	2	5	4	9	9
Wheelwright	–	2	2	–	–	5	10	3
Winecooper	–	–	–	–	–	–	13	15
Others*	1	1	–	1	–	–	–	2
Totals	**53**	**64**	**46**	**67**	**85**	**85**	**92**	**119**
Percentages	**4.2**	**4.5**	**3.2**	**4.2**	**4.8**	**4.8**	**4.5**	**6.4**

* 1500–24 cowcher. 1525–49 carver & joiner. 1575–99 skepmaker. 1675–99 cabinetmaker; body-maker.

F. Metal trades

Occupation	1500–24	1525–49	1550–74	1575–99	1600–24	1625–49	1650–74	1675–99
Armourer	11	13	15	14	16	15	6	7
Bellfounder, bellmaker	1	1	–	–	–	–	1	–
Blacksmith	8	20	21	33	29	6	43	43
Bladesmith	6	2	4	2	1	–	–	–
Braisier	1	3	1	–	6	9	3	5
Cardmaker	3	2	3	–	–	–	–	–
Coppersmith	–	–	–	–	–	2	6	6
Cutler	3	4	8	7	2	2	4	7
Founder	10	7	8	10	4	–	–	–
Girdler	8	8	11	11	8	3	6	14
Goldfiner, goldsmith	8	19	30	13	21	15	12	25
Gunmaker, gunsmith	–	–	–	1	–	2	9	–
Hardwareman, ironmonger	3	3	3	1	1	–	–	–
Lastmaker	1	1	–	–	1	–	1	1
Locksmith	3	16	11	13	21	15	16	2
Lorimer	–	–	–	3	1	–	–	–
Marshal, smith	19	11	11	2	1	–	–	–
Mettleman	–	2	3	–	–	2	–	–
Pewterer	13	23	18	21	19	12	29	18
Pinner	4	5	8	13	8	20	18	17
Pinner & wiredrawer	2	–	–	–	1	–	–	–
Plumber	4	5	2	6	1	2	2	3
Scissorsmith	–	–	–	–	–	–	3	–
Spooner	–	–	–	–	–	–	1	2
Spurrier	10	6	9	4	4	6	4	2
Tinkler	1	–	2	1	–	–	–	–
Whitesmith	–	–	–	–	–	–	12	33
Wiredrawer	2	3	–	2	–	–	–	1
Others*	4	–	–	2	–	–	–	1
Totals	**125**	**154**	**168**	**159**	**145**	**111**	**176**	**187**
Percentages	**9.8**	**10.9**	**11.5**	**9.9**	**8.2**	**6.3**	**8.6**	**10.0**

* 1500–24 blacksmith, locksmith and lorimer; bladesmith and blacksmith; goldsmith and haberdasher; locksmith and bladesmith. 1575–99 combmaker; gunsmith and locksmith. 1675–99 brascaster.

G. Distributive trades

Occupation	1500–24	1525–49	1550–74	1575–99	1600–24	1625–49	1650–74	1675–99
Apothecary	2	2	2	10	12	15	14	17
Bookseller	–	–	–	–	–	–	–	4
Burnleder, waterleder	2	1	–	–	1	–	–	–
Chandler	2	–	1	–	4	6	8	16
Chapmen, cornchapmen	4	6	2	–	–	–	–	–
Cornmerchant	5	24	2	–	–	–	–	–
Draper	2	14	28	40	38	40	33	17
Draper tailor	–	–	–	4	2	–	–	–
Drover	–	–	–	2	–	–	–	–
Grocer, vitualler	5	42	25	20	27	26	44	45
Haberdasher	35	4	–	37	46	30	22	14
Haberdasher & chandler	3	2	3	–	–	1	–	–
Linendraper	–	1	–	5	2	4	–	–
Mercer	8	9	6	34	46	53	65	42
Merchant	94	109	111	157	126	169	76	54
Merchant tailor	–	–	–	–	–	–	10	77
Mercator	–	–	–	–	–	–	30	22
Salter	1	–	–	–	–	–	1	–
Sandeder	4	–	–	–	–	–	–	–
Spicer	3	–	–	–	–	–	–	–
Stationer	2	3	5	1	1	3	9	4
Tallowchandler	–	–	–	4	9	10	10	5
Vintner	10	6	8	8	18	18	20	9
Waxchandler	7	9	–	–	–	–	–	–
Woollen draper	–	–	–	–	–	–	1	2
Others*	6	1	1	–	–	1	1	2
Totals	**195**	**233**	**194**	**322**	**332**	**376**	**344**	**330**
Percentages	**15.3**	**16.5**	**13.3**	**20.0**	**18.9**	**21.4**	**16.8**	**17.6**

*   1500–24 chapman & haberdasher; grocer & vintner; haberdasher & questor; linen merchant; vintner, haberdasher & innholder; waxchandler & stringer. 1525–49 draper & painter. 1550–74 merchant draper. 1624–49 merchant adventurer. 1650–74 lanius. 1675–99 druggist; tinker.

H. Transport

Occupation	1500–24	1525–49	1550–74	1575–99	1600–24	1625–49	1650–74	1675–99
Carrier	3	5	6	4	–	–	–	–
Craneman	4	1	–	–	–	–	–	–
Marriner, seaman	–	–	–	–	–	–	46	42
Panyerman	1	16	15	30	18	8	1	1
Porter	7	13	11	16	12	7	5	7
Shipman	14	–	–	–	–	–	3	–
Sledman	7	1	6	3	1	2	2	–
Waterman	1	2	–	–	–	–	–	3
Others*	2	–	–	–	–	–	–	–
Totals	**39**	**38**	**38**	**53**	**31**	**17**	**57**	**53**
Percentages	**3.1**	**2.7**	**2.6**	**3.3**	**1.8**	**1.0**	**2.8**	**2.8**

*   1500–24 porter & labourer; shipman & fishmonger.

I. Food and drink

Occupation	1500–24	1525–49	1550–74	1575–99	1600–24	1625–49	1650–74	1675–99
Alehousekeeper	–	–	–	–	–	–	–	2
Baker	43	51	78	76	70	91	88	82
Berebrewer, brewer	5	9	10	6	–	2	6	12
Butcher	44	49	61	60	75	58	70	61
Cook	14	22	17	17	22	26	12	17
Fisher	46	38	14	5	–	–	–	–
Fishmonger	14	21	15	30	21	29	22	22
Fruiterer	–	–	–	–	–	–	1	1
Innholder, innkeeper	12	21	40	70	71	39	31	32
Inholder & haberdasher	2	–	–	–	–	–	–	–
Maltster	–	1	3	1	3	2	–	2
Milner, miller	30	43	29	29	37	53	40	38
Others*	4	–	–	1	1	–	–	3
Totals	**214**	**255**	**267**	**295**	**300**	**300**	**270**	**272**
Percentages	**16.8**	**18.0**	**18.3**	**18.3**	**17.1**	**17.1**	**13.2**	**14.5**

*   1500–24 innholder & smith; maltman & fisher; milner & milnwright; saucemaker. 1575–99 alebrewer. 1600–24 custordmaker. 1675–99 confectioner; distiller; sugar baker.

J. Professional

Occupation	1500–24	1525–49	1550–74	1575–99	1600–24	1625–49	1650–74	1675–99
Alderman	4	–	2	–	3	1	6	8
Attorney	–	–	–	–	–	–	–	3
Baccalarius, lerneyman	1	1	1	–	–	–	–	–
Barber	19	18	3	2	13	12	18	24
Barber & chandler	1	–	1	1	–	–	–	–
Barber & waxchandler	2	1	–	–	–	–	–	–
Barber surgeon	1	–	2	2	4	11	22	25
Barber surgeon & waxchandler	1	1	–	–	–	–	–	–
Baronet	–	–	–	–	–	–	2	1
Clerk	28	10	7	1	2	3	–	1
Doctor	3	1	–	–	1	–	–	–
Generosus legisperitus	1	–	1	2	–	–	5	5
Litteratus & haberdasher	2	–	–	–	–	–	–	–
Notary, notarius publicus	3	–	7	–	–	–	–	–
Notary and merchant	1	1	–	–	–	–	–	–
Parish clerk	5	6	2	–	–	–	–	–
Scrivener	7	3	9	1	2	–	–	–
Surgeon	3	2	3	–	2	2	4	2
Others*	–	–	1	–	1	–	1	–
Totals	**82**	**44**	**39**	**9**	**28**	**29**	**58**	**69**
Percentages	**6.4**	**3.1**	**2.7**	**0.6**	**1.6**	**1.7**	**2.8**	**3.7**

*1550–74 horseleche. 1625–49 schoolmaster. 1650–74 militis.

K. Miscellaneous

Occupation	1500– 24	1525– 49	1550– 74	1575– 99	1600– 24	1625– 49	1650– 74	1675– 99
Armiger	–	1	–	–	–	1	2	–
Bookbinder	1	1	1	–	–	–	–	7
Clockmaker, watchmaker	–	–	–	–	6	9	12	9
Combmaker	–	–	–	–	–	–	–	2
Dancing Master	–	–	–	–	–	–	2	–
Dutchman	–	–	7	–	–	–	–	–
Gardiner	–	–	–	–	–	–	–	4
Gentleman	4	5	13	2	2	3	9	5
Generosus	2	2	2	–	4	3	–	–
Hornbreker, horner	4	3	1	–	2	1	2	3
Husbandman	–	1	–	–	2	–	–	–
Instrumentmaker	–	–	–	2	2	3	–	1
Labourer	9	32	16	9	10	48	77	105
Milnwright	–	–	–	–	–	–	1	2
Musician	–	–	1	4	17	8	9	4
Painter stainer	9	13	11	12	6	10	9	18
Pardoner, questor	3	–	–	–	–	–	–	–
Paver	–	1	1	–	–	1	–	3
Pipemaker	–	–	–	–	–	–	4	5
Potter	8	8	7	4	–	1	4	–
Potter & bellmaker, bellfounder	2	1	–	–	–	–	–	–
Roper, ropemaker	2	6	6	8	3	5	2	10
Sopeboiler	–	–	–	–	2	–	–	–
Spencer	3	–	–	–	–	–	–	–
Vidua	–	2	1	–	–	–	–	–
Wayte	–	1	1	–	–	1	–	–
Yeoman	6	–	16	6	–	5	13	4
Others*	6	1	3	1	2	–	–	10
Totals	**59**	**78**	**87**	**48**	**58**	**99**	**146**	**192**
Percentages	**4.6**	**5.5**	**6.0**	**3.0**	**3.3**	**5.6**	**7.1**	**10.2**

*   1500–24 asshbryner, labourer & tapiter; textwriter; lumer; florisher; turner & scribner; unus attorm. 1525–49 sprosedrysser. 1550–74 harper; lawndrer; messenger. 1575–99 writer. 1600–24 comsolmaker; syvemaker. 1674–99 capmaker; chemist; coachmaker; furrier; gardiner; limminer; printer; rugmaker; sadletreemaker; tobacco cutter.

Sources: For the period 1500–1649 the analysis follows Sakata (1982b), which in turn is based on Pound (1966). For the period 1650–99 the entries have been extracted from Collins (1900).

INDIVIDUAL PARISH CONTRIBUTIONS TO THE YORK AGGREGATE SERIES

Parish	Baptisms	Burials	Marriages
All Saints North Street	1578–1642, 1650–1700	1578–1642, 1650–74, 1676–1700	1578–1642, 1650–1700
All Saints Pavement	1561–86, 1590–1700	1561–84, 1591–1700	1561–76, 1593–1700
Holy Trinity Goodramgate	1583–1700	1583–1700	1583–1700
Holy Trinity Kings Court	1616–49, 1654–1700	1616–44, 1646–48, 1654–1700	1616–43, 1654–1700
Holy Trinity Micklegate	1587–1623, 1626–47, 1650–1700	1587–1623, 1626–44, 1654–1700	1587–1647, 1651–57, 1664–1700
St Crux	1561–1700	1561–1700	1561–1700
St Cuthbert	1684–1700	1684–1700	1684–1700
St Denys with St George	1561–75, 1582–1700	1561–75, 1582–1700	1561–75, 1582–1700
St Helen Stonegate	1568–71, 1577–80, 1583–1647, 1690–1700	1568–1640, 1642–48, 1690–1700	1573–1644, 1690–1700
St John Ousebridge	1580–84, 1589–1641, 1644–85	1580–84, 1589–1641, 1644–1700	1580–1641, 1644–85
St Lawrence	1613–37, 1671–80, 1695–1700	1613–37, 1671–80, 1695–1700	1613–37, 1671–80, 1695–1700
St Margaret Walmgate	1561–64, 1566–73, 1575–1614, 1616–1700	1561–64, 1566–73, 1575–1614, 1616–79, 1683–1700	1561–64, 1566–73, 1575–1614, 1616–42, 1667–1700
St Martin Coney Street	1561–1700	1561–1700	1561–1700
St Martin cum Gregory	1589–1609, 1612–1700	1589–1609, 1612–1700	1589–1609, 1612–1700
St Mary Bishophill Junior	1603–44, 1647–1700	1603–44, 1647–1700	1603–44, 1647–1700
St Mary Bishophill Senior	1661–69, 1671–1700	1661–69, 1671–1700	1661–1700
St Mary Castlegate	1605–1700	1604–1700	1604–1700
St Maurice	1651–1700	1651–1700	1651–1700
St Michael le Belfrey	1566–1700	1566–1700	1566–1700
St Michael Spurriergate	1603–15, 1618–1700	1603–13, 1618–1700	1603–15, 1618–1700

Parish	Baptisms	Burials	Marriages
St Olave	1561–1644, 1654–1700	1561–1603, 1605–15, 1617–1644, 1654–1700	1561–1644, 1654–61, 1665–1700
St Sampson	1641–54, 1664–1700	1641–54, 1664–1700	1641–54, 1664–1700
St Saviour	1576–84, 1591–1700	1576–84, 1591–1700	1576–84, 1591–1700
Bedern	1682–1700		
Minster Yard	1634–1700	1634–1700	1634–1700

BIBLIOGRAPHY

ADAIR, R. (1991), 'Regional variations in illegitimacy and courtship patterns in England 1538–1754' (unpublished University of Cambridge PhD thesis).

ADEY, K. R. (1973), 'Seventeenth-century Stafford: a county town in decline', *Midland History* **2**, 152–67.

ALLDRIDGE, N. (1986), 'The population profile of an early modern town: Chester 1547–1728', *Annales de Démographie Historique*, 115–31.

ALLISON, K. J. (1955), 'The wool supply and the worsted cloth industry in Norfolk in the sixteenth and seventeenth centuries' (unpublished University of Leeds PhD thesis).

ALLOTT, S. (1978), *Friends in York*, York.

APPELBY, A. (1978), *Famine in Tudor and Stuart England*, Liverpool.

ARKELL, T. (1982), 'Multiplying factors for estimating population totals from the Hearth Tax', *Local Population Studies* **28**, 51–7.

ARKELL, T. (1992), 'A method for estimating population totals from the Compton census returns', In K. Shurer and T. Arkell (eds), *Surveying the People*, Matlock, 97–116.

ARMSTRONG, W. A. (1974), *Stability and Change in an English County Town*, Cambridge.

ARMSTRONG, W. A. (1981), 'The trend of mortality in Carlisle between the 1780s and 1840s: a demographic contribution to the standard of living debate', *Economic History Review*, **34**, 94–114.

AVELING, J. C. H. (1970), *Catholic Recusancy in the City of York 1558–1791*, (Catholic Record Society).

BABBAGE, S. B. (1962), *Puritanism and Richard Bancroft*, London.

BARRY, J. (ed.) (1990), *The Tudor and Stuart Town 1530–1688*, London.

BARTLETT, J. N. (1959), 'The expansion and decline of York in the later middle ages', *Economic History Review*, **12**, 17–33.

BEIER, A. L. (1985), *Masterless Men: The Vagrancy Problem in England 1560–1640*, London.

BEN-AMOS, I. K. (1991), 'Failure to become freemen: urban apprentices in early modern England', *Social History*, **16**, 155–72.

BEN-AMOS, I. K. (1994), *Adolescence and Youth in Early Modern England*, New Haven.

BENGTSSON, M. (1995), 'Infant and child mortality in an urban environment', In A. Brändström and L.-G. Tedebrand (eds), *Swedish Urban Demography during Industrialization*, Umeå, 13–63.

BERRY, B. M. and R. S. SCHOFIELD (1971), 'Age at baptism in pre-industrial

England', *Population Studies*, **25**, 453–63.

BORSAY, P. (1989), *The English Urban Renaissance*, Oxford.

BOULTON, J. (1987a), *Neighbourhood and Society: A London Suburb in the Seventeenth Century*, Cambridge.

BOULTON, J. (1987a), 'Neighbourhood migration in early modern London', In P. Clark and D. Souden (eds), *Migration and Society in Pre-industrial England*, London, 107–49.

BOULTON, J. (1990), 'London widowhood revisited: the decline of female remarriage in the seventeenth and eighteenth centuries', *Continuity and Change*, **5**, 323–55.

BOULTON, J. (1992), 'The Marriage Duty Act and parochial registration in London, 1695–1706', In K. Schurer and T. Arkell (eds), *Surveying the People* Matlock, 222–52.

BOULTON, J. (1993), 'Clandestine marriages in London: an examination of a neglected urban variable', *Urban History*, **20**, 191–210.

BOURGEOIS-PICHAT, J. (1952), 'An analysis of infant mortality', *Population Bulletin of the United Nations*, **2**, 1–14.

BRODSKY, V. (1981), 'Single women in the London marriage market: age, status and mobility, 1598–1619', In R. B. Outhwaite (ed.), *Marriage and Society: Studies in the Social History of Marriage*, London, 81–100.

BRODSKY, V. (1986), 'Widows in late Elizabethan London: remarriage, economic opportunity and family orientations', In L. Bonfield, R. M. Smith and K. Wrightson (eds), *The World We Have Gained*, London, 122–54.

BROOKES, F. W. (1954), 'York and the Council of the North', *St. Anthony's Hall Publications*, **5**.

BUCKATZCH, E. J. (1949–50), 'Places of origin of a group of immigrants into Sheffield 1624–1799', *Economic History Review*, **2**, 303–06.

CHAPMAN, C. R. (1991), *Pre-1841 Censuses & Population Listings in the British Isles*, Dursley.

CLARK, G. (1987), 'A study of nurse children, 1550–1750', *Local Population Studies*, **39**, 8–23.

CLARK, P. (1972), 'The migrant in Kentish towns 1580–1640', In P. Clark and P. Slack (eds), *Crisis and Order in English Towns*, London, 117–63.

CLARK, P. (1979), 'Migration in England during the late seventeenth and early eighteenth centuries', *Past and Present*, **83**, 57–90.

CLARK, P. (1985), 'A Crisis contained? The condition of English towns in the 1590's', In P. Clark (ed.), *The European Crisis of the 1590's*, London, 44–66.

CLARK, P., K. GASKIN and A. WILSON (1989), 'Population estimates of English small towns' (Working Paper No. 3, Centre for Urban History, University of Leicester).

CLARK, P. and P. SLACK (1976), *English Towns in Transition 1500–1700*, Oxford.

CLARK, P. and D. SOUDEN (eds) (1987), *Migration and Society in Pre-industrial England*, London.

CLARKSON, L. A. (1971), *The Pre-industrial Economy in England 1500–1750*,

London.

CLAY, J. W. (ed.) (various years), 'Paver's marriage licences', *Yorkshire Archaeo-logical Journal*, **7** (1883), 289–304; **9** (1885), 362–79; **10** (1886), 35–50, 169–204, 445–60; **11** (1887), 209–45; **12** (1888), 116–22, 143–58, 269–84; **13** (1889), 371–86; **14** (1890), 220–38, 458–506; **16** (1892), 1–37; **17** (1893), 155–91; **20** (1894), 68–97; *York Archaeological Society Record Series Vol. 1*, **40** (1908); *Vol. 2*, **43** (1911); *Vol. 3*, **46** (1912).

COALE, A. J. and P. DEMENY (1983), *Regional Model Life Tables and Stable Pop-ulations,* 2nd edition, Princeton.

COLLINS, F. (ed.) (1900), 'Register of the Freemen of the city of York, vol. 2 1559–1759', *Surtees Society*, **102**.

COLLINSON, P. (1983), 'The Jacobean religious settlement: the Hampton Court conference', In H. Tomlinson (ed.), *Before the English Civil War*, London, 27–52.

COOPER, T. P. (1928–29), 'Some old York inns with special reference to "The Star" Stonegate', *Associated Architectural Societies' Report and Papers*, **39**, 273–318.

CORFIELD, P. (1977), 'Economic growth and change in seventeenth-century Eng-lish towns', In *Open University Course A322, unit 10 English Urban History 1500–1700*, Milton Keynes, 31–71.

CORFIELD, P. (1982), *The Impact of English Towns 1700–1800*, Oxford.

CORSINI, C. A., and P. P. VIAZZO (eds) (1993), *The Decline of Infant Mortality in Europe: 1800–1950: Four National Case Studies*, Florence.

COWGILL, U. M. (1967), 'Life and death in the sixteenth century in the city of York', *Population Studies*, **21**, 53–62.

COWGILL, U. M. (1970), 'Marriage and its progeny in the city of York 1538–1751', *Kroeber Anthropological Society Papers*, **42**, 47–87.

COX, J. C. (1910), *The Parish Registers of England*, London.

CRAWFORD, P. (1983), 'From the women's view: pre-industrial England, 1500–1750', In P. Crawford (ed.), *Exploring Women's Past* , London, 49–85.

CREIGHTON, C. (1965), *A History of Epidemics in Britain* (2 Vols., 2nd edition) London.

DAVIES, R. (ed) (1863), 'The life of Marmaduke Rawdon of York', *Camden Soci-ety*.

DAVIES, R. (1873), 'The plague at York in the seventeenth century', *Yorkshire Philosophical Society Annual Report* 4–34.

DEFOE, D. (1971), *A Tour through the Whole Island of Great Britain*, Har-monsworth (first published 1724–26).

DICKENS, A. G. (1961), 'Tudor York', In P. M. Tillot (ed.), *A History of the County of Yorkshire. The City of York*, London, 117–59.

DOBSON, M. J. (1987), 'A chronology of epidemic disease and mortality in south-east England, 1601–1800', *Historical Geography Research Series*, **19**.

DOBSON, M. J. (1989), 'The last hiccup of the old demographic regime: population stagnation and decline in late seventeenth and early eighteenth-century south-east England', *Continuity and Change*, **4**, 395–428.

DOBSON, M. J. (1992), 'Contours of death: disease, mortality and the environment in early modern England', *Health Transition Review*, **2** (Supplement), 77–95.

DOBSON, R. B. (1973), 'Admissions to the Freedom of the city of York in the later Middle Ages', *Economic History Review*, **26**, 1–22.

DRAKE, M. (1961–62), 'An elementary exercise in parish register demography', *Economic History Review*, **14**, 427–45.

DUNCAN, S. R., S. SCOTT and C. J. DUNCAN (1994), 'Smallpox epidemics in cities in Britain', *Journal of Interdisciplinary History*, **25**, 255–71.

DUPÂQUIER, J. (1979), *La Population Français aux XVIIe et XVIIe Siècles*, Paris.

DUREY, M. (1974), 'The first spasmodic cholera epidemic in York, 1832', *Borthwick Papers*, **46**.

DYER, A. (1973), *The City of Worcester in the Sixteenth Century*, Leicester.

DYER, A. (1981), 'Seasonality of baptisms: an urban approach', *Local Population Studies*, **27**, 26–34.

DYER, A. (1985), 'Epidemics of measles in a seventeenth-century town', *Local Population Studies*, **34**, 35–45.

DYER, A. (1991), *Decline and Growth in English Towns 1400–1600*, Basingstoke.

EDWARDS, J. K. (1969), 'Norwich Bills of Mortality – 1701–1803', *Yorkshire Bulletin of Economic and Social Research*, **21**, 94–113.

ENFIELD, W. (1773), *An Essay Towards the History of Liverpool*, Warrington.

EYLER, J. M. (1979), *Victorian Social Medicine*, Baltimore.

FILDES, V. (1980), 'Neonatal feeding practices and infant mortality during the 18th century', *Journal of Biosocial Sciences*, **12**, 313–24.

FILDES, V. (1985), *Wet Nursing*, Oxford.

FINLAY, R. (1980), 'Distance to church and registration experience', *Local Population Studies*, **24**, 26–40.

FINLAY, R. (1981a), 'Natural decrease in early modern cities', *Past and Present*, **92**, 169–74.

FINLAY, R. (1981b), 'Parish registers: an introduction', *Historical Geography Research Series*, **7**.

FINLAY, R. (1981c), *Population and Metropolis*, Cambridge.

FORBES, T. R. (1971), *Chronicle from Aldgate* (New Haven).

FORSTER, G. C. F. (1961), 'York in the 17th century', In P. M. Tillot (ed.), *A History of the County of York, The City of York*, London, 160–206.

FORSTER, G. C. F. (1969), 'Hull in the 16th and 17th centuries', In K. J. Allinson (ed.), *A History of the County of York: East Riding Vol. 1. The City of Kingston upon Hull*, Oxford, 90–173.

FRIEDRICHS, C. R. (1985), 'Immigration and urban society: seventeenth-century Nördlingen', in E. Francois (ed.), *Immigration et Société Urbaine en Europe Occidentale XVIe–XXe Siecle*, Paris, 65–77.

FRIEDRICHS, C. R. (1995), *The Early Modern City 1450–1720*, London.

GALLEY, C. (1991), 'Growth, stagnation and crisis: the demography of York 1561–1700' (unpublished University of Sheffield PhD thesis).

GALLEY, C. (1993), '"One face, one voice, one habit, and two persons!" The survival of twins in early modern society', *Local Population Studies*, **51**, 73–6.

GALLEY, C. (1994), 'A never-ending succession of epidemics? Mortality in early-modern York', *Social History of Medicine*, **7**, 29–57.

GALLEY, C. (1995a), 'A model of early modern urban demography', *Economic History Review*, **48**, 448–69.

GALLEY, C. (1995b), 'Assessing infant mortality in the industrial north' (unpublished paper).

GALLEY, C., N. WILLIAMS and R. WOODS (1995), 'Detection without correction: problems in assessing the quality of English Ecclesiastical and Civil Registration', *Annales de Démographie Historique*, 161–83.

GIBSON, J. and M. MEDLYCOTT (1992), *Local Census Listings 1522–1930*, Birmingham.

GLASS, D. V. (1950), 'Graunt's life table', *Journal of the Institute of Actuaries*, **76**, 61–4.

GLASS, D. V. (1951), 'A note on the under-registration of births in Britain in the nineteenth century', *Population Studies*, **5**, 70–88.

GLASS, D. V. (1965), 'Two papers on Gregory King', In D. V. Glass and D. E. C. Eversley (eds), *Population and Society*, London, 159–220.

GLASS, D. V. (1966), *London Inhabitants within the Walls*, London.

GLASS, D. V. (1972), 'Notes on the Demography of London at the end of the Seventeenth Century', in D. V. Glass and R. Revelle (eds), *Population and Social Change*, London, 275–85.

GLASS, D. V. (1973a), *Numbering the People*, Farnborough.

GLASS, D. V. (1973b), *The Development of Population Statistics*, Farnborough.

GLASS, D. V. (1973c), *The Population Controversy*, Farnborough.

GOLDBERG, P. J. P. (1986), 'Marriage, migration, servanthood and life-cycle in Yorkshire towns of the later Middle Ages: some York cause paper evidence', *Continuity and Change*, **1**, 141–69.

GOLDBERG, P. J. P., (1990), 'Urban identity and the poll taxes of 1377, 1379 and 1381', *Economic History Review*, **43**, 194–216.

GOLDBERG, P. J. P., (1992a), 'Marriage, migration and servanthood: the York cause paper evidence', In P. J. P. Goldberg (ed.), *Women is a Worthy Wight*, Stroud, 1–15.

GOLDBERG, P. J. P., (1992b), *Women, Work, and Life Cycle in a Medieval Economy*, Oxford.

GOOSE, N. (1986), 'In search of the urban variable: towns and the English economy, 1500–1650', *Economic History Review*, **39**, 165–85.

GOOSE, N. (1994), 'Urban demography in pre-industrial England: what is to be done?', *Urban History*, **21**, 273–84.

GRAUNT, J. (1973), *Natural and Political Observations made upon the Bills of Mortality* (first published 1662), reprinted in P. Laslett (ed.), *The Earliest Classics: John Graunt and Gregory King*, Farnborough.

HAJNAL, J. (1965), 'European marriage patterns in perspective', In D. V. Glass and D. E. C. Eversley (eds), *Population and History*, London, 101–43.

HALLEY, E. (1692), 'An estimate of the degrees of mortality of mankind, drawn from curious tables of the births and funerals at the city of Breslaw; with an attempt to ascertain the price of annuity on lives', *Philosophical Transactions of the Royal Society*, **17**, 596–610.

HANSON, J. S. (ed.) (1936), 'The Catholic Registers of Little Blake Street Chapel, now St Wilfred's, York 1771–1838', *Catholic Record Society*, **35**, 1–197

HARDING, V. (1990), 'The population of London, 1550–1700: a review of the published evidence', *London Journal*, **15**, 111–28.

HARLEY, D. (1995), 'From providence to nature: the moral theology and godly practice of maternal breastfeeding in Stuart England', *Bulletin of the History of Medicine*, **69**, 198–223.

HAYGARTH, J. (1981), 'Observations on the Bills of Mortality in Chester for the years 1772 and 1773', reprinted in J. H. Cassedy (ed.), *Mortality in Pre-industrial Times: The Contemporary Verdict*, Farnborough.

HECHT, J. (1987), 'Johann Peter Süssmilch: a German prophet in foreign countries', *Population Studies*, **41**, 31–58.

HENRY, L. (1968), 'Some comments on Ursula M. Cowgill's article, "Life and death in the sixteenth century in the city of York"', *Population Studies*, **22**, 165–9.

HERLIHY, D. (1977), 'Deaths, marriages, births and the Tuscan economy', In R. D. Lee (ed.), *Population Patterns in the Past*, London, 135–64.

HERLIHY, D. and C. KLAPISCH-ZUBER (1985), *Tuscans and their Families: A Study of the Florentine Catasto of 1427*, New Haven.

HEY, D. (1986), *Yorkshire from AD 1000*, London.

HEY, D. (1991), *The Fiery Blades of Hallamshire*, Leicester.

HEYNSHAM, J. (1973), 'Collected Bills of Mortality for Carlisle, 1779–1787', reprinted in D. V. Glass, (ed.), *The Development of Population Statistics*, Farnborough.

HIBBERD, D. J. (1981), 'Urban inequalities: social geography and demography in seventeenth-century York' (unpublished Liverpool University PhD thesis).

HIBBERD, D. J. (1983), 'Data-linkage and the Hearth Tax: the case of seventeenth-century York', In N. Alldridge (ed.), *The Hearth Tax: Problems and Possibilities*, Hull, 59–84.

HEYNSHAM, J. (1983), 'Data-linkage and the Hearth Tax: the case of seventeenth-century York', In N. Alldridge (ed.), *The Hearth Tax: Problems and Possibilities*, Hull, 59–84 .

HILL, B. (1994), 'Rural–urban migration of women and their employment in towns', *Rural History*, **5**, 185–94.

HOLMAN, R. J. (1980), 'Apprenticeship as a factor in migration; Bristol 1675–1726', *Bristol and Gloucester Archaeology Journal*, **97**, 85–92.

HOSKINS, W. G. (1976), 'English provincial towns in the early sixteenth century', in P. Clark (ed.), *The Early Modern Town*, London, 91–105.

HUCK, P. (1994), 'Infant mortality in nine industrial parishes in Northern England 1813–1836', *Population Studies*, **48**, 513–26.

HULL CITY RECORD OFFICE (1990), *The People of Hull in 1695 and 1697*, Hull.

HULL, C. H. (ed.) (1964), *The Economic Writings of Sir William Petty, Vol. 2*, New York.

HUMPHERY-SMITH, C. R. (1984), *The Phillimore Atlas and Index of Parish Registers*, Chichester.

HUTCHINSON, J. and D. M. PALLISER (1980), *York*, Edinburgh.

JEUB, U. N. (1993), *Parish Records*, Umeå.

KÄLVEMARK, A.–S. (1977), 'The country that kept track of its population', in J. Sundin and E. Söderlund (eds), *Time, Space and Man*, Stockholm, 221–38.

KEARNS, G., 'The urban penalty and the population history of England', In A. Brändström and L.-G. Tedebrand (eds), *Society, Health and Population during the Demographic Transition*, Stockholm, 213–36.

KEYFITZ, N., 'Do cities grow by natural increase or by migration?', *Geographical Analysis*, **12**, 142–56.

KEYFITZ, N. and D. PHILIPOV, 'Migration and natural increase in the growth of cities', *Geographical Analysis*, **13**, 287–99.

KING, G. (1973), 'The LCC Burns journal', In P. Laslett (ed.), *The Earliest Classics*, Farnborough.

KITCH, M. J. (1986), 'Capital and kingdom: migration to later Stuart London' In A. L. Beier and R. Finlay (eds), *London 1500–1700. The Making of the Metropolis*, London, 224–51.

KUCZYNSKI, R. R. (1938), 'British demographers' opinions on fertility, 1660 to 1760' In L. Hogben (ed.), *Political Arithmetic*, London, 283–327.

KUSSMAUL, A. (1981), *Servants in Husbandry in Early Modern England*, Cambridge.

KUSSMAUL, A. (1990), *A General View of the Rural Economy of England 1538–1840*, Cambridge.

LANDERS, J. (1990a), 'Age patterns of mortality in London during the "long eighteenth century": a test of the "high potential" model of metropolitan mortality', *Social History of Medicine*, **3**, 27–60.

LANDERS, J. (1990b), 'Fertility decline and birth spacing among London Quakers' In J. Landers and V. Reynolds (eds), *Fertility and Resources*, Cambridge, 92–117.

LANDERS, J. (1992), 'Historical epidemiology and the structural analysis of mortality', *Health Transition Review*, **2** (Supplement), 47–75.

LANDERS, J. (1993), *Death and the Metropolis*, Cambridge.

LANGTON, J. and P. LAXTON (1978), 'Parish registers and urban structure', *Urban History Yearbook*, 74–84.

LASLETT, P. (1972), 'Mean household size in England since the sixteenth century', In P. Laslett and R. Wall (eds), *Household and Family in Past Time*, Cambridge, 125–58.

LASLETT, P. (1988), 'The institution of service', *Local Population Studies*, **40**, 55–60.

LASLETT, P. and K. OOSTERVEEN (1973), 'Long-term trends in bastardy in England', *Population Studies*, **27**, 255–86.

LAW, C. M. (1967), 'The growth of urban population in England and Wales,

1801–1911', *Transactions of the Institute of British Geographers*, **41**, 125–43.

LAXTON, P. and N. WILLIAMS (1989), 'Urbanization and infant mortality in England: a long-term perspective and review', in M. C. Nelson and J. Rogers (eds), *Urbanisation and the Epidemiological Transition*, Uppsala, 109–35.

LAYCOCK, T. K. (1844), *Report on the State of York, in Reply to the Questions Circulated by the Health of Towns Commission*, London.

LEE, R. D. (1985), 'Population homeostasis and English population history', *Journal of Interdisciplinary History*, **15**, 635–60.

VAN LEEUWEN, M. D. H. and J. E. OEPPEN (1993), 'Reconstructing the demographic regime of Amsterdam 1681–1920', *Economic and Social History in the Netherlands*, **5**, 61–102.

LEWIS, F. (1993), 'The demographic and occupational structure of Liverpool: a study of the parish register, 1660–1750' (unpublished University of Liverpool PhD thesis).

LONG, M. and M. PICKLES (1986), 'An enquiry into mortality in some mid-Wharfedale parishes in 1623', *Local Population Studies*, **37**, 19–35.

LYNCH, K. A. (1991), 'The European marriage pattern in the cities: variations on a theme by Hajnal', *Journal of Family History*, **16**, 79–96.

MACFARLANE, A. (1977), *Reconstructing Historical Communities*, Cambridge.

MACFARLANE, A. (1986), *Marriage and Love in England 1300–1840*, Oxford.

McNEILL, W. H. (1980), 'Migration patterns and infections in traditional societies', In N. F. Stanley and R. A. Joske (eds), *Changing Disease Patterns and Human Infections*, London, 27–36.

MALTHUS, T. R. (1970), *An Essay on the Principle of Population*, London (reprint of 1st edition, published 1798).

MALTHUS, T. R. (1973), *An Essay on the Principle of Population*, London (reprint of 7th edition, published 1872).

MARCHANT, R. A. (1969), *The Church under the Law*, Cambridge.

MAYHEW, G. (1976), *Tudor Rye*, Falmer.

MEADS, D. M. (ed.) (1930), *Diary of Lady Margaret Hoby 1599–1605*, London.

MERCER, A. (1990), *Disease, Mortality and Population in Transition*, Leicester.

MOSLEY, W. H. and L. C. CHEN (1984), 'An analytic framework for the study of child survival in developing countries', In W. H. Mosley and H. C. Chen (eds), 'Child survival: strategies for research', *Population and Development Review*, **10** (Supplement), 25–45.

MURRAY, H., S. RIDDICK and R. GREEN (1990), *York through the Eyes of the Artist*, York.

NEWELL, C. (1988), *Methods and Models in Demography*, Chicester.

NEWMAN, P. R. (1978), 'Two York City regiments, 1642–1644', *York Historian*, **2**, 24–30.

OEPPEN, J. (1993), 'Back projection and inverse projection: members of a wider class of constrained projection models', *Population Studies*, **47**, 245–67.

OLLARD, S. L. and P. C. WALKER (eds) (various years), 'Archbishop Herring's Visitation Returns, 1743', *Yorkshire Archaeological Society Record Series Vol. 1*,

71 (1927); *Vol. 2*, **72** (1929); *Vol. 3*, **75** (1929); *Vol. 4*, **77** (1930); *Vol.5*, **79** (1931).

OUTHWAITE, R. B. (1995), *Clandestine Marriage in England, 1500–1850*, London.

PALLISER, D. M. (1973), 'Epidemics in Tudor York', *Northern History*, **7**, 45–63.

PALLISER, D. M. (1974), 'The union of parishes at York 1547–86', *Yorkshire Archaeological Journal*, **46**, 87–102.

PALLISER, D. M. (1979), *Tudor York*, Oxford.

PALLISER, D. M. (1982), 'Civic mentality and the environment in Tudor York', *Northern History*, **18**, 78–115.

PALLISER, D. M. (1983), *The Age of Elizabeth*, London.

PALLISER, D. M. (1985), 'A regional capital as magnet: immigrants to York 1477–1566', *Yorkshire Archaeological Journal*, **57**, 111–23.

PALLISER, D. M. (1990), 'Domesday York', *Borthwick Papers*, **78**.

PALLISER, D. M. and M. PALLISER (1979), *York as they saw it*, York.

PATTEN, J. (1973), 'Rural–urban migration in pre-industrial England', *Oxford School of Geography Research Papers*, **6**.

PATTEN, J. (1976), 'Patterns of migration and movement of labour in three pre-industrial East Anglian towns', *Journal of Historical Geography*, **2**, 111–29.

PAULSON, R. (1975), *The Art of Hogarth*, London.

PELLING, M. (1982), 'Occupational diversity: barbersurgeons and the trades of Norwich, 1550–1640', *Bulletin of the History of Medicine*, **56**, 484–511.

PELLING, M. (1988), 'Child health as a social value in early modern England', *Social History of Medicine*, **1**, 135–64.

PERRENOUD, A. (1970), *La Population du Genèva du Seizeème au Début du Dix-Neuvième Siècle*, Genèva.

PERRENOUD, A. (1982), 'Croissance ou décline? Les mechanisms du non-renouvellemnet des population urbaines', *Histoire, Economie et Société*, **4**, 581–601.

PHYTHIAN-ADAMS, C. (1979), *Desolation of a City: Coventry and the Urban Crisis of the Late Middle Ages*, Cambridge.

PICKARD, R. (1947), *The Population and Epidemics of Exeter in Pre-census Times*, Exeter.

PICKLES, M. F. (1996), 'Labour migration: Yorkshire, c. 1670–1743', *Local Population Studies*, **57**, 30–49.

POUND, J. F. (1966), 'The social and trade structure of Norwich 1525–1575', *Past and Present*, **34**, 49–69.

POUND, J. F. (1971), 'The Norwich Census of the Poor 1570', *Norwich Record Society*, **40**.

POUND, J. F. (1988), *Tudor and Stuart Norwich*, Chichester.

PRESSAT, R. and C. WILSON (eds) (1985), *The Dictionary of Demography*, Oxford.

PRICE, R. (1771), *Observations on Revisionary Payments*, Vol. II, London.

RALPH, E. and M. E. WILLIAMS (eds) (1968), *The Inhabitants of Bristol in 1696*, Bristol.

RAMSAY, G. D. (1986), 'The recruitment of some London freemen in the mid-sixteenth century', *Economic History Review*, **31**, 526–40.

RAPPAPORT, S. (1989), *Worlds within Worlds: Structures of Life in Sixteenth-century London*, Cambridge.

REED, M. (1981), 'Economic structure and change in seventeenth-century Ipswich', In P. Clark (ed.), *County Towns in Pre-industrial England*, Leicester, 87–141.

REHER, D. S. (1990), *Town and Country in Pre-industrial Spain*, Cambridge.

REID, R. R. (1921), *King's Council in the North*, London.

RICHARDSON, R. C. and T. B. JAMES (eds) (1983), *The Urban Experience*, Manchester.

RICKMAN, J. (1973), 'Observations on the results of the Population Act, 41 Geo. III', reprinted in D. V. Glass (ed.), *The Development of Population Statistics*, Farnborough.

ROYAL COMMISSION ON HISTORICAL MONUMENTS (1972), *An Inventory of the Historical Monuments in the City of York, Vol. 2: The Defences*, London.

ROYLE, E. (1985), 'Nonconformity in nineteenth-century York', *Borthwick Papers*, **68**.

RUGGLES, S. (1992), 'Migration, marriage, and mortality: correcting sources of bias in English family reconstitution', *Population Studies*, **46**, 507–22.

RUSSELL, J. C. (1948), *British Medieval Population*, Albuquerque.

SAITO, O. (1990), 'The changing structure of employment and its effects on migration patterns in eighteenth- and nineteenth-century Japan', In A. D. van der Woude, A. Hayami and J. de Vries (eds), *Urbanization in History*, Oxford, 205–19.

SAKATA, T. (1982a), 'Some original materials concerning the plague of York in 1604', *Osaka Gakuin Review of Economics and Business*, **8** 59–109.

SAKATA, T. (1982b), 'Economic change in late medieval and early modern York' (in Japanese), *Hikaku Toshishi Kenkyu*, **1**, 12–44.

SAKATA, T. (1988), 'Demographic and economic trends in late medieval and early modern York: an analysis of rent rolls and Freemen's Register', *The Bulletin of St Margaret's*, **19**, 49–71.

SASAKI, Y. (1985), 'Urban migration in Tokugawa Japan: the city of Takayama 1773–1871', In S. B. Hanley and A. P. Wolf (eds), *Family and Population in East Asian History*, Stanford, 110–32.

SCHOFIELD, R. S. (1970), 'Age-specific mobility in an eighteenth century rural English parish', *Annales de Démographic Historique*, 261–74.

SCHOFIELD, R. S. (1984a), 'English marriage patterns revisited', *Journal of Family History*, **10**, 2–20.

SCHOFIELD, R. S. (1984b), 'Traffic in corpses: some evidence from Barming, Kent, 1788–1812', *Local Population Studies*, **33**, 49–53.

SCHOFIELD, R. S. (1989), 'Family structure, demographic behaviour, and economic growth' In J. Walter and R. S. Schofield (eds), *Famine, Disease and the Social Order in Early Modern Society*, Cambridge, 279–304.

SCHOFIELD, R. S. and E. A. WRIGLEY (1979), 'Infant and child mortality in England in the late Tudor and early Stuart period', In C. Webster (ed.), *Health, Med-*

icine and Mortality in the Sixteenth Century, Cambridge, 61–95.

SCHOFIELD, R. S. AND E. A. WRIGLEY (1981), 'Remarriage intervals and the effect of marriage order on fertility', In J. Dûpaquier (ed.), *Marriage and Remarriage in Populations of the Past*, London, 211–27.

SCOTT, D. A. (1990), 'Politics, dissent and Quakerism in York 1640–1700' (unpublished University of York DPhil thesis.

SELLARS, M. (1913), 'Social and economic history', In W. Page (ed.), *Victoria County History of York, Vol. 3*, London, 435–48.

SHARLIN, A. (1978), 'Natural decrease in early modern cities: a reconsideration', *Past and Present*, **79**, 126–38.

SHARLIN, A. (1981), 'A rejoinder to an article by R. Finlay', *Past and Present*, **92**, 175–80.

SHARPE, J. A. (1980), 'Defamation and sexual slander in early modern England: the church courts at York', *Borthwick Papers*, **58**.

SHARPE, P. (1991), 'Literally spinsters: a new interpretation of local economy and demography in Colyton in the seventeenth and eighteenth centuries', *Economic History Review*, **44**, 46–65.

SHORT, T. (1750), *New Observations on City, Town and Country Bills of Mortality*, London.

SHORT, T. (1767), *Comparative History of the Increase and Decrease of Mankind*, London.

SJOBERG, G. (1960), *The Preindustrial City*, New York.

SLACK, P. (1977), 'The English urban landscape', *Open University Course A322, Unit 3 English Urban History 1500–1780*, Milton Keynes, 79–110.

SLACK, P. (1985), *The Impact of Bubonic Plague in Tudor and Stuart England*, London.

SLACK, P. (1988), *Poverty and Policy in Tudor and Stuart England*, London.

SLACK, P. (1989), 'The response to plague in early modern England: public policies and their consequences', In J. Walter and R. Schofield (eds), *Famine, Disease and the Social Order in Early Modern Society*, Cambridge, 167–87.

SMITH, R. M. (1978), 'Population and its geography in England 1500–1730', In R. A. Dodgson and R. A. Butlin (eds), *An Historical Geography of England and Wales*, London, 199–237.

SMITH, R. M. (1981a), 'Fertility, economy and household formation in England over three centuries', *Population and Development Review*, **7**, 595–622.

SMITH, R. M. (1981b), 'The people of Tuscany and their families in the fifteenth century: Medieval or Mediterranean?', *Journal of Family History*, **6**, 107–28.

SMITH, R. M. (1986), 'Marriage processes in the English past: some continuities' In L. Bonfield, R. M. Smith and K. Wrightson (eds), *The World We Have Gained*, Oxford, 43–99.

SMITH, S. R. (1973), 'The social and geographical origins of the London Apprentices, 1630–1660', *Guildhall Miscellany*, **4**, 195–206

SÖDERBERG, J., U. JONSSON and C. PERSSON (1991), *A Stagnating Metropolis: The Economy and Demography of Stockholm, 1750–1850*, Cambridge.

SOUDEN, D. (1984a), 'Movers and stayers in family reconstitution populations', *Local Population Studies*, **33**, 11–28.

SOUDEN, D. (1984b), 'Migrants and the population structure of later seventeenth-century provincial cities and market towns', In P. Clark (ed.), *The Transformation of English Provincial Towns*, London, 133–68.

SOUDEN, D. (1987), '"East, west – home's best": regional patterns of migration in early modern England', In P. Clark and D. Souden (eds), *Migration and Society in Pre-industrial England*, London, 292–332.

SOUTHALL, H. and D. GILBERT (1996), 'A good time to wed?: marriage and economic distress in England and Wales, 1839–1914', *Economic History Review*, **49**, 35–57.

STANGELAND, C. E. (1966), *Pre-Malthusian Doctrines of Population*, New York (first published 1904).

SUNDIN, J. (1995), 'Culture, class, and infant mortality during the Swedish mortality transition, 1750–1850', *Social Science History*, **19**, 117–45.

SUTHERLAND, I. (1972), 'When was the Great Plague? Mortality in London 1563 to 1665', In D. V. Glass and R. Revelle (eds), *Population and Social Change*, London, 287–320.

SWANSON, H. (1989), *Medieval Artisans*, Oxford.

TATE, W. (1969), *The Parish Chest*, Cambridge.

THWAITES, W. (1984), 'Women in the market place: Oxfordshire c. 1690–1800', *Midland History*, **9**, 23–42.

TILLOT, P. M. (ed.) (1961), *A History of the County of Yorkshire: The City of York*, London.

TODD, B. J. (1985), 'The remarrying widow: a stereotype reconsidered', In M. Prior (ed.), *Women in English Society, 1500–1800*, London, 54–92.

TODD, B. J. (1994), 'Demographic determinism and female agency: the remarrying widow reconsidered … again', *Continuity and Change*, **9**, 421–50.

UNWIN, R. W. (1981), 'Tradition and transition: market towns of the Vale of York, 1660–1830', *Northern History*, **17**, 72–116.

VANN, R. T. and D. E. C. EVERSLEY (1992), *Friends in Life and Death*, Cambridge.

VÖGELE, J. P. (1994), 'Urban infant mortality in Imperial Germany', *Social History of Medicine*, **7**, 401–25.

DE VRIES, J. (1984), *European Urbanization 1500–1800*, London.

WALL, R. (1977), 'Regional and temporal variations in English household structure from 1650', In J. Hobcraft and P. Rees (eds), *Regional Demographic Development*, London, 89–113.

WALL, R. (1978), 'The age at leaving home', *Journal of Family History*, **3**, 181–202.

WALL, R. (1987), 'Leaving home and the process of household formation in pre-industrial England', *Continuity and Change*, **2**, 77–101.

WAREING, J. (1980), 'Changes in the geographical distribution of the recruitment of apprentices to the London companies 1486–1750', *Journal of Historical Geog-*

raphy, **6**, 241–9.

WARMINGTON, A. R. (1990), 'The Corporation of York in peace and war', *York Historian*, **9**, 16–26.

WEBB, C. C. (1981), *A Guide to Genealogical Sources in the Borthwick Institute of Historical Research*, York.

WEBB, J. (1966), *Poor Relief in Elizabethan Ipswich*, Ipswich.

WEIR, D. R. (1983), 'Rather never than late: celibacy and age at marriage in English cohort fertility, 1541–1871', *Journal of Family History*, **9**, 340–54.

WEITZMAN, A. J. (1975), 'Eighteenth-century London: urban paradise or fallen city?', *Journal of the History of Ideas*, **26**, 469–80.

WENHAM, P. (1970), *The Great and Close Siege of York, 1644* , Kineton.

WEST, F. (1974), 'Infant mortality in the East Fen parishes of Leake and Wrangle', *Local Population Studies*, **13**, 41–4.

WHITE, W. (1782), 'Observations on the bills of mortality at York', *Philosophical Transactions of the Royal Society*, **72**, 35–43.

WHITEMAN, A. (ed.) (1986), *The Compton Census of 1676: A Critical Edition*, London.

WHITEMAN, A. (1992), 'The Compton census of 1676', In K. Shurer and T. Arkell (eds), *Surveying the People*, Matlock, 78–96.

WIDDRINGTON, T. (1897), *Analecta Eboracensia*, London.

WILLEN, D. (1988), 'Women in the public sphere in early modern England: the case of the urban working poor', *Sixteenth Century Journal*, **19**, 559–75.

WILLIAMS, N. (1992), 'Death in its season: class environment and the mortality of infants in nineteenth-century Sheffield', *Social History of Medicine*, **5**, 71–94.

WILLIAMS, N. and C. GALLEY (1995), 'Urban–rural differentials in infant mortality in Victorian England', *Population Studies*, **49**, 401–20.

WILSON, B. M. (1967), 'The Corporation of York, 1580–1660' (unpublished University of York MPhil thesis).

WILSON, C. (1982), 'Marital fertility in pre-industrial England' (unpublished University of Cambridge PhD thesis).

WILSON, C. (1984), 'Natural fertility in pre-industrial England, 1600–1799', *Population Studies*, **38**, 225–40.

WILSON, C. (1986), 'The proximate determinants of marital fertility in England 1600–1719', In L. Bonfield, R. M. Smith and K. Wrightson (eds), *The World We Have Gained*, Oxford, 203–30.

WILSON, C. and R. WOODS (1991), 'Fertility in England: a long-term perspective', *Population Studies*, **45**, 399–415.

WOODS, R. I. (1979), *Population Analysis in Geography*, London.

WOODS, R. I. (1982), *Theoretical Population Geography7*, London.

WOODS, R. I. (1985), 'The effect of population redistribution on the level of mortality in nineteenth-century England and Wales', *Journal of Economic History*, **45**, 645–51.

WOODS, R. I. (1989), 'What would one need to know to solve the "natural population decrease problem" in early modern cities', in R. Lawton (ed.), *The Rise and*

Fall of Great Cities, London, 80–95.

WOODS, R. I. (1993), 'On the historical relationship between infant and adult mortality', *Population Studies*, **47**, 195–219.

WOODS, R. I. and P. R. A. HINDE (1987), 'Mortality in Victorian England: models and patterns', *Journal of Interdisciplinary History*, **18**, 119–44.

WOODS, R. I., P. A. WATTERSON and J. H. WOODWARD (1988/89), 'The causes of rapid infant mortality decline in England and Wales, 1861–1921', *Population Studies*, part 1, **42** (1988), 343–66; part 2, **43** (1989), 113–32.

WOODS, R. I. and N. WILLIAMS (1995), 'Must the gap widen before it can be narrowed? Long-term trends in social class mortality differentials', *Continuity and Change*, **10**, 105–37.

WOODS, R., N. WILLIAMS and C. GALLEY (1993), 'Infant mortality in England – 1550–1950 – Problems in the identification of long-term trends and geographical and social variations', In C. A. Corsini and P. P. Viazzo (eds), *The Decline of Infant Mortality in Europe 1800–1950: Four National Case Studies*, Florence, 35–50.

WOODS, R., N. WILLIAMS and C. GALLEY (1997), 'Differential mortality patterns among infants and other young children: the experience of England and Wales in the nineteenth century', In C. C. Corsini and P. P. Viazzo (eds), *Infant and Childhood Mortality. The European Experience, 1750–1990*, The Hague, 57–72.

WOODWARD, D. (1975), 'The impact of the Commonwealth Act on Yorkshire parish registers', *Local Population Studies*, **14**, 15–31.

WOODWARD, D. (1995), *Men at Work*, Cambridge.

VAN DER WOUDE, A. M. (1982), Population developments in the northern Netherlands (1500–1800) and the validity of the "urban graveyard" effect', *Annales de Demographie Historique*, 55–75.

WRIGHT, S. J. (1985a), '"Churmaids, huswyfes and hucksters": the employment of women in Tudor and Stuart Salisbury', In L. Charles and L. Duffin (eds), *Women and Work in Pre-industrial England*, London, 100–21.

WRIGHT, S. J. (1985b), 'Easter books and parish rate books: a new source for the urban historian', *Urban History Yearbook*, 30–45.

WRIGHT, S. J. (1989a), '"Holding up half the sky": women and their occupations in eighteenth-century Ludlow', *Midland History*, **14**, 53–74.

WRIGHT, S. J. (1989b), 'A guide to Easter books and related parish listings', *Local Population Studies*, part I, **42** (1989), 18–31; part II, **43** (1989), 13–27.

WRIGLEY, E. A. (1966a), 'Family limitation in pre-industrial England', *Economic History Review*, **19**, 82–109.

WRIGLEY, E. A. (1966b), 'Family reconstitution', In E. A. Wrigley (ed.), *An Introduction to Historical Demography*, London, 96–159.

WRIGLEY, E. A. (1967), 'A simple model of London's importance in changing English society and economy', *Past and Present*, **37**, 38–70.

WRIGLEY, E. A. (1969), *Population and History*, London.

WRIGLEY, E. A. (1972), 'Mortality in pre-industrial England: the example of Colyton, Devon over three centuries', In D. V. Glass and R. Revelle (eds), *Population and Social Change*, London, 243–73.

WRIGLEY, E. A. (1973a), 'Clandestine marriage in Tetbury in the late 17th century', *Local Population Studies*, **10**, 15–21.

WRIGLEY, E. A. (ed.) (1973b) *Identifying People in the Past*, London.

WRIGLEY, E. A. (1977), 'Births and baptisms: the use of Anglican registers as a source of information about the numbers of births in England before the beginning of Civil Registration', *Population Studies*, **31**, 281–312.

WRIGLEY, E. A. (1978), 'Parasite or stimulus: the town in a pre-industrial economy', In P. Abrams and E. A. Wrigley (eds), *Towns in Society*, Cambridge, 295–309.

WRIGLEY, E. A. (1985a), 'The means to marry: population and economy in pre-industrial England', *Quarterly Journal of Social Affairs*, **1**, 271–80.

WRIGLEY, E. A. (1985b), 'Urban growth and agricultural change: England and the continent in the early modern period', *Journal of Interdisciplinary History*, **15**, 683–728.

WRIGLEY, E. A. (1987), 'No death without birth: the implication of English mortality in the early modern period', In R. Porter and A. Wear (eds), *Problems and Methods in the History of Medicine*, London, 133–50.

WRIGLEY, E. A. (1990), 'Brake or accelerator? Urban and population growth before the industrial revolution', In A. D. van der Woude, A. Hayami and J. de Vries (eds), *Urbanization and History*, Oxford, 101–12.

WRIGLEY, E. A. (1994), 'The effect of migration on the estimation of marriage age in family reconstitution studies', *Population Studies*, **48**, 81–97.

WRIGLEY, E. A. and R. S. SCHOFIELD (1981), *The Population History of England, 1541–1871: A Reconstruction*, London.

WRIGLEY, E. A. and R. S. SCHOFIELD (1983), 'English population history from family reconstitution: summary results', *Population Studies*, **37**, 157–84.

INDEX